Lost Subjects, Contested Objects

Lost Subjects, Contested Objects

*Toward a
Psychoanalytic
Inquiry of Learning*

Deborah P. Britzman

State University of New York Press

Published by
State University of New York Press, Albany

© 1998 State University of New York

Printed in the United States of America

For information, address State University of New York Press,
State University Plaza, Albany, N.Y., 12246

Production by Marilyn P. Semerad
Marketing by Dana E. Yanulavich

Library of Congress Cataloging-in-Publication Data

Britzman, Deborah P., 1952–
    Lost subjects, contested objects : toward a psychoanalytic inquiry
of learning / Deborah P. Britzman.
       p.   cm.
    Includes bibliographical references (p.   ) and index.
    ISBN 0–7914–3807–4 (hc : alk. paper). — ISBN 0–7914–3808–2 (pb :
alk. paper)
    1. Learning.   2. Psychoanalysis.   3. Ethics.   4. Critical
pedagogy.   I. Title.
LB1060.B765   1998
370.15'23—dc21
                                   97–35166
                                        CIP

10 9 8 7 6 5 4 3 2 1

Contents

Acknowledgments

That psychoanalysis would have something to say to me, that my educational residence would be lost and refound, not so much by moving to another country, but by learning within this move to be addressed by the strange address of psychoanalysis, continues to surprise. Perhaps something outside must be encountered as strange for that other intimate strangeness—the psychical—to be admitted. Then, one might begin to raise some interminable questions for education: How does one become susceptible, interested really, to the call of culture, friendship, love, or theory? How is it that one decides to interfere with the self? How do the old consolations lose their usefulness? And why can anyone risk the insufficiency of interpretation to make something more from the strange logic of a dream? This work of learning to meet these elusive subjects without the consolations of answers or the legitimation of institutions is what I am asking of readers.

Over the course of writing this book, I have benefited from lovely conversations, strange arguments, interesting symposiums, loving friendships, thoughtful students, and, I hope, being mixed up with the fictions of the analysts, writers, artists, and even characters in literature. Many thanks go to Roger I. Simon and Don Dippo, both of whom, in very different and gracious ways, pushed this work and helped me continue in the slow transition from living in the United States to living in Canada. I am forever indebted to the gift of William Haver's friendship. His influence in my readings of the Freuds, and indeed, much of my thinking about "the dignity of having an everyday" mark many of the ideas presented here. Over the years, my friendship with Maxine Greene and my engagement with her work have made my own possible. I thank Patti Lather and John Willinsky, who offered important questions to this work. My colleagues at York University—in the Faculty of Education and in the Graduate Programs of Social and Political Thought and Women's Studies—have been generous with their time, encouragement, and even for some, with their incredulity toward the question of psychoanalysis in education. Special thanks for commenting on this work, go to Dan Yon, Rinaldo Walcott, Sharon Todd, Dennis Sumara, and Brent Davis. This book also has benefited from the keen editorial eyes of Adriena

Benzaquen, Kate Kaul, and Jen Gilbert, although the blind spots are my own. I thank as well Lois Patton, acting director of State University of New York Press for her offer of invaluable advice and rigorous expectations. Finally, over the course of writing this book, Alice J. Pitt has given her time and her keen analytical insight with grace, humor, and the gift of love. I thank her most of all.

Earlier versions of a few chapters were published elsewhere. I thank the following publishers for granting permission to reprint and revise this early work: An earlier version of chapter 2, under the title "On Doing Something More" is included the forthcoming *A Light in Dark Times: Conversations in Relation to Maxine Greene*, edited by Janet Miller and Bill Ayers (New York: Teachers College Press); a shorter version of chapter 4 under the same title will appear in the forthcoming *Sexualities and Social Action: Inside the Academy and Out*, edited by Janice Ristock and Catherine Taylor (Toronto: University of Toronto Press); and, a shorter version of chapter 5, printed from *Off White* edited by Michelle Fine et al. (1997) by permission of the publisher, Routledge: New York and London; excerpt originally published under the title of "Difference in a Minor Key: Some Modulations of History, Memory and Community."

Introduction

Toward a Psychoanalytic
Inquiry of Learning

> If the other is not to be sold off, it must be
> sought incognito, among lost things.
>
> —Adorno, *Mahler: A Musical Physiognomy*

The definition of education we will grapple with is one that startles in difficulty and implication. It belongs to Anna Freud, known for her attempts to consider in tandem the demands of psychoanalysis and the demands of education. She takes the child's point of view, arguing that education wants something from the child: "Step by step education aims at the exact opposite of what the child wants, and at each step it regards as desirable the very opposite of the child's inherent instinctual strivings."[1] The wishes of education clash with the wishes of the child. As Miss Freud gradually comes to reach her startling definition of education, she names the relation between the teacher and the student "a never-ending battle" (101). Here we have the institutional drama of teaching and learning as it plays out through the intimate staging of attention, affection, surprise, and chance. Learning and teaching, it turns out, are epic in their force, pressure, twists, reversals and returns. Anna Freud's punch line is that education can be defined as all types of interference. And perhaps from the point of view of the educator—who, after all, was also a child—the definition itself is felt as interference.

This would not be the first time psychoanalytic discussion has seized upon a notion of interference as a volatile and organizing dynamic. Indeed, one might read the entire psychic topology of the ego, the id, and the superego as variations on this theme. We will bring this interference to education as well.

1

Throughout the chapters of this book, I will be drawing primarily upon the course of such analysts as Sigmund Freud and Anna Freud, bringing their views to contemporary educational problems in an encounter with "difficult knowledge" to explore what psychoanalysis offers to education. We will explore continually the question, the status, and the directionality of interference. We will do so through the play of affect and its attachments, primarily focusing upon love and hate in learning, as we consider the movements, mingling, and force of two simultaneous directions that are difficult to distinguish from one another even as they collapse into one another: the inside or the psychic, and the outside or the social. Before moving on to these troublesome discussions, the thought of education as constituting all types of interference requires some explanation. With what am I comparing this view?

When one attempts to define education, the following associations may take center stage: change, progress, betterment, advancement. We find these terms both in radical and in conservative views, for it is almost impossible to separate the arguments over social engineering, nation building, and economics from the wishes and the institutions of education. We might add that education wishes to be deliberate—conscious really—and that its design and institutional form proceed from the assumption of building incremental knowledge upon the edifice of the learner. That bits and pieces of knowledge may be terrorizing to students and teachers and that the commonly accepted view that learning proceeds from simplicity to complexity may not be comforting, is hardly thought. Instead the big stage of education attempts to build the little stage of individual development. These chapters do not engage this all-too-common story of normal development. The notion of development at work here is far more unruly and fragile. We shall define development, along Anna Freud's lines of development, as "new editions of very old conflicts" (88).

It would be foolish to insist that education does not make a difference in the lives people live or that knowledge does not matter. But it also would be foolish not to question what sort of difference works within the difference of education. One central difference can be found in Raymond Williams' dictionary entry on "educated," which engages with the social tensions from which education is made.[2] Williams argues that the definition of modern education could emerge only when an idea of "uneducated" became thinkable. More directly, it was through the legislation of compulsory education that the categories of educated/uneducated began to circulate in public discourse. This distinction is now central to contemporary definitions of education that rely upon rationality, certainty, measurement, and control. There must be, in this view, a certain knowledge and a certainty in knowledge, that can be recognized, developed, examined, and urged through incremental measurement, grading schemes, age distribution, and diplomas, and that rest upon fantasies of what every educated person should know.[3] The wish is that how one learns, what one learns, and why one learns may be consciously deliberated and controllable, and that, if learning does not occur, that too may be explained and corrected (or at least that the failure will be accompanied by a suitable category to contain it). This condensed wish makes it almost impossible to separate the question of education from the will to power, the desire for mastery, and the quest for an omnipotent knowledge unencumbered by psychical life.

Whereas Raymond Williams had in mind the burgeoning educational apparatus of the late nineteenth century, our consideration will be how education might be imagined in the twilight of our own. We are not concerned with building a bridge to the new century as much as with placing into question the contingent arrangements of time in learning. But with this trope of time, of what becomes in retrospect a certain historicity, we can ask why the wish that condenses education with mastery has not gone away, even as many do acknowledge that the wish for mastery has gone awry. The recognition that the insistence upon mastery raises as many problems as it attempts to settle may partly explain why across the different scenes of institutional education, even in those disciplines whose historical movements have denied their implication in the education of children and in the discipline of education, the subject of pedagogy has emerged as the new object of incitement. The field of education and the fields of humanities and social sciences are preoccupied with the promise and dangers of pedagogy.

In the social sciences and humanities, the turn to pedagogy indicates an acknowledgment that the dilemmas of the university classroom and of what becomes of knowledge in that space are too big to ignore. Specifically, this is a question for university classrooms that center the contested histories of civil rights, identity politics, social change, and cultural discontentment. Various texts, in which pedagogy appears as politics, as culture war, as impersonation, as that which is coming to an end, as deconstruction, as borders, as machine, and as in ruins return to that primal classroom scene to sort through the miniature deliberations between educational design and social justice.[4] Their arguments vary widely in metaphor, in theoretical stance, in appeal, and in remedy, but they all seem to share an underlying thematic anxiety that continues the long debate over which knowledge is important for which social subjects. And while this critical literature continues to press for new forms of signification offering subjects new narratives for conceptualizing the world, its centering of knowledge, however inadvertently, sustains through reversal the binary pointed out by Raymond Williams between the educated and the uneducated. Not surprisingly, figures of consciousness—whether in the form of the teacher, the student, or the text—loom large in discussions over critical issues in higher education such as power, authority, and agency. But in centering consciousness and in critiquing the normative force of institutional education, we have not yet left a notion of development as progress, nor have we centered the primal scene of learning. Lost in the fault lines of debates on knowledge is the question of education as psychic event.[5] What else happens when the subject that is the learner meets and uses the object that is knowledge? Shall we admit that something other than consciousness interferes with education?

Educational studies seem to take a different tact even as, in their maneuvers, they end with the same plea. Their preoccupation is still the question of incremental knowledge, as if the time of education could set precisely the time of learning. Their assumptions are still that learning proceeds by way of direct apprehension, that experience is always conscious experience, and that identity organizes political consciousness. We can find the same insistence upon the need to fix the learner through the centering of identity, the focus upon the building of self-esteem, and the offering of role models and heros. Perhaps for the sake of polemics, but certainly to draw attention to the issues of violence in education, some studies refuse to distinguish the arbitrary violence of the street from the defensive and aggressive dynamics of the classroom. And it seems as though the only audiences that can be imagined are those who are in agreement with such remedies and those who refuse them. The proposed remedies and narrative styles constitute an attempt to make visible the significant exclusions and monocultural prejudices that largely structure educational encounters throughout North America. Still, what cannot be thought about in this literature is that more is at stake than beginners and that education does not solely reside in the teacher's efforts, the good curriculum, and the question of locating the source of empowerment.[6]

Education is best considered as a frontier concept: something between the teacher and the student, something yet to become. The work of learning is not so much an accumulation of knowledge but a means for the human to use knowledge, to craft and alter itself. But as we shall see throughout this volume, the view of the human psychoanalysis offers to education is difficult and fragile. Analyst Michael Balint poses the human as "an intimate mixture of extremes" made from the conditions of growing up. Balint names three extremes: "(1) extreme dependence [upon others]; (2) extreme bliss—the satisfied child is still the prototype of happiness; and, (3) extreme swings of emotion from love to hate, from complete confidence to dire suspicion or paralyzing fear."[7] These, it will be argued throughout, are also the extremes of learning, of history, of the social bonds, and of love. As dynamics, these extremes repeat in epistemology in the very construction and use of knowledge. And like matters of love, this strange mixture of extremes cannot, as Freud suggests, "be measured by the same standards as other things; it is as though they were written on a page by themselves which would not take any other script."[8]

New, unacknowledged problems emerge, having to do with the question of how one learns from one's own difficulties and pleasures in learning as one learns as well something from the difficulties and pleasures of others. By not admitting this tension, the advocacies of educational studies still seem lopsided, weighed down by the force of the social bearing down upon subjects, even as this work also contributes to discussions of feminist pedagogy, antiracist curriculum, and multicultural education. However, given that strange mixture of extremes, even when the weight of the social is acknowledged, there is no easy measure as to how its burdens and obstacles are noticed, felt, and used. One of the most puzzling effects of these progressive initiatives, that must now be addressed, is that these transformatory gestures are implicated in the repressed of resistance, resentment, and accusation. New editions of the old educated/uneducated conflict return, this time in the guise of high and low consciousness.

When all these fields are considered most generally, when education *writ large* questions its relation to social justice with the suggestion that education can be made from the proper teacher, the proper curriculum, or the proper pedagogy so that learning will be no problem to the actors involved, we might note that for there to be a learning there must be conflict within learning. In this view, we have changed the directionality of interference: from interference that bears down upon the learner to those within the learner. Learning is a problem, but it has to do with something other than the material of pedagogy. We might begin to pry apart the conditions of learning from that which conditions the desire to learn and the desire to ignore. We might wonder how one comes to be susceptible to the call of ideas. Within this other space, we might think of learning as a dynamic psychical event, made from our capacity for extremes. What seems lost in these very different discussions on pedagogy is the sense that learning is a relearning of one's history of learning—new editions of old conflicts—and that it is precisely this unconscious force that renders the work of learning so difficult in intimacy and in public. If learning is a relearning and hence an unlearning of old strategies (as opposed to a repetition of one's own history of learning in the guise of new strategies), then the questions at stake in educational efforts are simultaneously those that can think the force of history within the force of learning. The chapters that follow reside within such contradictions by setting into tension instances of cultural history embodied in a series of debates within communities with comments on psychic histories embodying that other debate, the world of internal conflicts. What attaches the psychical to the social and the social to the psychical are matters of love and hate in learning. Each of the chapters that follow meditates on this interminable "inside/outside" encounter, an encounter here named "education." The question of interference, then, raises something more: How does education live in people and how do people live in education?

Any notion of education depends upon a theory of knowledge, but one of the central arguments in this text is that such a theory must begin within the tensions exercised when the knowledge offered through pedagogy meets the knowledge brought to pedagogy. These are the passionate tensions of love and hate, of learning to love and of love of learning. Within this exercise, yet another sort of history must be admitted: that of the unconscious. When ontology meets epistemology, when the subject of education can be extended to what is barely perceptible but still exerts its own force, the appearance of education can become complicated by its own others: the incognito, the unapparent, the contested, indeed the "what else" and the "elsewhere" of learning. In positing education as a question of interference (as opposed to an engineered development), we have a very different epistemology and ontology of actions and actors: one that insists that the inside of actors is as complicated as the outside, and that this combination is the grounds of education. Not only does the world impinge cruelly upon the subject, and not only does the subject's inner world constitute the be-all of understanding and misunderstanding: the subject lives both dilemmas in ways that cannot be predicted, authorized by another, or even deliberately planned and separated.

"The distinction," writes analyst Andre Green, "between external and internal reality is basic yet vague. Internal reality is not just the reality of the wish, it is also the reality of the body as a place of need. External reality is also not so simple."[9] We are back to the intimate question of interference, but now as a sort of frontier between the wish and the need, between the social body and the physical body. Such vagueness itself makes distinction a question. For while the body must secure its boundaries, it can do so only through attachment. If it is the desire to attach—to touch and to be touched—that inaugurates the subject, this inchoate desire, as we shall see, makes our subject and its distinctions fragile. Neither internal nor external reality is simple. To tolerate this insight is just the beginning of what Freud calls "working through" or learning.

We have a view of our subject and a view of learning that raise interminable questions: If education is all types of interference, can one even point to an originary moment? With what does education interfere? What interferes with education? What types of interference can we consider, and how much interference becomes felt as too much? What desires structure the demands to interfere? Is there a difference between the ways a subject interferes with herself and the ways education interferes with the subject? Can there be an ethic of interference? And if the sorts of interference in which we are interested concern the questions of the psychical and social dynamics of love and hate in learning, how do these forces interfere with the subject of education, however defined?

More Interference

The questions offered above are set in motion, and bothered by, psychoanalytic insight. So far, we have been grappling with a characterization of the inside and outside of education and of the stakes opened when education is defined as constituting all types of interference. Now we must turn to a different movement of interference: the interference within the subject. In psychoanalytic views, the most incredible interference is, oddly, the most indirect. And this indirection seems to shape how Sigmund Freud justifies the concept of the unconscious: indirection requires indirection.[10]

Freud's concept of the unconscious is paradoxical, for while the unconscious is something one cannot know directly, its workings interfere with what is taken as direct experience and with what is valued as intentionality. Nonetheless, Freud argues, it is necessary to put forth such a concept because "a gain in meaning is a perfectly justifiable ground for going beyond the limits of direct experience" (167). Something inside interferes with the limits of consciousness and the ego's strategies of perception. Knowing that this interference is difficult to accept—because it goes against the wish that consciousness is all, that individuals are masters of their thought, that cognition precedes affect, and that affect should not contradict attitudes—Freud works by way of an analogy that opens even more dilemmas than his first insistence on moving beyond the rules for direct experience. To approximate the otherness that he calls "the unconscious," Freud takes a detour through a conscious wish, by way of a sliding parenthetical remark: "(It would no doubt be psychologically more correct to put it in this way: that without any special reflection we attribute to everyone else our own constitution and therefore our consciousness as well, and that this identification is a *sine qua non* of our understanding)" (169). A special reflection is necessary if we are to move to the fragility of understanding others and disrupt the wish for a continuity and sameness that attributes to others the same state of mind. Something interferes with conscious identifications.

The problem is that, while projecting his or her own state of mind onto others, the one who projects misplaces the projection. Freud offers the example of how easy it seems to be critical of others but how difficult it is to recognize in the self the very same difficulties that one knows so well. Oddly, the self's projection is resisted: "Furthermore, experience shows that we understand very well how to interpret in other people (that is, how to fit into their chain of mental events) the same acts which we refuse to acknowledge as being mental in ourselves. Here some special hindrance evidently deflects our investigations from our own self and prevents our obtaining true knowledge of it" (169–70). This "special hindrance," more akin to a censor, is not yet the unconscious. But the resistance at stake is not only that perception is not everything but also that it must be made from flaws. It is through this resistance to the limits of self-knowledge that Freud returns the repressed: the curious incognito of the unconscious, the place of lost subjects, and the place of re-finding lost objects.

With what does the unconscious interfere? Or better, where does the unconscious interfere? Freud presents two types of interference, both in the form of an ambivalent wish. The unconscious wishes to do whatever it wants without regard for others, consequences, social convention, logic. One might call this wish the "force of Eros." But this interferes with the ego's wish to forget, ignore, and turn away from that which the ego cannot stand or bear to know. In this conflicted design, what is refused cannot go away but is instead repressed, only to return through indirection, in new and disguised forms such as negation, dreams, slips of the tongue, baffling and bungled actions, jokes, fantasy, irreverence. In these ways the ego is reminded of its own lost wishes and of the fragility of its standing in the social world. These odd hauntings interfere with conscious attitudes. Our subject is made ambivalent through its own conflicted demands and wishes. The two types of interference represent two senses of a wish: the ego's wish to ignore and to flee from what is felt as unpleasure and danger, and the unconscious wish for something without consequence. But there is even more, for what makes the unconscious other to the conscious are its curious qualities: the unconscious knows no time, no contradiction, indeed no negation. It is other to education and, unlike the ego, it tolerates all.

A Suspicious Meeting

Psychoanalysis considers in tandem two directions of interference: those within, that animate and try to resolve psychical conflict, and those without, such as education, culture, and law, which animate and attempt to resolve conflict as well. Each dynamic of interference makes the subject fragile in, and susceptible to, education, social pressures, and the subject's own wandering desires. Again we are back to Michael Balint's notion of the human as constituted from its own "intimate mixture of extremes." But unlike education, which depends upon its wish to persuade the subject to transcend conflict in order to learn, psychoanalysis insists that there is no outside to conflict;[11] hence the problem of learning becomes how the social and the individual can come to tolerate ethically the demands of the self and the demands of the social. And psychoanalysis, which defines development as new forms of old conflicts, extends this struggle to knowledge itself.[12] Knowledge as well is made from the flaws of its own capacity for extremes. Psychoanalysis asks education to refuse to secure itself through the consolations of certainty, rationality, and progress but, at the same time, to continue to risk itself without the old guarantees. When Freud noted that there are three impossible professions—government, healing, and education—he named not just the failings of central institutions to shape everyday lives in their own image but also the inadequate gambles of their knowledge. "There is no help for it," Freud wrote in one of his last essays.[13] And then, in "Analysis Terminable and Interminable," Freud returns to his own impossible profession, "in which one can be sure beforehand of achieving unsatisfactory results" (248). Such admissions on the limits of practice and on the strange occurrence of being theoretically right and practically wrong offer no consolation. For many in education feel that these demands are too much and thus view psychoanalysis with suspicion.

However much each field of practice may appear to discourage the other, the modern history of psychoanalysis cannot be considered outside of the modern history of education. After all, both begin with notions of childhood, learning, and sociality. One might notice that both consider questions of suffering, but their views on its sources are opposed. In psychoanalysis the sources of suffering are interminable. One can suffer from memories, fantasy, and anxiety as easily as one can suffer from social impediments. And while certain forms of education attempt to address the cruel obstacles made from conditions of injustice, social inequalities, and social aggression, Freud's thought does not promise a utopic social engineering. Indeed, one of the most frequent sentences found in Freud's writings is this: "Ladies and gentlemen, I can offer you no consolation." And then, Anna Freud offers her readers a different sort of caution: "We must not demand too much from one another."[14]

Still, psychoanalysis has a history of attempting to bring its insights to educational efforts. Anna Freud's *Four Lectures on Psychoanalysis for Teachers and Parents* suggest that a psychoanalytic orientation to learning and teaching can offer teachers a different way of conceptualizing not just the question of the child's psychic development, but more crucially the teacher's understanding of her or his own development as it plays through, repeats, and becomes elaborated within the teacher's relations with individual children, school knowledge, other adults, and, of course, the teacher's own self. Miss Freud tells her audience of three contributions psychoanalysis makes to pedagogical understanding. It is a means to criticize educational methods; a means to extend the teacher's knowledge of the complications of social relations; and, perhaps, something of a "repair [to] the injuries which have been inflicted upon the child during the process of education" (129).

With this last point we are back to the question of education as constituting interference, reminiscent of an earlier warning raised by Sigmund Freud that the best education can do is less harm.[15] This ethical question—what Jacqueline Rose calls "an ethics of failure"[16]—is what makes the project of education interminable and explains why, perhaps, Anna Freud placed the question of interference as the central dynamic of education. For, if education must interfere with psychic and social development, with the pushes and pulls of superstitious and stereotypical thought, and with a narcissism that so easily becomes attached to and defended by all sorts of prejudices,[17] then how does education decide which force of interference shall matter? How can education recognize and repair not just the harm done by others but the harm that occurs under the name of education? How can education recognize and repair its own harm? Freud offers a balance, as precarious as his metaphor, in which each side is weighed down by its own hazards: "Education has to find its way between the Scylla of non-interference and the Charybdis of frustration."[18] Between Scylla's transformation from nymph to monster and Charybdis's drowning movements the interference of education is lost and found.

Anna Freud implies these hazards and the need for education to grapple with its ethicality. Education, she seems to say, must address two directions at the same time: the turning of education back upon itself to view how its practices affect its structures, and the turning of education upon the learner to notice how its practices affect its subjects. This mode of address is different from the plea to apply psychoanalysis to students, something Miss Freud acknowledges when she insists that the move to fix quickly may actually be a symptom of resistance to change! People do not give up their libidinal positions easily, and when encountering differences, they seem to work hard to assert their own continuity. Anna Freud expects denial, *and* she expects that people can surpass those first anxious attempts at making a limit, at refusing to learn. What is surprising is that she considers these first responses necessary because the ego must attempt to defend itself from what at first glance seems senseless, dangerous, or worrisome.[19]

Imagine some statements of defense, or resistances, that Anna Freud seems to anticipate: What does this have to do with me? That's all very well and good but what about this? I wish you would just go away. Everything is not just psyche! You want to put me on the couch! It might be nice in theory, but who has the time? Can't a mistake just be a mistake! So, what's new, I already knew that! Then bring these curious sentences into tension with what Anna Freud has to say:

> Examining the small mistakes in the everyday life of human beings, such as forgetting, losing, or misplacing things, misreading or mishearing, psychoanalysis succeeded in demonstrating that such errors are always based on an intent of the person who makes them. Previously these occurrences had been explained, without much thought, as the results of lack of attention, fatigue, or mere chance. Psychoanalytic investigation established that, generally speaking, we forget nothing except what we wish to forget for some good reason or other, though that reason is usually quite unknown to us. . . . People would not take so much trouble to lock up something worthless![20]

Just as education constitutes all types of interference, so too does psychoanalysis. Psychoanalysis reminds one of the failure of knowledge, the work of forgetting, the elusiveness of significance, the incidental, the coincident, the bungled action, and the psychic creativity of selves: how the self crafts its meanings of the self in the world, what these meanings do to the psyche, and what the psyche does to these meanings. Psychoanalysis interferes with education's dream of mastery, for, through its methods, it catches subjects in the fault lines of inattention: free association, wondering over the elusive significance of the thing furthest from one's mind, and interpretation of dreams. It risks insight from knowledge devoid of social authority and intelligibility. And so we might wonder how the dream of education says something about its underside: the desire for omnipotence, transcendence, innocence, domination.

When the psychoanalytic definition of education is brought to education, education may begin the slow acknowledgement of its own ethical implication: education must interfere. There is nothing else it can do for it demands of students and teachers that each come to something, make something more of themselves.

The problem is that the demand can be felt as too much and too little. The demand can come too early and too late. After all, consider what education asks of students: to listen, to pay attention, to stop talking, to hold the whisper, to stay with the subject, to concentrate, to risk a mistake, to correct a mistake, to talk in front of their peers, to take a test, to go play, to be serious, to stop laughing, to consider things which would not occur to the self, to debate a belief, to encounter strange theories; indeed, it asks students to confront perspectives, situations, and ideas that may not be just unfamiliar but appear at first glance as a criticism of the learner's view. In all these demands, education seems to be asking selves to risk their resistance even as educators have difficulty tolerating the forms working through resistance takes. These demands directed outward return to the teacher in contested forms: as questions, hostile notes, gossip, hurt feelings, forgotten details, failure, incomplete sentences, baffling behavior, falling asleep, sexual innuendo, boredom, slips of the tongue, jokes, irrelevant comments, silence, indeed as all other sorts of ambiguous and puzzling gestures. Our educational demand actually comprises two: we demand that the self consider its own wishes, desires, and needs—to think for itself—precisely in the same moment that we demand that the self think about the requirements of others. Education must set in motion something more than it wants.

A Note on the Ego's Means of Defense

Whereas her father, Sigmund Freud, sketched out the curious movements of the instincts known as love and hate, Anna Freud centered questions of the ego's elaboration and its mechanisms of defense, for the bodily ego is made from its relations with others and in its capacity to touch and be touched.[21] The inside and outside pressures the ego feels and observes put the ego into question. Because it cannot flee from itself, the ego requires its own strategies of existence. The ego has indirect means for encountering and defending itself from the interference known as education. And these means return to structure the ego. Anna Freud focused on ten "special methods," or strategies, the ego makes in order to modulate and release conflict and unpleasure. The mechanisms of defense are the ego's fragile attempt to secure its own boundaries, to mediate its capacity for extremes, and quite precariously, to make a relation.

What seems curious about these defenses is not their content—for the content keeps changing—but the motility of their guises in dynamic movement: their twists, turns, reversals, returns, and hence their movements of relationality. A mechanism of defense is a relation, but one that moves back and forth, from psychic reality to social reality. This motility is the condition for ideas or contents to unattach from the force of their affect and then reattach to, and hence disguise, the affect in a new idea. The affect, however, "constitutes a challenge to thought."[22] Its time is contradictory: the affect comes too early and too late. We can substitute one idea for another, and even though these two ideas appear at first glance to be opposed, the same affect can be repeated within a new idea. Why does one care so much that a mistake has been made, that a word has been forgotten, that one is misunderstood? What seems most at stake for psychoanalysis is the underlying or latent wish disguised in the tolerable idea. These stakes form the basis of Freud's method for interpreting the dream. It is not just that we mean the opposite of what we say or dream, but that ambivalence in desire complicates what each of us can tolerate knowing. The present concern, the obsession, the care, the hatred, all these things point elsewhere. The study is with the dynamic and the tricks of its content.

The defenses of the ego are thus not a question of Why? but of *where*? Where is the desire of the defense?[23] With the directional indicator of where, we can consider the prepositional movements of defense: against, in, on, around, behind, in front of, beside, with, and under. After all, the movements of the defenses are curious and volatile symptoms of other relations, other histories, other desires, indeed otherness itself. The ten defenses Anna Freud formulates offer us plenty of directions: regression, repression, reaction formation, isolation, undoing, projection, introjection, turning against the self, reversal, and sublimation. Anna Freud would come to add two more to the ego's socially oriented strategies: altruism and identification with the aggressor. The ego's learning, it turns out, is neither linear nor progressive but entangled in its capacity to touch and to be touched. We are not concerned with positing stages or chronology, for in psychoanalytic method more than one chronology occupies the same space, and, because of ambivalence, we can hold two opposite understandings precisely in the same place. We become torn.

Psychoanalysis presents the bodily ego as very busy. In Freud's second psychic topology, the ego is named a "frontier creature"[24] and is twice constituted: through its attempts to mediate, placate, and even trick something besides itself and something within itself, the id and the superego, and through its capacity to be touched by its relations with others in the world. Because the ego works through perception, observation, reality testing, projection, and hallucination, it must struggle with the question of boundaries and with the question of education. Over and over, the ego must solve the problem of love. What belongs to the ego, and what belongs to the object? Is it me, or is it them? How do I know that what I think is happening is actually happening? What if I can not believe what I see? How do my actions become puzzling to me? How do I recognize my self when my self is at the same time conflictive, ambivalent, and caught between my own demands and the demands of others? Again, what belongs to the ego, and what belongs to the object? More pertinent, in a place called "education," what belongs to the teacher, and what belongs to the student? Where do the teacher's emotional ties become entangled in pedagogy? Where is the student? We are back to the question of interference, or, put in a slightly different way, the question of an implication that reaches elsewhere. But where?

Self-Subversive Narratives of Education

We can now make our exploration more specific and borrow a method from the writer Samuel R. Delany. In his autobiography, *A Motion of Light in Water*, Delany offers readers a story of his first day in the prestigious Bronx High School of Science. Actually, Delany comes to tell this story in three dimensions of time: the ethnographic (or the place of detail), the reflective (or the consideration of the significance of anxiety), and the uncanny (or the force of secrets). The first time of the story's telling is filled with ethnographic details: fifteen-year-old Delany enters the classroom on that first day, peruses his new classmates, complies with the teacher's request that the students rearrange themselves through alphabetizing their seating order, and then listens to the teacher's next request, that classmates nominate someone for the student government organization. A boy named Chuck, whom Delany has just met, nominates Delany. And of the four nominations, Delany wins the election. In this telling, perhaps too good to be true, too easy to tell, everything happens well: his new peers acclaim him, he meets a new friend, and his teacher seems friendly.

In the second telling of the story, the details return with the difference of anxiety. The first ethnographic telling is mulled over with a retrospective observation: "What strikes me is how quickly the written narrative closes [more important details] out—puts [them] outside of language" (25). Our narrator wonders, What if the story could dare to admit those other moments, those movements of otherness one might term "anxiety"? But where is the anxiety? Remember the anxiety of that first day? Will I be liked? Will I like the others? Can I sit next to the one I'm attracted to? Will he like me? Will I be popular? Do I look alright? Does he know what I'm thinking? Am I as smart as the school? Delany imagines these worries and desires as arranged in parallel columns. Two realities coexist but one is more difficult. The ethnographic detail does not add up to make the whole story. And there is something more than the ethnographic detail can bear to admit.

Delany's second story is caught in the fault lines of our first victorious ethnography. There resides an older story buried and preserved in the ethnographic present. What our fifteen-year-old Delany notices that first day and cannot bear to leave alone is Chuck's beautiful hand. Noticing the beauty of Chuck's hand, Delany begins to fall in love. In this second telling, what is told is Chuck's body: his height, the color of his shirt, the fall of his hair, the tone of his skin, the way he sighs. In the momentary chaos of students finding their seats, our narrator loses sight of Chuck and in this loss feels the loneliness of that first day and his own strangeness. There is a brief panic: Had I only imagined him? If I see him again, will I see the same Chuck I first saw? But through the coincidence of alphabetical seating, Delany finds himself in a seat to the left of Chuck. And then their hands can finally meet; the surprise comes in the form of a handshake. The touching of the hands leaves behind a trace. Yes, it is that same Chuck who nominates Delany. Does that mean he likes me in the way I like him? The movements of anxiety—that strange dialogue Delany sets up between the id and the ego—momentarily rest, until the next worry troubles the telling.

There is always more to the story. The excess found in the third sense of time, the uncanny, also occupies what both tellings have not yet said. Still, the uncanny can be examined only in bits and pieces, for while its haunting persistence depends upon its being buried, its return is not yet home. In commenting on the second retelling and in re-finding the lost quota of affects that return, Delany maintains that the first story does not explain the second try at retelling. Readers are offered an interminable question: "Why speak of what's uncomfortable to speak of?" (29). Delany is worried about how his story will be understood, how his imagined readers may lend their own continuities to his fragile retelling. In this curious architecture where the imagined boundaries of the inside and the outside refuse to be known, Delany tests his narrative experiment with the following paradox: "If it *is* the split—the space between two columns (one resplendent and lucid with the writings of legitimacy, the other dark and hollow with the voices of the illegitimate)—that constitutes the subject, it is only after the Romantic inflation of the private into the subjective that such a split can even be located" (29-30).

The space that signifies the split between falling in love and recounting that first day as if there were no fall marks the loss of subjectivity. The discomfort is the symptom of that split, between the aggression of social rejection over the form of love and an Eros that desires contact and hence must risk the self.

Our turn to literature is also something psychoanalytic inquiry encourages, for in both narratives "the resplendent and the hollow" coexist in the same space. Two fictions meet: the fiction that is the theory and the fiction that is the subject. What surprises the meeting, how the coincidence stubbornly points elsewhere, is part of the paradox Delany offers. Because the paradox is necessary to the poetics of the self, it is not to be solved but rather located in the in-between space of potential relations. Where is the paradox? For Delany's story is not just about the ego's capacity to reality test, to hallucinate, or to observe, actions which would still keep us in the domain of the first story, the unaffected ethnography. That first ethnography would not yet be a fiction if we bring to bear on the question of fiction what Michel de Certeau noticed about the fiction we call "psychoanalysis:" "fiction as being a knowledge jeopardized and wounded by its own otherness (the affect, etc.)."[25] We might name the wound the "unconscious." We might name the knowledge "education." And so, de Certeau's strange pursuit can be set in tension with the question raised by our narrator: "Why speak of what's uncomfortable to speak of?" This question interferes as well, for how does the uncomfortable live within the comfort? How does the comfort defend against the uncomfortable? These questions occupy the uncanny third time of interference, that simultaneous moment of defense, recognition, and undoing that makes the ego so vulnerable. Freud called the work of learning a "working through." What did Delany learn from himself that he had not known before? How does Delany learn to allow his unconscious wishes to coexist with his conscious attitudes? The way Delany interferes with himself is also an education.

In Delany's first retelling, the teacher, Mr. Tannenbaum, is barely there, except for two ethnographic details. The first detail is that "he smiled if you made a joke, sometimes in spite of himself" (22). The second, that because of (or maybe in spite of) the prestige of the school, the teachers respected the students. Perhaps these details are related. In spite of something that tells the teacher not to laugh, the teacher laughs, and in this laughter offers a recognition of something other to the pressures of getting work done. The teacher laughs at the pressures of getting work done, for what else is a joke but the means to release a pressure, a way to tell oneself something that can be borne only with laughter? The otherness of teacher and student returns in the form of laughter, and this mutual recognition is the allowance of respect.

There is a story of another teacher. We return again to Anna Freud's lectures to parents and teachers. And just as Delany's method suggests the need to excavate the lost subjects in a story until what is uncanny can be engaged, Anna Freud relates a story of education by way of this need. This teacher's story again must pass through a story of the student. The first bearable ethnographic details add up to a happy ending. A governess went to work with a family who had three children. The oldest and the youngest were doing well in their studies and had the admiration and love of their parents. The middle child was the source of trouble: he was falling behind in his reading skills and was viewed as unmotivated in self-improvement. His parents and siblings encountered him as if he were an extra and heavy appendage, a burden that asked too much. The governess focused all her efforts on this child, and after some time he caught up to take his place as a valued member of the family. As soon as the child succeeded, the governess left her charge and sought new work.

Years later, the governess happened to engage an analyst, she happened to engage herself in psychoanalysis. And thus the ethnographic story—the rescue fantasy—could at last be interfered with. The governess can lift the veil of the discomfort that is also there. The happy story told that the governess had left the position because she had achieved her educational success. The otherness of the story is that the governess could not tolerate the child's success, for her emotional tie, the love she could bear to transfer onto the child, was made from her own childhood sense of being unsuccessful. She could only identify with the child when the child mirrored her own view of herself. Anna Freud poses the unspeakable this way: "All the love and care which she had lavished upon him meant that she was really saying to herself: 'That is the way I ought to have been treated to make something of me'" (130). As long as the child was falling behind and depended upon the governess's efforts, she could identify with the child and perhaps, in living through his failure, could find again her own lost self. Through her pedagogical efforts the governess found a way to perform the actions she wanted to have performed on herself. But the student's progress interfered with her actions of love. When the child improved and somehow was seen to earn the parents' love, the governess left. The governess experienced the child's success as a self-betrayal of her own unloved self. And this she could not tolerate.

Now in retelling, perhaps twice, the story of the governess, Anna Freud interferes with the unaffected ethnographic story of education: that fine educational successes should not be looked at too closely and that there is nothing more to pedagogical efforts than the teacher's desire for educational success. But we are being asked to tolerate what jeopardizes the ethnographic details of the governess. What does it mean for each teacher to notice a student and to ignore others? Why this student and not that student? How does what the teacher notice return in the form of the teacher's self or even seem to turn against the teacher? And how do those who are ignored come under the sign of the teacher? How does the teacher come to have an emotional tie to the student and where does that tie become entangled? If, as Anna Freud reminds us, the students can be more than "more or less suitable material on which to abreact [the teacher's] unconscious and unsolved difficulties" (131), then ethically the teacher is obligated to explore those other dimensions, that other story, the story of one's own otherness. Just as education demands something from the student, the kinds of interference we are exploring here demand something of the teacher.

Whereas Delany's story begins to hint at the vulnerable time of falling in love, our governess's proffers that curious moment of falling out of love, when love changes its content, when love turns to hate, and when love is lost. The same year Sigmund Freud justified the unconscious, he also articulated a view of the vicissitudes of the instincts.[26] He works with four kinds of vicissitudes or transformations of instincts: reversal into the opposite, turning round upon the subject's own self, repression, and sublimation (126). These movements are reminiscent of some of the ego's strategies of defense. Most interesting to our discussion is Freud's observation that "the change of the *content* of an instinct into its opposite is observed in a single instance only—the transformation of *love and hate*" (original emphasis, 133). The transformation of love and hate, and the view that both of these emotional ties can be directed at the same object, bring Freud to the concept of 'ambivalence.' For Freud, there are three positions in the dynamics of love: love and hate; loving and being loved; and unconcern or indifference (133). We can see fragments of the movements that occupy Delany and the governess, and indeed throughout this volume we will continue to explore such twists and turns: different combinations of unconcern, hate, and being loved and loving. Perhaps we can even observe in our own educational experiences traces of these lost subjects and their uncanny return, their coming back at the self in the form of contested objects; that is, if we care to study how we come to attach ourselves to as well as to ignore particular ideas, theories, and people. We also might come to a time in which what jeopardizes the ethnographic telling of education are the vicissitudes of love and hate.

The reversals of love and hate do not mean that these affects are equal in status. While each depends upon intra-psychical and subjective processes, neither is comparable to experiences of anger, indifference, or frustration, all of which are transformable when obstacles are removed by mutual action. Analyst Michael Balint argues: "Hate is a measure of inequality between object and subject; the smaller the inequality, the more mature the subject, the less is [the] need for hate."[27] Love, or what both Michael and Alice Balint call "mature love" requires the lover to tolerate the other's equality or right to have a separate and idiomatic existence. For Michael Balint, how one comes "to solve the problems of love without resorting in any way to hate" (149) determines the capacity to take pleasure in the other's otherness and the self's otherness. And how one comes to tolerate times when love is lost, indeed, when love loses its way, is also a part of the problem of love. These problems were also those of Delany and the governess.

Anna Freud also would be concerned with these dynamics. But because of her interest in education, her own psychoanalytic emphasis moved from the instincts and their vicissitudes to the ego's mechanisms of defense. This shift may have had to do with the institution of education, for there the ego must defend itself from all types of interference even as education attempts to educate the ego. The governess's story exemplifies a common defense employed by teachers, which seems to respond to one of education's impossible demands upon the teacher: to act for the student. Anna Freud calls this strategy "altruistic surrender:" the mechanism which somehow allows the ego to live through the other, to find "some proxy in the outside world to serve as a repository."[28] The student, the curriculum, the institutional mandate—all these objects can become, for the teacher's ego, a proxy. As it turns out, through this proxy the ego can find still the gratification it denies itself; through some distance, it can enjoy still what it appears to deny itself. This too was the governess's (other) story. While she could not lavish the love she required onto herself, she could find some proxy and then discard it as soon as it became other to herself. These curious turns were almost the same ones in Delany's story, had he stayed in the confines of the ethnographic detail that foreclosed and jeopardized recognition of his own otherness.

Anna Freud first describes the mechanism of altruistic surrender as a tentative answer to the curious phenomenon of sports fans. She tries to make sense of how the sports fan comes to be so invested in games he or she does not play. How to explain the manic triumphalism of the victory or the sad despair at watching one's favorite team lose the game? How do individuals get so caught up in lives they cannot live? What is this sacrifice for the ego? How does altruistic surrender turn around upon the self and come to be seen as an attack upon the ego? (And here we must note a familiar statement of the ingrate: "I did everything for you, and now you do this to me!") We can see this reversal of love into hate at work in the governess's story.

Anna Freud suggests that the defense mechanism of altruistic surrender is rooted in early conflicts with authority over some form of the child's desire for instinctual gratification. That first parental authority, asking that the self hold its desires in abeyance and identify with the aggressor's demand to find a more suitable substitute, is transferred onto other authorities, like education or the teacher. What is interesting is that the ego can manage still to find a way to reach the forbidden gratification. The problem is that the strategy of gratification then can be experienced as a turning back onto the ego and become its opposite: a hatred toward both the self that complies and the other who seems to ask for such compliance. Altruistic surrender transforms into another defense: identification with the aggressor, which is actually an identification with the actions of aggression. While in common parlance *the aggressor* is a term given over to the one who performs physical violence on another, in psychoanalytic discourse this term also is given over to the violence of authority. This is what Delany struggles over when he asks himself, "Why speak of the uncomfortable?" Part of the answer must be to locate "the where" of discomfort, and of course the split.

We can now return to a fuller version of Delany's third uncanny telling: "What damages might [this other story] do to women, children, the temperamentally more refined, the socially ignorant, the less well-educated, those with a barely controlled tendency toward the perverse . . . ? Since publishing it in most cases explains little or nothing of the public narrative, why not let it remain privy, personal, privileged—outside of language?" (29).

Samuel Delany cannot keep outside of language what is inside himself. One boy falls in love with another boy. The authority says: Keep this love to yourself and therefore renounce it. Surrender your desires for the sake of the social. Undo, do not touch, isolate yourself. While one may not think of the closet as a mechanism of defense, the altruistic surrender it requires, the proxy the closet becomes, covers that first identification with the aggressor. The defense mechanism of altruistic surrender, and as Delany poses it, the demand to identify with the aggressor's wish, with the authority who says no to that love, will diminish the ego. Delany must announce his love even if it costs him social disparagement. The directionality of interference is different in our governess's story, which begins with the finding of a proxy for the self. But this proxy seems to turn against her desire to preserve the loss. The governess falls out of love (again) with herself. If she is to love again, she too must announce that her love changed its content, becoming hate both for the boy and for her self. If the governess is to love again, she must learn to tolerate her own capacity for extremes.

An Outline of the Book

We have come full circle to the psychoanalytic definition of "the cure": the capacity to risk love and work. When each of us explores the otherness of the self, when each might decide that the uncanny in the social is also a site of learning, when each explores those lost subjects that jeopardize knowledge, the only purpose is to risk work, love, and learning. How one works, how one loves, how one learns, and how one makes room in the conceptualization of these themes are the stakes in the following chapters, and of course when a certain psychoanalysis meets a certain education. These fields of practice are brought to bear on each other because, at their respective best, they are concerned with the vulnerabilities, fragilities, and capacities of learning. And while the teacher's work must be different from the work of the analyst, the teacher is ethically obligated to formulate theories of learning that can tolerate the human's capacity for its own extremes and its mistakes, resistance, belatedness, demands, and loss without creating more harm. The work of education must be a working through of education. For this work to begin, the story of education must pass through —but not merely repeat— the ethnographic, the reflective, and the uncanny.

The reader will notice that the story of psychoanalysis offered in each of these chapters is not the one that typically has come to be supposed in order to be discarded: this story is not Eurocentric, not sexist, not homophobic, not racist; it is not analysis for the purposes of social adaptation and to berate the one who cannot adapt, and indeed not to posit something as normal or pathological. And while these histories, however, pressure and structure the demands and the repressed of education, in the exploration of some of their returning fragments the following chapters will consider the question of "working through" difficulties. The bad story of psychoanalysis does not interest us here for we need not, and should not, imagine psychoanalysis as literally mapping on to a sociology of the body, as a series of literal sentences, as apparent language, or even as capable of separating the psyche from the social. While all of us may be experts in dismissing ideas, we might turn our suspicions back upon our own expertise.

Our concern is with the unapparent, but we pass through the all-too-apparent of contemporary education and through the ways institutional design and social pressures put the conflicts that are so central to learning outside of the learner, the curriculum, and the pedagogy. In our own times, the pressures of social discourses such as "family values," new and old racism, homophobia, and nationalism weigh heavy in education and return to prop up social policy, curriculum design, admission criteria, censorship, and, of course, disputes over the currency of identity as category, nature, or no body. The chapters that follow focus on the problem of how conceptualizations of teachers, students, and the excess knowledge between them are lived as dilemmas and as difficult knowledge. But I also suggest that we may come to know our own dilemmas as elegant problems, necessary to the work of learning to love and love in learning. The lost subjects in the title refer to the repressed psychic events of teaching and learning, which return to haunt education in the form of its contested objects: as conflicts, as disruptions, as mistakes, and as controversies. Given the demands for widening the curriculum to include the relevances, desires, and histories of those who can matter, of communities, perspectives, and expressions that signal comfort and discomfort simultaneously; given the deep implication of education in the space of identity, life chances, and the capacity each of us holds to participate meaningfully in our respective lives; given all the chances education risks, the lost subjects considered here may raise some new questions for those grappling with the interminability of education and for those interested in conceptualizing a theory of learning that can tolerate the vicissitudes of love and hate in learning, that can begin with a generous curosity toward the subject's passionate capacity to attach to the world.

Chapter 1 continues to admit the strange relations between education and psychoanalysis: the arguments, registers, and limits that are made evident when the demands of psychoanalysis meet the demands of education. It examines how psychic topology becomes an event in learning and in public discourse about education, and then it moves to a discussion of "angst" in education. Chapter 2 discusses the philosophy and methods of Maxine Greene and her urging of an education that can get lost in the fictions of literature and the arts. In chapter 3 we consider the tensions inherent in conceptualizations of sex education in the time of AIDS and identity politics and in the strange relations between sexuality and curiosity. Chapter 4 offers a queer theory of pedagogy and discusses whether or not identities can be more than a site of mastery. There, we consider the question of reading practices. Chapter 5 is concerned with the issue of how relations of difference within communities structure relations of love and hate between communities, and then explores what such lost subjects have to say to the antiracist curriculum. Chapter 6 is a meditation on loss and the work of mourning in education as it wrestles with learning from the difficult histories of reception and pedagogy in Anne Frank's *Diary*. Taken together, all the chapters consider the specificities of identity, history, and difficult knowledge, in psychic time—an uncanny time in which the larger arguments of history, whether known or not, lives in the small history of the subject.

Perhaps we might have a theory of dreams. With it, we might risk interpretations of the operatic dreams of education. The metaphors and associations I am after, and perhaps that are after me, return to Freud's first method of free association—the things furthest from the mind—an association that might be interested in freedom and its interminable symptoms. "What we actually mean by free association," writes analyst Karen Horney, "is the purposelessness of mental productions. There is no immediate purpose other than this: letting things emerge."[29] We can refind these lost things in education as well. In the chapters that follow, my interest in a certain psychoanalysis is closer to what Adam Phillips calls a "post-Freudian Freudianism,"[30] a time to consider a learning in which there can be no experts, in which curiosity is incited and the demand of education meets those other demands and then does something more. The "post" is that strange time of learning when one can get lost in thoughts: when the inside meets the outside and the outside meets the inside. We can return to one of Sigmund Freud's last inconsolable essays, "Analysis Terminable and Interminable," in which he speaks of "the slow progress of analysis" (219) and then returns to the ego's mechanisms of defense to consider again the instincts of love and hate. Freud returns the question of education back to the educator: "Instead of an enquiry into how a cure by analysis comes about . . . the question should be asked of what are the obstacles that stand in the way of such a cure" (221). In his "post-Freudian" fashion, Adam Phillips, in *Terrors and Experts*, poses more difficulties: "There may, sometimes, be a cure for symptoms, but there is no cure for the unconscious, no solution for unconscious desire. Knowledge can't put a stop to that, only death can" (7).

Chapter One

The Arts of Getting By

What is argued within the constitution will not be that
which is argued within art, or within the arts of
getting by, or on the couch or on the street.
Yet nor are these domains given boundaries—
the different arguments cross, recross, regroup
and seek to have effect. . . . The "freedom" or
"tyranny" of a society is in part to be measured
by the capacity to tolerate or crush the
difference between domains.

—Adams, *The Emptiness of the Image*

This chapter belongs to a place that Elisabeth Young-Bruehl comically terms "a
different planet of discourse," the indirection of psychoanalysis.[1] We will mag-
nify the question of learning, perhaps the most intimate for each of us, because the
contentions noted above are lived psychically, in an imaginary state of perpetual
emergency. In that other place, freedom and tyranny coexist in a volatile combination and regroup impulsively, but now in a theory of learning. Across the spectrum of education, the arguments between the domains of law and life return in
smaller events such as the curriculum, the school rule, the university grade, the
peer relations, the community demand, the teacher's intervention, and the student's refusal. Practices such as these lend their intrigue to all kinds of ambivalent
relations that act upon and within the work of learning. A fugitive moment is also
at stake, something more impertinent than the old story of adaptation, conformity,
and compliance to the law, something quite elusive, called here "the arts of getting by." What, in education, do the arts of getting by mean to that other art, the art
of learning? How do learners work through, and get stuck in, all the conflictive

23

representations and theories of learning offered by the course of their life in education? What obscure relations work within the capacity to think, to live, to love, and to dream as if learning were the self's own work of art?

If these tiny questions are to become as urgent as the large ones we typically ask of education, we must pause to question why the daily worry over "getting by"—rather than the study of the "arts of getting by"—has overwhelmed educational discourse. The loneliness of the former phrase returns as accusation, excuse, and anxiety, and can make only literal, and inconsequential to learning, such familiar survival strategies as slipping between the cracks of attention, doing just enough so as not to draw attention to oneself, doing less than what might be done, squeaking by, indeed making oneself disappear right before the teacher's eyes. These furtive movements might be thought of as the learner's means to defend herself or himself against the demands of educators or, more pertinently, against the demands of learning. And the turning inward, a turn away from what is perceived as a threat from the outside, may well be just a fragile place to begin thinking, if the educator's response to these moves is not to become a further diminishment. To view the learner's strategies in this way—as being at odds with the demands of law and life—and to consider what else might happen to these psychic acts across the spectrum of education, requires a conceptualization of learning that can bear its own otherness.

If one could write the history of education's response to the psychic events of learning, the result might be the history of the woeful disregard of the work of conflict in learning. Listen to an early formulation of the argument between law and life offered by Siegfried Bernfeld who, in a 1925 polemic, characterized the ambivalent views on education of a public caught between "a tolerance for the ideas of education [and] a resolute and cold disbelief in its programs, means, and promises."[2] As Bernfeld saw it, the tension is stronger than what emerges from the banal statement that in theory education is a good idea, that is, until it collapses from the weight of its own practice. One might say the same thing of theories of childhood or, for that matter, adulthood. We shall put into suspicion the implicit theory of learning that forces such sentiments. For if the vicissitudes of learning—in all of its detours, hesitations, ambivalences, and mistakes—are viewed as intolerable, as an interruption, or as the outside to the real work of education, then learning can be confined only to the small corner of correction, adjustment, and accumulation. Yet even what is placed outside of education, what seems lost to education, somehow makes its way back to education, this time in the form of objection: as wrong answer, irrelevancy, whisper, secret, and according to Bernfeld, "cold disbelief."

Bernfeld's depiction of his hot and cold public is not the same as what we might say in our present, a time when still, it seems, education both in theory and in practice is looked upon incredulously. No, ours is not the same ambivalence Bernfeld presses, even though today the arguments over "theory and practice" and over what should count as education debated in schools and in universities are reminiscent of how, in Michel Foucault's terms, everything becomes dangerous.[3] Bernfeld places ambivalence at the very heart of the promise of education, within the work of learning itself. This dynamic is captured in the anxious title of his polemic: *Sisyphus or the Limits of Education.* The image it offers seems to set into commotion sheer desire and interminable tasks, perhaps lending some insight into the phrasing "between a rock and a hard place." In this forgotten text, educational theory cannot be distinguished from educational practice. This is because, as Bernfeld states at the beginning, "No theory of education can resolve the antinomy between the justified will of the child and the justified will of the teacher; on the contrary, education consists of this antinomy" (xxvii).

If the consolation of theory cannot diminish the antinomy between the teacher and the learner, neither can, for Bernfeld, the resolution we call "practice." The interminable question becomes how to make learning a work of art within and from the stuff of antinomy. Bernfeld arrives at this antinomy by way of a definition of education that confounds the boundary between school and life and between the educated and the uneducated discussed in the Introduction. Education, writes Bernfeld, is "the reaction of society to the fact of development" (90). Much later, Young-Bruehl would define adolescence in the same way, as "the sum of prejudices directed at puberty in a given societal time and place."[4] And while each definition resonates with Anna Freud's view of education as constituting all forms of interference, for these narrators of education the reaction formation at stake is the adult's attempt, through educational efforts, to master and to ignore "the fact of development." What "facts" are we considering?

Bernfeld argued that adults cannot tolerate the immature learner—its mistakes, fantasies, accidents, and detours—for this immature learner reminds adults of their former selves and present failings, even as this learner stands in as a measure to the achievements of adults. In our time, analyst Aldo Carotenuto terms this lack of tolerance for the anxiety that inaugurates learning "the frustration of insignificance."[5] Carotenuto's phrasing refers to the ways individuals defend themselves against acknowledgment of the import of their own limits, vulnerabilities, and culs-de-sac in their own quest for meaning and relationality. The quest is frustrated by the impatient response of both teachers and students when something cannot measure up, indeed when what is given up is the capacity to tolerate learning.

What then is lost when insignificance or meaninglessness cannot be tolerated? Analyst Alice Balint suggests that the fear of insignificance mobilizes the ego's defense.[6] The ego defends its own narcissism in an attempt to preserve its wish to be omnipotent. Having to learn something is actually felt as an injury to narcissism, for learning reminds the learner that the ego is not all. But when the experience of insignificance is ill-served, the very problem that learning requires—the making of significance from the drama of helplessness—does not go away. Rather the insignificance returns, as a threat that comes toward the learner.

The system of education is not designed to notice that learning occurs in belated time, and that accidents, chance, and frustration may well be the effects and not the derailing of any deliberate action on the part of the adult. According to Alice Balint, these blind spots, where "only the exertions of the educator are considered," shut out the serious work of the learner.[7] Nor is this system capable of working through the conflicts it unleashes when its own mistakes cannot be admitted and debated. Part of the antinomy that emerges from this place of loss can be observed in the adult's defensiveness, in acting as if the work of learning is only an authentication of, or an answer to, the question of the adult's capacity to control, to predict, and to measure. While such a stance often is not associated with the psychic demands of narcissism, the dynamics underlying the push to be certain and to control set in motion new forms of anxiety that render unthinkable the chance to understand without recourse to mastery.

What exactly happens to the work of learning that surprises this defensive logic? First, the educator cannot recognize the learner's logic—and learners know this. From the learner's vantage, the adults cannot understand, cannot remember, their own antinomies, awkwardness, and hesitations in learning even as they may also represent something like what the learner wishes to become. Perhaps, from the learner's vantage, what seems most unfair is that while educators demand that students tolerate the postponing of immediate gratification for the sake of the hard work of learning, educators feed their own immediate gratification by setting the time of learning to the clock of their own efforts! Bernfeld calls this clash of time, the vulnerabilities at stake when two histories of learning are at stake, "the fact of development," which precipitates the frustrated Sisyphus: big Sisyphus and little Sisyphus. And because in Bernfeld's account two justified wills meet, it is difficult to determine who exactly stars in the role of Sisyphus.[8]

At first glance, Bernfeld's observations may seem relevant only to compulsory education, for it is there that the struggles between adults, adolescents, and children loom so large and are magnified in discourses of development and growth. While in higher education the terms of learning become less rhapsodic and even seem to disappear into the dreary language of excellence, expertise, and competence, the antinomy between the teacher and the student over the course of knowledge is strangely reminiscent of a longer and barely acknowledged history of learning. The thousands of hours everyone spends in compulsory education do not suddenly dissolve into nothingness when one enters university, when one goes to work, when one falls in love. Indeed, by the time one enters university either as a teacher or as a student, one is already haunted by conflictive versions not just of education but also of what it means to learn and what efforts get to count as learning. Even though the manifest story of higher education is a story of reason and rationality, the latent content is more contentious: justified wills continue to clash as new editions of old learning conflicts are played out. Our Sisyphus may age, but its theory of learning still resides somewhere between the mystical thinking of childhood dependency and the superstitions of institutional design. Perhaps for this reason we can stretch, across the spectrum of education, Alice Balint's insistence that "education begins at an age at which it is too early for us to be able to count on understanding."[9]

There is a long tradition of attempts to understand the curious time of learning. Siegfried Bernfeld's text was an early attempt to combine a Freudian frame (or, "the crowded couch") that emphasized the question of group psychology and libidinal ties with a Socialist politic (or, "the crowded street") that demanded an equitable distribution of material comfort and meaningful work. In his investigation of the limits of education, Bernfeld considered two fragile contours: the big relation between education and social justice and the reasons for its precariousness and the limits between children and adults, just as interminable and perhaps similar, which structure not only relations between these subjects but also within each self.

In considering the limit between education and social justice, Bernfeld works backward, and here he is at his most polemical. Education becomes limited when it is indistinguishable from hatred and discrimination. Bernfeld breaks his narrative with a fictional interlude that introduces the reader to the delusions of "Citizen Machiavelli," minister of education, in charge of planning for an authoritarian education. The surprise for us is that this citizen's insight into group psychology allows him to posit a suitable object of derision and position educators as the "leaders" able to bind the community of education with ties of love and hatred. Says the citizen: "We put our youth and then the entire population in a state of panic fear: a sinister power threatens them and we come forward as their saviour and leader. Read Professor Freud's *Group Psychology* and you will be convinced that my plan will succeed" (76). Later, the citizen recommends that the Jews be appointed to serve as the threat to group cohesion. Only in terrible retrospect can Citizen Machiavelli be understood as a precursor to the ties education would establish with national socialism and fascism.

We will return to the "state of panic fear" to contrast it to the angst that pushes a difference within learning and that, perhaps, can bear to grapple with the interminability of education and social justice. But now let us consider, by way of a contrast, how Bernfeld's example questions the leader's manipulation of the follower's libidinal ties. Analyst Hans Sachs may be helpful in that he considered the question of affects in learning. Sachs opposed the work of leaders to the work of artists: "The leader retains all of his narcissism; he too wants to dominate the affects of his followers . . . in order to use them as instruments for his own purposes. . . . [The artist] wants their affects, but without ulterior motive."[10] With this comparison we can raise the question of what education wants from its subjects. In the confrontation between the ulterior motive and the desire for whatever, we not only have two different models of pedagogy but also the two considerable questions of subjectivity and its passions. For education must after all address the affects if teachers and students are to attach to knowledge and each other. But the teacher, in this view, can be more like an artist to consider her or his work as crafting the conditions of libidinality in learning as opposed to hardening her or his authority.

Bernfeld, too, is interested in something beyond the cruel twists of social determination, ulterior motive, and "state of panic fear." Because his book is about limits of education, Bernfeld also must situate himself within the contradiction between, on the one hand, authority and its discontent, and, on the other hand, the frontier of desire and its articulation. Pressing the intimate antinomy of psychic resiliency, Bernfeld notes that both aggression and love can "endure a thousand repressions and though altered in shape and aim, ineluctably press toward satisfaction" (21–22). In this view, the instincts are infinitely flexible and variable in both aim and object. This is the creative possibility that addresses education and that education might address. And yet the mode of address at stake is not settled by immediate gratification. For if psychic resiliency is claimed, it then becomes impossible ever to know how "the system of accidents" (110) that compose the life of an individual is actually affected by the deliberations of pedagogy or culture. Even the suppositions of psychoanalysis, itself a belated form of knowledge, can make sense only retrospectively of "the system of accidents," or psychic life. But, for Bernfeld, the limits of education have many tributaries: a given political system, a given culture, a given educational theory and practice, and then a given psychological make-up of adults and children. He added one more tributary: the psychological make-up of "that variant of adulthood—the teacher" (xxi). Here the facts of development meet the development of a fact and the antinomy known as education can begin.

We might venture to place Bernfeld in a specific history, a moment when education and psychoanalysis seemed almost to converge. Still, not all convergence is desirable, for to maintain a difference between these two domains also may allow the actors involved more room to maneuver. For a time, however, this chapter returns to some early figures in this history, notably Siegfried Bernfeld, August Aichhorn and Anna Freud, to consider the challenges they offered to education and to theories of learning. The return is not an exercise in dusting off suitable historical antecedents that can then render our contemporary present continuous with our past. As suggested in the opening of this chapter, to act as if education is or even should be a site of continuity and a movement toward resolution shuts out consideration of how discontinuity, difference, and learning might be the conditions of passionate subjectivity.

Moreover, the figures under study here, perhaps now just a footnote in a curious history, are too contradictory, too situated in their own historical antinomies to console through the trope of continuity. They warned their public against the function of leaders in educational discourse and may even allow us to suspect our own contemporary discourses on leadership. Even with these warnings, the analysts's own flaws and blind spots should make contemporary readers quite suspicious of some of the categories presented and urged. Our return to them is not limited by the need to disapprove of their theories so much as it is an attempt to suggest the need to trouble our own. For psychoanalytic discourses on learning not only proffer a conceptualization of the vicissitudes of organizing psychical experience; more crucially, this "different planet of discourse" provides the means to deepen concern for what the crafting of dignity has to do with the arts of learning. In our selective account, we shall try to stay close to the intimacies of relations that go under the question of education, placing in question the curious events of psychic structure and educational design. Then we will attempt to comment differently on our own contemporary limits, our own arts of getting by.

Education and Psychoanalysis?

The bringing together of education and psychoanalysis has a difficult history, in which each field's consideration of the time of development confounds the desire for any synthesis. We meet, again, two justified wills. The relations between these fields seem to perform the psychoanalytic definition of learning and development: new editions of old conflicts.[11] In my own attempt to study these relations, I began with a rather romantic question: Why can education not tolerate psychoanalysis? My answer, however—that education cannot tolerate the unconscious and hence the flaws of any perception—did not, at first, temper my desire to elevate psychoanalysis with the wish that its insights would rescue education. My surprise was that this rescue fantasy is not outside of the history between these two fields. But my question, like all beginning romances, ignored the antinomy within each field, and how the arguments within returned to structure the arguments between them. If either field is offered as "cure" one loses the elusiveness of the subject in question. One loses the question.[12]

The tensions each dynamic opens are the starting point for analyst Michael Balint, who critiques psychoanalytic phobia of pedagogy. Balint argues that analytic critiques against education have concerned themselves only with one kind of pedagogy, that which considers "the restrictions imposed by society on the individual, such as those in regard to cleanliness, feelings of shame and disgust, pity, aesthetics, morals, reverence, etc. These are the feelings which draw their strength from the superego."[13] But in reducing pedagogy to the education of the superego, analytic discourse has not yet addressed its own pedagogical potential and hence has not considered a more creative notion of pedagogy. Balint goes on to argue that, in the pedagogical orientation to analysis, the analyst must discern that more than the superego is at stake in learning. In fact, Balint posits the view that, because learning has much to do with becoming experienced, it is the bodily ego that pedagogy and analysis must address. And yet, as we shall see, the bringing into tension of education and psychoanalysis, as "two justified wills," often seems to dissipate into a battle of superegos.

The attempt to historicize the relation between education and psychoanalysis typically has been organized through study of its central figures,[14] study of social trauma, like war and discrimination,[15] study of childhood,[16] accounts by analysts of their work with children,[17] and studies on the question of learning.[18] While psychoanalysis must be interested in education because childhood and learning are the material of its theories, the psychology that has most affected educational efforts and the education of educators wavers between the desexualized pole of Skinnerian behaviorism and the rhapsodic boundlessness of humanistic psychology.[19]

As a discourse and a set of institutional structures, education has a history of refusing to conceptualize the dynamical interference known as the unconscious,[20] an invention that, in the words of Nicholas Rand, "introduced a principle of noncoherence at the root of identity . . . [and regards this noncoherence] as the very foundation of any form of identity."[21] The unconscious is a paradox, other to education and to consciousness, other to the wish to stabilize and to divide the outside from the inside. Unlike the ego, the unconscious does not require reality as a test of its wishes. But the noncoherence that inaugurates the subject's fragility in identity and in the social is not itself the problem. Rather, what places education at stake is its response to the question of the unconscious.

Both for psychoanalysis and for education, there is something deeply disturbing about psychoanalytic theories of learning (which are indistinguishable from theories of the self): how learning is put into question; how the work of learning puts the self into question; how this work can reverse its content and turn against the learner; and, how learning becomes entangled in the vicissitudes of unhappiness, suffering, conflict, accident, and desire. In analytic views, learning is a psychic event, a moment when the difference between affect and cognition, between perception and interpretation, between desire and defense, and between being and having cannot be determined. Nor can there be a fine fit between either the desire for knowledge and the thing to be learned or the knowledge offered and the lives that are lived. Something unravels the narrative's coherence, something interferes with the individual intention, something resists knowledge. Adam Phillips thus puts the analytic dilemma called "learning": "In psychoanalysis, at least, answers are not a cure for questions."[22]

These tensions of learning are illustrated in Freud's 1925 essay, "On Negation." At first glance, the concept of 'negation' signals a way to refuse an idea and thus sever relationality. Freud offers complications, by-passing the "no" to restore a relation and magnifying the ideas that surround the no. Then, negation becomes an ambivalent form of thought, capable of subverting and resisting itself: a thought caught within the fault lines of its own acts, a simultaneous yes and no. "Negation," Freud writes, "is a way of taking cognizance of what is repressed; indeed it is already a lifting of the repression; though not, of course, an acceptance of what is repressed" (235–36). Our subject is caught between intellect and affect, between judgment and its consequences. Freud also reverses the order of judgment, suggesting that judgment does not begin with the ego's capacity to reality test, but rather with the ego's pleasure principle. Negation, he speculates, is a repetition of the oldest form of intellectual judgment, the separation of good and bad, a form that precedes and inaugurates the next division: the ego's capacity to distinguish between the inside and the outside, the subjective and the objective, and the interest in attributing judgment to reality testing. In this strange order of perception, the ego's capacity to judge and the ego's work of attempting to satisfy instinctual pressure occur simultaneously. Just as instinct belongs to the pressures of Eros and Destruction, judgment belongs to affirmation and destruction. The odd time of grammar embodied in the statements, "I didn't (ever) think of that" or "I would never think that," allows the ego to experiment with a form of thought besides itself and within itself. In this view, negation is quite a central strategy of perception, and Freud then tentatively concludes: "on our hypothesis, perception is not a purely passive process" (238). If negation is a means for the ego to take in the good and expel the bad, we also might say that perception must be a passionate relation, an attempt to attach or bind and undo or unbind the precarious boundaries played out in the name of reality testing. If the ego's work of perception is so entwined within its capacity to make judgments, these judgments, as both psychoanalysis and education suggest, still can be surprised through interpretation. But then, even interpretation cannot be mistaken, to return to Adam Phillips's point, for a cure for questions. Indeed, we must read around the idea and the affect.

Surely psychoanalysis renders its own consolations and the consolations of education inconsolable. It does so in the ways psychoanalytic thought studies the actions of learning and the actions involved in the refusal to learn. Analysts are as curious as to why meaning holds together as they are in their explorations of why meaning falls apart. There is an interest in studying why it is so difficult to learn from experience, how encrypted secrets return in the strange form of jumbled discourse, why the making of enemies and friends is so important in life, and even how becoming bored takes effort.[23] The study of learning is a study of how individuals attach, displace, forget, and disengage knowledge. And with these moves, the study of learning is inseparable from the study of love.[24]

The paradox is that learning is provoked in the failure to learn. The ego first attempts to extend itself through what Alice Balint called "identificatory thinking,"[25] the strategy of taking in what is, after all, other to itself. The move to take in what is outside, however necessary, is insufficient and flawed, because identificatory thinking is the ego's means to console itself, to defend itself against its own anxiety. Balint maintains that identificatory thinking is not yet understanding. In her words, "identification tends to do away with the separation between the ego and the external world, while it is a necessary condition of loving that we should recognize the fact that something else exists outside ourselves" (322–23). Learning is not a "mental mimicry" (326) but an interminable experiment, a crafting of identification into understanding.

Even one of the forms of thought most valued in education—intellectualization—is viewed with suspicion, not because one should not abstract thought, or because thinking is somehow beside the point, but because, when analysts consider how individuals intellectualize their lives, their social, and their political commitments, they consider such actions as the ego's attempt to defend itself. Something more than an idea is at stake in intellectualization.

Anna Freud names intellectualization—or the ways one abstracts thoughts, raises the big questions, and becomes preoccupied with or lost in theoretical constructs—one of the ego's special ways of defending itself against a quantity of instinctual pressure.[26] She describes intellectualization as "the thinking over of instinctual conflict" (161), having come to this view in her work with adolescents. In the analytic context, Miss Freud noticed that while some of her young analysands had terrific ideas, these ideas did not influence their actions. Instead, the intellectualization of their lives was a form of intense self-absorption and a defense against their worries. Because intellectualization is an ego defense, it can serve as a means to berate others, to punish others with moral discourse. The trouble Anna Freud raised with her concept of 'defense,' however, is not that we need more adequate reasons to think or that we need to search for an authentic intellection somehow capable of constructing a thought that can exceed the thinker's own psychical dynamics; rather, she wondered how individuals come to consider the ethics of intellectualization and become implicated in their own views, denouncements, and desires. Can education be a place where thoughts not only are troubled but are troubled to explore how our thoughts get us in and out of trouble?

This strange collection of preoccupations is similar to an assumption Lyotard pointed out in his discussion of the difference between "data" (the accumulation of information stored in machines) and "thought" (the self's capacity to grapple with the making of significance): "Thinking and suffering overlap."[27] In psychoanalytic terms, for the self to be more than a prisoner of its own narcissism, the self must bother itself. It must learn to obligate itself to notice the breaches and losses between acts and thoughts, between wishes and responsibilities, between dreams and waking life. To think is to haunt one's thoughts, to be haunted by thoughts.

Such a strange orientation may bother two curative views of thought in education that banish doubt, ambivalence, and the irreducibility of loss: reflective practice and critical thinking. Whereas reflective practice has been reduced to the utility of correcting practices and devotes itself to propping up the practitioners' control and mastery, critical thinking skills valorize the quest for a rationality that can settle the trouble that inaugurates thought. The problem is that thought is not reducible to finding the proper data. Moreover, these two solutions to thought must ignore a kind of thinking that is other to social utility, the logic of otherness called "daydreams," "fantasy," and "playing with ideas." These forms of thought are without alibi, agreement, or social sanction. Possessing their own psychical value, these little epics allow the self new risks, imaginative elaborations, and attachments. In education, however, this unanticipated work typically is relegated to irrelevancy, to losing the point, to being off the subject, to wasting time.

Psychoanalytic views on thinking and learning press the argument over whether education can be a place for individuals to associate freely, to render thinking interminable, to confront the obligations that are made in learning, and to approach the difficult relation between affect and thought. But there is also something more that makes analytic views of learning so difficult for education, having to do with what the unconscious might mean in dynamics in learning: the ways history repeats itself, the ways desire attaches to and roams away from ideas, the ways interpretation and perception must entangle and be fundamentally flawed. Surprising questions then can be asked, such as the one offered by Christopher Bollas in his consideration of history: "Do we have to choose between the imagined and the happened? Are they opposed?"[28]

A History of Antinomy?

The different understandings of how learning is conceptualized, when learning begins, and where learning breaks down have played havoc in attempts, on the part of educators and psychoanalysts, to bring these fields closer. Ekstein and Motto described three co-extensive dynamics in such attempts: (1) when the projects of psychoanalysis and education were posed as indistinguishable; (2) when the project of psychoanalysis was used as a means to critique educational methods; and (3) when the project of psychoanalysis was offered as a means to cure the neurosis either of the teacher or of the student.[29] We will add a few more attempts to this characterization: (4) when the differences between the projects of psychoanalysis and education were highlighted by attention to culture; and (5) when the project of psychoanalysis began to focus on questions of creativity in education and in psychic elaborations.

In the early relations between education and psychoanalysis, analysts in and close to Freud's circle argued that the dynamical qualities of each field were indistinguishable. This is because psychoanalysis has centered two relations that structure the earliest forms of object relations in learning: those of love and those of authority. Freud made a name for the exchange of love and authority for learning: transference. Transference is perhaps the most central dynamic of time and space that organizes and stalls the practices of learning. The compromised and condensed time of transference catches the "then and there" of the past and the "here and now" of the present.[30] As a mode of address, the message is derivative of something else, reminiscent of another scene but uncanny in its present urgency. As a means to question how individuals attempt understanding, the concept of 'transference' must be imprecise for its relational reach exceeds conscious intentions and its movements are back and forth and conjure a panorama of affective ties and their libidinal history.

Psychoanalysis assumes that libidinal ties are reminiscent of an earlier history of an individual's ties to and strategies with significant others that are re-animated in new situations. Put more directly, the infantile strategies of attempting to rescue or secure the love one wants from another do not go away but are instead elaborated throughout a life. Still, in the attempt to put the question of love more directly, something escapes notice. Analyst Otto Fenichel noticed that what is actually demanded in the demand for that first love is closer to the child's (unconscious) desire to be the parent rather than to have the parent's love. The child desires the parent's position: "The child's longing for love and affection [from those first others] is simultaneous longing for participation in their omnipotence."[31] If we consider this dynamic in an educational context, we might say that the student desires to be as important and as all knowing as she/he imagines the teacher to be; the student desires the teacher's omnipotent position. Enacted here is what Alice Balint termed "identificatory thinking," a means of clinging not yet replaced with understanding.

The terms of transference suggest something yet to be resolved, something that, perhaps by its very nature, resists resolution. What is transferred to the new encounter is not the content of the old relationship but the dynamical force of affects—including the resistance to the relation. Along with the transference of love and authority onto a new figure (and here the figure can be an idea as well as an actual person), transferred as well are the old conflicts and resistances made from the experience of giving oneself over to the need for love, and of having to give love when one does not wish to. We are considering the struggles against submitting to authority—not wanting to give oneself over to love, being unable to tolerate the helplessness that love requires— and, the desire to be the authority for the other. In addition to the transference that conditions the condition of learning, Freud distinguished in that relation a residue made from a new anxiety he called "transference neurosis," a problem analysis actually induces.

Transference neurosis begins when the problem becomes the analysis, that is to say, when the problem becomes not what is to be learned but the act of learning itself. This move differs from the demand to be critical, for even in that demand one's own denials and aggressions can remain through the mask of intellectualization. In educational terms, transference neurosis inaugurates a new kind of anxiety. Something more is placed at stake than the specific learning at hand: a theory of learning, an implication in the investigation into how one learns.[32] If, as Karen Horney argues, "in every neurosis there is a check on vitality,"[33] transference neurosis is an invitation to explore the conditions required to restore one's lost vitality.

There are, however, crucial differences in how authority and love become symbolized in transferential relations of learning played out in formal education. In Freud's view, the teacher unconsciously reminds the student of her or his own parental authority, and through the figure of the teacher the student again encounters the desire for the teacher's knowledge and love. In Shoshana

Felman's account of the transference in university classrooms, the student desires the teacher's knowledge, for this knowledge is viewed as securing the position of authority.[34] Felman argues that this illusion, itself a symptom of the desire for omnipotence, must be broken if the learner is to render as a problem and as a question her or his own relation to and desires in knowledge. The learner must confront the fragility of all knowledge and the meaning of the wish for mastery. The source of authority may be seen as residing in the teacher's body or in the body of knowledge that seems to possess the teacher; but in both cases, because the relation is built from the old dynamics of previous relations, as a transferential relation, learning is defined ambivalently, as a new edition of old conflicts between wanting to have the love and knowledge of another and wanting to be the knowledge and love for the other. Our first movement of psychoanalysis and education, then, highlighted the transference as the imaginary grounds of learning. For this romance to be accepted, however, significant differences between the fields were ignored.

The differences between education and psychoanalysis structured the second and the third strange relationships. One might say that the romance came to a bitter end, for in the next movements the project of psychoanalysis viewed itself as a corrective force to educationally induced neurosis. Analysts continued to insist that education repressed instinctual drives, although, in early formulations of the conflict between pleasure and reality, the questions of how one can moderate internal conflict, how one interprets pleasure and reality, and how the individual comes to participate well with others were ignored.[35] The concept of transference was extended to a consideration of the teacher's own countertransference of her or his childhood conflicts onto the screen of the student, the curriculum, and pedagogical strategies. Obstacles to learning were examined as the second and third movements focused on educational neurosis and its structure of denial. Anna Freud was quite clear about the effects of denial in educational design when she noted that analysts "cannot help but see education from its worst aspect."[36] Even more explicit is another of her observations: "psychoanalysis so far has stood for limiting the efforts of education" (123). We have, in this last wish to limit education, not the limit of education but the thought that education limits learning.

Within the field of education, there were comparable critiques that centered upon what Karen Horney called "neurotic trends," or the persistent, repetitious, and routinized ways students and teachers disassociate from implicating themselves in their own psychic events.[37] This after all is the common defense mechanism of the family romance. The consideration of specific disturbances of educationally induced neurosis, defined along the lines articulated by Young-Bruehl as "rigid, compulsive, irrational [and] maladaptive behaviours,"[38] allowed for the critique of mass experiences such as conformity in education, repression of sexuality, and curriculum glosses over the difficulties and conflicts in life. Christopher Bollas would come to see these educational forms of repudiation as "the violence of innocence" or "the subject's denial of the other's perspective," and the refusal to see this disregard as a provocation of suffering.[39] But such critiques also were being made from within education: in Willard Waller's first sociology of education, Louise Rosenblatt's arguments for the use of literature to explore instinctual conflicts and to learn to refuse fascist world views, and Maxine Greene's existential account of anomie and commitment in teaching.[40]

In one of the early attempts by an educator to grasp the vicissitudes of psychical dynamics from the vantage of the teacher's world, Arthur Jersild studied how teachers consider anxiety, aggression, hostility, loneliness, meaninglessness, and discouragement. Jersild pressed the point that, while experienced individually, these affects are intimately tied to, and provoked by, the structure of educational thought. Even though anxiety is not a key concept in education or in theories of learning, Jersild maintained that "the history of education . . . is in part a history of [people's] efforts to evade or to face anxiety."[41] This returns us momentarily to Bernfeld, and we might as well define education as the society's response to psychic design. But the evasions—or, to use Bollas's terms, "the violence of innocence"—are slippery. More often than not, as Jersild came to find, the denials that sustain the fronts one puts up to evade anxiety are usually those that are socially acceptable, even as they serve precariously to block out the threatening and difficult truths of ordinary fragilities. Here are two of Jersild's observations on daily life in education: "There is anxiety when the aggressive people who habitually dominate educational meetings suspect (by the intensity of their impatience when other people are talking), but dare not face the thought, that they talk so much because of a compulsion to talk rather than because they have so much to contribute. There is anxiety, likewise, if those who do not talk, but would like to, feel tense and aggrieved but do nothing about it" (28).

To consider the ways neurotic action abounds in its disguises, Jersild asked educators to confront how unconscious conflict lives in, and seems to be disclaimed by, their conscious activity. The question he posed to educational conduct was quite interminable, and it had to do with how actions defend the actor from acknowledging her or his own unhappiness and from viewing the ripples of her or his dissatisfaction. In posing social behavior as signalling both a manifest and a latent content, Jersild began to interpret the dream of education as a wish to forget the fragility of its own institutional design and dreams, the fragility of its subjects.

Our early analysts, those closest to Freud's analytic circle or analyzed by that circle, might be in agreement with Jersild's consideration of what living a life in education means. This, after all, was one of their great problems. Within the first three dynamics noted, the attempt to bring psychoanalytic insight to education began in a very specific historical context: war, genocide, and, for some, a life in exile. The early analysts' theories emerged from a deep meditation on the immense capacity for human cruelty and on the vulnerabilities made in suffering. Today we might view these theories as a form of protest against social breakdown and the twentieth-century events of the mass psychosis called "war."[42] The questions raised in these theories rendered the design of education without an alibi: What is the relation between education and social aggression? What are the social bonds and obligations of education? Can psychical conflict be educated to exceed its repetitions? These projects to bring psychoanalysis and education into closer contact continued to waver between the view that education can address the vicissitudes of the instincts and the view that education can address only the ego and its own vicissitudes of defense. Alice Balint would formulate the problem of address differently: "The relation between the ego and the external world is after all the main problem of all educative measures."[43]

Questions of the location of potential relations—between the self and the others and the self in the contiguity of cultural experiences—characterize the fourth movement of psychoanalysis and education. D. W. Winnicott's concept of 'cultural experience' and his attempt at finding its location was a means to consider what he thought of as a forgotten question both in psychoanalysis and in education: "What is life about?"[44] Winnicott named cultural experience as a third area, something in-between psychic reality and outside reality, something "derivative of play" (102). Whereas Winnicott attended to the human's capacity to craft and to live within potential spaces, analyst Maud Mannoni considered the significance of language as a site of relationality and cultural experiences.

Maud Mannoni's note on the difficult relations between psychoanalysis and education brought her to a more systemic look at the institutional culture and psychology of education.[45] She argued that there were significant differences between the work of teaching and the work of analysis. These differences occasionally would be noted by an earlier generation, but they were not considered in their ethnographic glory until anthropologists (such as Margaret Mead) and analysts influenced by the cultural specificities of psychical structure (such as Eric Erikson) began to study education and childhood as widely varying cultural and historical dynamics.[46]

Mannoni points out that the analyst and the analysand are in intimate relation; the room where such dialogue is made takes its rules from the reading of fiction, where even the most minute and obscure detail may surprise with its relevancy. The classroom has a different set of concerns even as its fictions become animated in teaching and learning. Classroom discourse, however, is not dependent upon free association. Education demands that everyone get to the point. Nor are individual psychic dynamics the entire story of exchange in classroom settings. Whereas many of the early analysts argued for the need for teachers to be analyzed, Mannoni believes it was not practical to ask that teachers be analyzed for them to participate well in the education of others. It might do just as well if a psychoanalyst works within educational institutions and begins, together with those involved in their places, to reconstruct collectively a psychic anthropology into the neurosis of institutions, those compromise formations made from the psychical conflicts of wishes, desires, and defense.[47] Everyone involved in the institution, Mannoni goes on to argue, might consider a few psychoanalytic concepts for the purposes of making more interesting group psychology and group dynamics in learning. Then, psychoanalysis might be worked with best as a means to explore the making and undoing of community. In Mannoni's words: "Psychoanalysis has meaning only if it can be conducted from a position where the analytic spotlight makes it possible to change the language of education" (251).

Our fourth movement begins with respect for psychoanalytic narrative, the language of education, and cultural experiences. In a small way, talk between individuals, as in the capacity to respond well and not diminish the contingent work of making relations, is the central tie both in analysis and in education. In larger ways, institutions organize the rules of talk through policy, the organization of knowledge, age groupings, and so on. In centering questions of language and play, and hence experiences of desire, meaning, and the capacity to use objects, we move closer, momentarily, to a fifth movement between psychoanalysis and education, called here "the arts of getting by." But even in these relations, psychoanalysis does not give up on the critique of education, for much in its method engages the breakdowns, the hesitations, the dreams, and the accidents that provoke unease, despair, and withdrawal from the risks of work and love. By our fifth movement, however, some of the old repetitions that populated earlier formulations of the relation between psychoanalysis and education—such as the normal and the pathological, adaptation and discontentment, and knowledge and ignorance, all of which, perhaps unconsciously, serve the elevation of a certain psychoanalysis over the obstacles and repressions of education—are understood differently. When the project of psychoanalysis began to focus on questions of creativity in education and in psychical elaborations, viewing these as a third area, questions of love and hate, of illusion and disillusion, of construction and destruction were brought closer to Winnicott's interminable question, "What is life about?" Writes Winnicott: "You may cure your patient and not know what it is that makes him or her go on living" (100). We can add, "You may educate your student but not know what it is that makes her or him go on with the work of learning."

This last concern in bringing a bit closer the relations of psychoanalysis and education emerges both from educators and from psychoanalysts. Contemporary analysts—such as Christopher Bollas in his exploration of the creative work of the human idiom, Adam Phillips in his meditations on the everyday strategies of making the details of a self, and Jessica Benjamin in her curiosity toward the strange return of domination in relations of love and hate—center the dynamical qualities of love and hate in learning a life. In education, Victoria Muñoz' study of the experiences of youth falling in and out of love for work examines how there is no single story of identity even as singular stories comment on the social's capacity and incapacity to tolerate the work of becoming somebody. The work of Alice Pitt, Sharon Todd, and Judith Robertson places the passionate genealogy of desire at the center of education.[48] These theorists open a reflection on the cultivation of, and the obstacles to, the creative force of the psyche and the creative forces of play. And perhaps they offer a way into Winnicott's strange question: "If play is neither inside nor outside, where is it?" (96). In so doing, they offer us stories of the arts of getting by. If such creative maneuvers of our subject are to be noticed, part of what educators will have to tolerate is a theory of learning that can creatively address and attempt to work through the vicissitudes of love and hate in learning. This requires a rethinking of the central questions that psychoanalysis poses to education and that education might pose to psychoanalysis.

From Neurotic Anxiety to Existential Angst

We know that Freud offered to education a different conceptualization of the persistent time of childhood and a view of learning that unsettled the notion of linear progress, upsetting the time we call "history." But those who responded to these ideas, because they practiced in education, focused their attention upon the social qualities of psychical life. Between 1925 and 1930, three early psychoanalytic educators, Siegfried Bernfeld, August Aichhorn, and Anna Freud, published books that responded to Freud's great emphasis on the centrality of early libidinal ties to learning, addressed most profoundly in his 1921 study, *Group Psychology and the Analysis of the Ego.*[49]

In that study, Freud struggled with affective questions that concerned individuals' susceptibility to culture, their libidinal or emotional ties to leaders, and the conservative nature of the group mind where individuals seem to lose easily their critical faculties. We find this emphasis in Bernfeld. While Freud's chief examples of group psychology stem from the organization of the church and the army, rather extreme forms of group obedience, he also mentions the school and children's concern for fairness with the roundabout observation that, within the family, children are forced to give up their hostility to one another because this would cost them the love of an adult. The fear of losing love is brought to the classroom: "So there grows up in the troop of children a communal or group feeling, which is then further developed at school. The first demand made by this reaction-formation is for justice, for equal treatment for all. We all know how loudly and implacably this claim is put forward at school. If one cannot be the favourite oneself, at all events nobody else shall be the favourite" (120). The demand to be equal is a sublimation of narcissism. In its most naive and aggressive moments, it also works as a means for individuals to keep each other in line, a formation quite common in compulsory school life. Freud viewed these demands for justice as an important transformation (a reversal of the content of hate into love) of an original hostility: rivalry, jealousy, and the demands of omnipotence. But he also called attention to the conflict such transformation requires and to the way original hostility may limit how groups imagine the qualities of equality and justice. And from this point, our psychoanalytic educators considered, in looking toward the questions raised in *Group Psychology*, whether and how education might engage its own conflictive dynamics, of which group psychology is the chief symptom.

The conflictive dynamics at stake are located on the frontier between the individual and the social. In education, the figure of the teacher attempts to guard this frontier with tactics that strangely resemble those of parents and leaders. Otto Fenichel reduced these strategies to three: "direct threat, mobilization of the fear of losing love, and the promise of special rewards."[50] What lends these threats and promises coherency, strength, and conviction is that they are the strategies that find and incite the superego as well. As repetitions, reminiscent of family dynamics, the strategies are not meant to invoke insight into the ethical dilemmas of thought or the harshness of life. Nor do these methods or strategies of address consider how they might sustain identificatory thinking as opposed to understanding. This is because the tricks invoke a rather rigid sense of guilt and fear, which then incite the ego's defenses.

In Freud's aside on the ways the students vie for the teacher's love, it seems as though the student must pass through the figure of the teacher on the way to knowledge. Freud named this passing moment "transferential relations of love."[51] The concept emerged from Freud's adult consideration of an accidental meeting on the street with a teacher from his past and of his surprise at how young the teacher seemed now that Freud, too, was an adult. Freud's theory of transference began with the puzzle of why as a student he viewed his teacher as so much older and wiser. Why do students take teachers so seriously that they even fantasize about the teacher's other life beyond the classroom? Freud's answer was that he transferred the love of his parents onto other adults; the libidinal ties of his youth were new editions of these old conflictive ties. What is transferred, then, are also the conflicts and ambivalences that love attempts to compromise. This may be why Freud, in one of his last lectures, notes the fact of transference as "on the one hand an instrument of irreplaceable value and on the other hand a source of serious dangers. The transference is ambivalent: it comprises positive (affectionate) as well as negative (hostile) attitudes towards [others]."[52] The love transferred is caught in its own dramatic acts, and sustaining this fragile tie without recourse to manipulation is just the beginning.

What Freud did not consider in the story of the accidental meeting is the teacher's view of the child and the adult that returns, years later, to register surprise. Our exploration of transference is still incomplete. There is another side to this story: the teacher's countertransference, or more simply what August Aichhorn calls the teacher's emotional response to the student.[53] And with this exchange, we might begin to understand why the three strategies educators depend upon seem so timeless, so obdurate, so reminiscent of the teacher's own childhood. Analyst J. B. Pontalis repeats, throughout his essay on countertransfer-

Countertransference

ence, the following axiom: "One cannot talk about countertransference in all truth, i.e. tell the truth about it."[54] Countertransference is a form of psychical representation of the analyst's resistance to the analysand. One cannot tell the truth about countertransference because the dynamic itself provokes a disavowal. What is resisted is the acknowledgment that the analysand affects the analyst's own feelings. We can see this in education when the teacher attempts to act as if the act of teaching could somehow be placed outside of the teacher's subjectivity, as if the teacher's own passion lost its force. Countertransference is there, in Pontalis's terms, when "our only protection and way out is to ascribe our own discomfort to the patient and to suppose that he *has an effect*— through silence, attacks, and absence *over* us and *within* us" (173–74). The countertransference induces the transference neurosis.

So far we have been considering the antinomy within and between the teacher's relations to the student. This strange course is the most charted throughout the relations between psychoanalysis and education. But there is a problem in positioning the teacher as the central moment in the student's learning. For in this view, what becomes lost is an analysis of one of the central fantasies of omnipotence in education: that there can be a direct link between teaching and learning and that both of these dynamics are a rational outcome of the teacher's conscious efforts. The supposition only returns us to Otto Fenichel's three strategies and serves as a disavowal of the very conflict that lends persistency to this wish for mastery. While the teacher creates her own countertransferential relations and may well imagine that the student somehow stands in for the teacher's old self, the insistence on the importance of the student and the teacher's libidinal ties to each other cannot be the whole story of education, if the story of education is to exceed the story of the family romance. The elevation of transferential love as the condition of learning places too much pressure on the teacher and the student and forecloses attention to other dynamics and antinomies in education. After all, not all teachers are charismatic figures; not all teachers' pedagogy depends upon their personality, even if the pedagogy is somehow tied to the teacher's identity; and not all students need the teacher to be an object of love or hate.

Bruno Bettelheim proffers a different sort of figure of the teacher, drawn from his work with parents.[55] The "good enough teacher" is one who transfers, in exchange for her or his love, not a learning but a demand that students learn to make their own demands in learning. The "good enough teacher" leans upon Winnicott's suggestion that the work of the "good enough" mother is composed of two different actions toward the infant, and upon the mother's own self: "active adaption to the infant's needs, an active adaptation that gradually lessens, according to the infant's growing ability to account for failure of adaptation and to tolerate the results of frustration."[56] The mother must help the infant in the illusion and in the disillusion of demand. The "good enough" teacher must engage the student's capacity for illusion and disillusion, the capacity to express and understand, and the capacity to tolerate times of being misunderstood and not understanding. The "good enough" teacher must also help herself in tolerating the results of her or his own frustration.

Bettelheim brought to education this notion of the teacher's work after studying a few heroic education texts, made popular in the early 1970s, in which the teacher seems to single-handedly move students from failure to success. This hero is quite familiar in educational lore, returning each year either to pick up an award or to play a starring role in a Hollywood film. For Bettelheim, the teacher as hero is more like a wish that disguises the larger social anxiety over the saving of children and adolescents and the teacher's desire for rescue fantasies.[57] For the "ordinary teacher," the problem is larger than the teacher's wish to be desired by the student: it is "how education can fortify the child's inner world to serve learning."[58]

With this move, Bettelheim seems a bit out of step with the first generation of child analysts.[59] Whereas his predecessors, such as Bernfeld and Aichhorn, were seen as charismatic and intuitive to the extent that their methodology could not in fact be taught, Bettelheim's discussion of psychoanalysis and education confronted the question of how desire for knowledge and the capacity for freedom might be cultivated within the experience of learning. He reminds teachers that their work cannot rest with sheer inspiration, the desire to love children, nor even, as did Aichhorn's work, depend upon the method of transferential relations of love. Perhaps closer to Bernfeld, who warned educators that the libidinal ties between them and the students are insufficient to the intellectual growth of all, Bettelheim argues that "diligence, concentration, and perseverance do not come about because of self-interest alone, but because of an irrational superego anxiety" (130). Something from within must pressure the learner. Fenichel describes this pressure as the beginning of a "twofold ethics," one set in tension when one feels oneself watched by an outside authority, and the other effective when one is alone.[60] What would education be like if it could engage in such a twofold ethic: watching itself as it watches others and watching itself when alone? Can a twofold ethic disturb the identificatory thinking that provokes "the violence of innocence"?

With the question of a twofold ethic, an ethic that can tolerate scrutinizing itself, we can tentatively posit that the work of education might attempt to transform neurotic anxiety into existential angst.[61] The move is to consider the vicissitudes of thought and suffering. Education might attempt to address the irrationality and violence of the superego (the irrationality that demands to be punished or to watch the punishments of others) and hence not exacerbate the superego's "compulsive character which manifests itself in the form of a categorical imperative."[62] Something from within must pressure the learner. But paradoxically, this pressure also must operate in the same ways the "good enough" teacher relates to the "good enough" student. Both positions must account for failure in ways that do not repeat its agony. This inside pressure must tolerate the illusion and disillusion that inaugurates learning.

Two problems are now apparent. One concerns the consequences of the educational imperative to settle meaning through its own insistence upon the proper definition, the correct answer, the stable reply, the passionless essay. What would education be like without its categorical imperatives? The other problem concerns the limits placed on learning when education addresses the superego as if it were synonymous to the law, or as if the superego were unaffected by its own history of love. "The irrational superego anxiety" that Bettelheim calls upon is provoked by the history of love from which the superego also draws. We are speaking here of the difference between two forms of anxiety: neurotic anxiety and existential angst. And while anxiety is the ego's special "expression of a retreat from danger,"[63] there is a difference in the qualities of that expression made from the ego's great decision as to what comes to count as a danger and a threat. Even these perceptions do not come out of nowhere. Erik Erikson speaks of "a community of egos," the way the social is lived in the individual, and then remarks on how "a kind of communality links egos in a mutual attraction. Something in the ego process then, something in the social process is—well, identical."[64] If education is to be a community of egos, a place where the ego ventures outward, the time of existential angst inaugurated in movement, then learning must begin with a question, must place the ego into question. We call this question "ethicality." To act ethically is already to place the act in question. For the ethical intention is no guarantee of ethicality. Indeed, the ethical cannot be guaranteed, only attempted and approached. We might say that existential anxiety, or the capacity for agony and concern, provides a possibility within which one attempts to do less harm in uncertainty, to risk the love of learning.

Bettelheim insists that learning is hard work and that, somehow, pleasure must be made from this reality principle. Educational design is challenged to figure ways for students and teachers to tolerate the difficulties of learning and to make insight from their own conflictive experiments in learning. Bettelheim is not arguing that education be based upon inhibition, rigidity, and cruelty, all authoritarian forms of fear that make irrational anxiety aggressive. He is concerned with how one learns to move from the early fear of losing the other's love—one of the central methods Fenichel notes—to "the fear of losing self-respect."[65] The paradox is that self-respect can be made only from relations with others, from "the community of egos," in that uncertain quest for freedom.

But the direction Bettelheim offers educators is more like an indirection. One has to do with taking Freud's elegant formulation of the goal of psychoanalysis to education: "Where id was, there ego shall be."[66] Before continuing with Bettelheim's consideration of how this sentence might implicate education, and further exploring the curious trajectory of love that it rests upon, we briefly return to the types of questions that provoked Freud's sentence. One question signaled the idea of *poiesis*, or the making and production of the ego. In an early discussion, Freud poses the ego as a bodily ego, undistinguished and capable of becoming.[67] The ego emerges from the id or unconscious, but its ties are not absolutely broken, nor are the boundaries ever solidified. Whereas the id is preoccupied with instincts, and from this bodily demand elaborates uncensored wishes, the ego's gradual work is to mediate the demands both of instincts and of the outside world. The ego's sole purpose is self-preservation.

Freud's early description of the relation between the ego and the id seems a bit bizarre in metaphor. At one instance he supposes that, unlike the id, the ego "wears a 'cap of hearing'—on one side only. . . . It might be said to wear it awry" (25). The ego hears selectively and through distortion. Freud likens the relation between the ego and the id to a horse and its rider: "Often a rider, if he is not to be parted from his horse, is obligated to guide it where it wants to go; so in the same way the ego is in the habit of transforming the id's will into action as if it were his own" (25). One might wonder about this sort of charge, but that would be beside the point; for the metaphor is not quite right, because the ego has difficulty distinguishing what is in charge.

To complicate matters even more, Freud introduces yet another part of the ego: its ideal, or what later will be called the "superego." This psychical agency emerges from the libidinal ties one has to parents and culture. Its poiesis occurs as the ego is developing, hence in its most fragile and dependent state. Now we have at stake the complicated question of social bond and the means by which authority is constituted. Freud considers this complication as sudden, violent, and leading to a dynamic outcome: "The character of the ego is a precipitate of abandoned object-cathexes and . . . it contains the history of those object-choices" (29). Thus the ego is transformed through its own history of love, by taking into itself the qualities of the loved object. The very poiesis of the ego sets in motion its ambivalence, fragility, and fault lines. We can now return to Freud's formulation of the work of psychoanalysis: "To strengthen the ego, to make it more independent of the super-ego, to widen its field of perception and enlarge its organization, so that it can appropriate fresh portions of the id. Where id was, there ego shall be. It is a work of culture—not unlike the draining of the Zuider Zee."[68] If education is that other work of culture, can it become a place where one's life continues its own work of art, a place where one encounters the vicissitudes of love, a place to refind the means whereby love of ideas can be made from the stuff of one's dreams, from the otherness offered from within, and from the otherness encountered in the world?

The transformation at stake, in order to risk love of work, was the movement noted by Ekstein and Motto: "from learning for love to love of learning." The shift of address is a practice that begins with the acknowledgment that, whereas transferential relations between the teacher and the student may be necessary for the student's interest in pleasing the teacher or in meeting the teacher's unconscious demands, the student also must be able to make her or his own demands to learn, in this process becoming curious about her or his own dynamics of learning. Then, the love that takes at first the form of dependency upon the teacher to ordain learning can become redirected, exceeding "identificatory thinking" that renders the ego rigid and incapable of participating in its own work of culture. The interminable goal is to craft a love and understand that it can tolerate the difference and the surprising relations that might be made between what we have been calling "the domains of law and life." But for this to occur the teacher must also reckon with her own psychic events.

The stakes of this movement—from learning for love to love of learning—gamble with how the student and the teacher risk engagement with new ideas, make new meanings, and question where the id can go. Identificatory thinking then might be wrested from its own impulses to deny the interminability of understanding. Then the ego or self might learn something from its capacity to take the libidinal object off its pedestal to create a new love that can tolerate the vicissitudes and vulnerability, the illusion and disillusion, that permits learning to be risked. What kind of love can be made in education? Can the ego's interest in the world be made more generous and flexible if the ego can work through, as opposed to becoming entangled in, its own libidinal ties? Can the ego decide to receive the address of its projections?

Bettelheim's second suggestion to educators stems from his insistence that education address the psychic events of learners. Here, Bettelheim confounds his earlier formulation of the goal of analysis by examining more specifically the demands of education, demands that are close to the ego's processes of reality testing and that draw upon the superego's reservoir of guilt. Following Anna Freud and August Aichhorn, Bettelheim claims that there can be no education without fear. The kind of fear at stake here is not the panic fear noted earlier by Bernfeld, in which the educator induces a "panic hatred" into the student for the purpose of binding a community. The fear these educators have in mind is called "anxiety," the angst made from the stuff of uncertainty and then the interest to do something creative in this pressure. Then as now, the question that structures debates on this matter is how much fear is too much? For, if where the id was there the ego shall be, the id is also the stuff from which the superego draws, namely libidinal ties to authorities. If we return for a moment to Freud's posing of the task of analysis, we can see that the point is not to strengthen the superego and overwhelm the ego. Nor is the goal social adaptation. Rather education must appeal to the ego's potential to love, to work, to touch and to be touched. But what is it for education to address itself to the ego when the ego is not exactly in charge?

August Aichhorn for example tried to solve the dilemma of inducing enough fear through his method called "the transference."[69] He worked with youth who had lost their way and whose actions he read as dynamic expressions of symptoms of being lost. To understand the wayward youth, one must understand the psychic content of the youth's expression and the psychic situation that moved it into form. Aichhorn maintained that moral lectures are of no use. He urged educators to take the side of the child, not the law. His method was to create a transferential relation through his authority and through his empathy with the youth's dilemmas. His authority was made by an uncanny ability to enter into, and identify with, the youth's logic and to surprise the youth with an offer to help make that logic stronger. George Mohr termed this method "matching wits," or "a subtle exploitation of the transference situation."[70] Aichhorn's case studies offer plenty of instances: one finds him allowing fights, helping a thief steal, assisting runaway escapes, and covering over mistakes. The method incites the symptom and induces new kinds of anxiety until the symptom can no longer serve its purpose of achieving satisfaction.

Aichhorn argued that, while these youths' anxious actions carried their own logic, the address of anxiety had to be redirected back to the self; hence he attempted to instill a new kind of fear of authority into these youths by embodying purposefully an ambivalent postion, offering promise and foreclosing destructive possibilities. In doing so, he tried to help the ego craft its own "two-fold ethics." Paradoxically, the youth must become her or his own authority. For this sort of redirection Aichhorn depended upon transferential relations of love. Reading his own recounting of interviews with youths, one gets a sense that Aichhorn directed to those he saw a strange combination of compassion and fear. He asked questions of himself, such as, What would I need to know in order to repeat the actions? In one interview Aichhorn advises a young man who stole money how to steal without getting caught. In another, Aichhorn asks a youth to empty his pockets and then takes back the stolen money. Rather than berating the youth, he asked what the youth would do in the evening. When the youth confessed he wanted to go to the movies, Aichhorn gave him some of the stolen money. While these approaches may seem shocking, the outcome was that the young, so surprised at not being punished, became both fearful and respectful of Aichhorn's knowledge. In a sense, Aichhorn did take the role of the superego. But not in order to berate the ego or to strengthen the superego's love of prohibition and censorship. Rather Aichhorn addressed the anxiety and redirected the address to a place where the ego can respond to that great decision as to what counts as danger without doing more harm to itself and to others.[71]

Aichhorn's context, however, is not the same context as the classroom. There the teacher must work in large groups, and transferential relations may not actually be even noticed, let alone cultivated. However, there is something one might draw upon from Aichhorn's practice, and this has to do with taking the side of the learner as opposed to the side of morality and the law. It has to do with considering the logic of the student and allowing this logic to guide the work of making education. Teachers might then see a great deal of their work as a problem of redirecting the address of anxiety (beginning with their own), as opposed to viewing the circulation of anxiety as an interruption of education. But in doing so, the teacher must become interested in embodying, purposefully, an ambivalent position, entertaining some promises, foreclosing others.

Anna Freud as well makes the point that there can be no education without anxiety. This is because anxiety serves to heighten the attention of the ego.

Anxiety
+ leeuny

The ego perceives a possible danger and then mobilizes its defenses. But the ego cannot be sure of the location of the threat, and this uncertainty, or existential angst, can become a pressure to refine and make vital the ego's attention. What if learning itself is viewed as a threat to the ego? What if learning is felt as a narcissistic injury? Might we say that this sort of anxiety, which incites the ego's defenses, prevents an encounter with a more interesting variety—existential angst? This other anxiety is the one Anna Freud had in mind. Still, if there can be no learning and no teaching without anxiety, what actually is anxiety in teaching and learning? If the ego shall become where the id once was, then, in such a curious switching of places, or in the curious reordering of the psychic event, where does the anxiety address? How does one move from the fear of losing the love of the other to the fear of losing one's own respect?

    I have been arguing that a great deal of anxiety in education is induced by a theory of learning that cannot tolerate the vicissitudes of love and hate in learning. This intolerance and the defenses made to protect it partly stem from a problematic signaled early on in the curious history of education and psychoanalysis, and partly stem from the curious history of the subject. Located perhaps in the fault lines of both subjects are questions that have to do with history and its boundaries or limits and with questions that have to do with cultural experiences and the making of a potential space of freedom. What belongs to the ego, and what belongs to the object? What do the dynamics of love and hate mean in the work of learning? When and where does learning begin, and how does learning break down, reverse its content, turn against the learner? Anna Freud, supporting her father's theory of infantile sexuality, insisted that just as sexuality begins in the beginning of life, so too does education. But precisely because education begins too soon—or to return to Alice Balint's observation, "before it can depend upon understanding"—the very basis of education, like the basis of learning, begins in helplessness and hence must work through its own breakdowns. In our own time, but turning to the institution of education, Bill Readings raises the question from the other side: How long does education take if it is taken as "systematically incapable of closure?"[72] Can pedagogy refuse to justify the institution and become curious about the antinomy known as education? Can pedagogy take the side of the learner?

    We can now return to our chapter's title, "the arts of getting by," for the phrasing has something to do with what is opened if the work of culture allows the work of desire, if the work of education allows for the making of what Hans Sachs called a "community of daydreams," interested in whatever. Karen Horney's discussion of how to analyze the self begins with the admission of the incompletion of such work.[73] She does not attribute self-analysis to a technique that can be taught and applied. Instead, self-analysis begins with qualities of attentiveness: "inner freedom, ingenuity, and finger-tip feelings."[74] Gillian Rose names this exploration "love's work, a reckoning with life." Self-analysis must be subjective and oddly singular, just like the vicissitudes of learning. There are no directions to follow, no grand plan to ensure consistency, no guarantees. But if, as Horney maintains, the work of self-analysis is to be a work of art, indeed, the arts of getting by one's own constraints, such work does not depend upon what Horney calls "an enigmatic artistic endowment" (266). What matters, both for self-analysis and for learning, is "one's interest or incentive. This remains a subjective factor, but is it not the decisive one for most of the things we do? What matters is the spirit and not the rules" (266). Can education be educated to tolerate this existential angst, to make its matter the question of the spirit?

With these difficulties we leave, for a time, the figure of the teacher and student and move on to the thing between them, another contested subject, curriculum objects. For there, perhaps the frontier between the domains of law and life, one might study the dramatic events of psychic movement, social context, historical mandates, institutional neurosis, and national preoccupations. One might study the unpleasures and pleasures of others in order to work through something like one's own. What would the curriculum be like if it could be like a study of existential anxiety, if it could provoke the risk to detect the twists and turns of psychic events, indeed, the vicissitudes of love and hate in learning? This is the subject of our next chapter.

Chapter Two

On Making Education Inconsolable

Around 1965, the year of publication for Maxine Greene's *The Public School and the Private Vision: A Search for America in Education and Literature*, Bill T. Jones, an African American choreographer, dancer, and MacArthur Foundation recipient, was a student in elementary school. He would not begin dancing until college, but throughout elementary and secondary education his interest was in theater. He recalls directing a high school production of Arthur Miller's *The Crucible*, a text often censored in U.S. schools. And he remembers a certain teacher: "I was fortunate enough to have a very feisty teacher, Miss Mary Lee Shappee, a white woman, who was an 'out' atheist. As an atheist, she considered herself slightly above everybody else in our small, bourgeois community, and she took a liking to me. She encouraged my skepticism and she emphasized, 'There's something more than this.' That was in the fourth grade."[1] Mary Lee Shappee and Bill T. Jones may or may not have read Professor Maxine Greene's 1965 text. But to juxtapose their experiences in education allows for a collective insistence on imagining "something more" than staying put in the logic of official knowledge. With the juxtaposition, itself a method engaged by Maxine Greene, there can be that contradictory sense of schooling as that great social accident *and* that haunted cultural sphere, where some are lucky enough to encounter "feisty teachers" while many more are left to fend off the temporality of the felt present—classroom time—that seems to move at a glacier rate. These latter stories of stoicism also abound. To bring into tension another voice, one might turn to Michel Foucault, who questioned the inconsolabilities of education in an interview he did with high school boys. Foucault's question still startles: "What is the most intolerable form of repression for those of you currently enrolled in a lycée [high school]."[2] This question haunts my own teaching and learning: the quest to study not just the intolerable but also what I cannot tolerate knowing. This unsentimental method is also practiced by Professor Greene, as she posits schooling as a potential space where histories of disparate groups meet and collide and where there can coexist moments when limits are exceeded, when an uncommon sociality can be invented in a common place.

Within Bill T. Jones's counter-memory of having been affirmed through the cultivation of skepticism, within Mary Lee Shappee's insistence on being known and on knowing others as an atheist during a time when daily Christian prayer was mandatorily broadcast in each public school classroom, within Michel Foucault's strange exploration of the intolerable, and within Maxine Greene's restless search for the moments and movements between literature and the lived, one should feel a sense of precarious danger and, perhaps, of transgressive pleasure. The danger has something to do with what Maxine Greene names, early on in her 1965 text, *the dream of public education*: "the validity of the claim that a community of common men could be created in an open world and that it could survive" (4).

But what of *the dream of public education*? Dreams, as Freud tells us, are wish fulfillments, fashioned unconsciously. "To dream while fulfilling a wish," analyst Andre Green writes, "is an accomplishment of the psychic apparatus, not only because the dream fulfills the wish, but because the dream itself is a fulfilment of the wish to dream."[3] The wish, however, can only offer unapparent knowledge made from the strange methods of dream work: condensation, substitution, distortion, displacement, reversal into its opposite. This method of dream work mirrors the vicissitudes of the instinct, or the ways the affect and the idea combine, ignite, argue, and resist. Dream work, writes Freud, "does not think, calculate or judge in any way at all; it restricts itself to giving things new form."[4] And yet, while the dream does not think, it is paradoxically a form of thought, but a thought without condition, "with the 'perhaps' omitted" (534). The thinking about the dream—the wish to interpret—is then made from the wish to dream. It is in this afterward, or the belated interpretation, that the omitted "perhaps" can return and the censorship that allows the dream to do its work can be exceeded and worked through.

Toni Morrison reminds us of the fragility of this confrontation. In her exploration of the white literary imagination, she reminds readers that the subject of the dream is the dreamer.[5] Dreams, Freud says, "are completely egotistical."[6] But what then is the subject of the public dream of education? As Maxine Greene interprets it, the dream is split within its own ambivalence: a dream for a community of those who have something in common and a wish for a thing in common that can make a community. If the dream is "completely egotistical" we must also admit the ego is never complete. Rather, the ego is a part of something beside itself and within itself. It must learn to include its own "perhaps" through its relation to its own otherness (the id and the superego) and in relation to the other's otherness. Whereas those who imagine themselves as already possessing a thing in common (a complete ego) present community as something to step into and comply with, the wish to make a thing in common (from the uncompleted ego) poses community as a question. Maxine Greene's interest is with a community that tolerates the question and that makes itself a question.

But if the thing in common is the capacity to live in a world which is not yet, then the dream of the open world is also one of transgression and pleasure. For to dream of an education that can open the world and still claim the possibility of community, education would have to understand that the only condition for community is difference. To dream an open world and to desire a community would require, as a condition of membership, not the renunciation of instinct but the refusal of the defense mechanisms that imagine difference as a problem to be overcome.[7] Essentially, this would mean that education needs to question its own desire for, and implication in, knowledge. And if, in fact, education could proceed without treating knowledge as category-maintenance work, and without shutting down its own attempt at opening the world, its problems would become more than just how it might recognize itself without criteria of standardization, prediction, norms, and deviancies. If education could fashion both a community and an open world, its problem would become how communities can be made from an inessential commonality. If I follow Maxine Greene's 1965 text, and my own reading of educators' fears of uncertainty, this interpretation of their dream bothers the hell out of "the schoolmen," the engineers of that great confinement and romance known as schooling.

Maybe the heart of Professor Greene's 1965 text is the *Bildungsroman* of schools. If it is a *Bildungsroman*, a building of selves and culture, a bringing up of education and life, and a battling between public personae and singular desires, it is not necessarily the heroic story of progress. By now, we should be wary of the promise of progress, not because development does not occur but because progress must forget the conflicts it requires. In part, the stuff of Professor Greene's narrative is built from the dreary reports of "the schoolmen" and their collective efforts to keep the lid on the radical anxieties and uncertainties of education and nation, all in the name of progress. There are, in Greene's early text, uncanny and often cruel stories of identities being both made from and repressed within the knowledge and sociality known as schooling. We read of these efforts in our own time, when education is thought to place a nation at risk, when new identity categories deposit deviancy into the bodies of adolescents, when the histories of inequalities are viewed as interruptions to the real business of curriculum, when the complications of lives lived are dismissed as irrelevant complaints. But from another vantage point, we also read how education makes the discontents.

Maxine Greene writes a *Bildungsroman* that can argue with itself. The arguments are made from the anxious stuff of artists' visions, fantasies, and dreams. The anxiety becomes what we in education call "the curriculum," the site where the artists deposit and perhaps bury their uncanny dreams. What is offered are stories of being lost and of losing things, of melancholy longings and perhaps, as Freud would say, of the work of mourning.[8] The literary part of Maxine

Greene's 1965 text troubles—then as now—even the best efforts of "the school-men." The trouble, as Toni Morrison would write years later, already resides buried in what is taken as a nation's founding literature: "For a people who made much of their "newness"—their potential, freedom, and innocence—it is striking how dour, how troubled, how frightened and haunted our early and founding liter-ature truly is."[9] The trouble, as Michel de Certeau tells us, is that fiction, in the psychoanalytic sense, is "knowledge jeopardized and wounded by its own other-ness . . . it is touched or wounded by the affect."[10] And the affect is something between the instinct and the idea, a threat to thought. The knowledge of literature, like that of dreams, is not authoritative. Shoshana Felman writes of the paradox: literature is "knowledge that is not in mastery of itself."[11] Herein lie the impossi-ble grounds of education's possibilities.

As Professor Greene tells them, the stories of compulsory education are at once stories of how culture works to divide and to unify, of how subjection is lived under the banners of freedom, of individuality, and of opportunity, and even of how "there was the 'single person' still to be accounted for."[12] But in writing within and against this incompleteness, and in managing to be both suspicious of and hopeful for what education is and can become, Maxine Greene parts company with the majority of her contemporaries, who then as now insisted, for their metaphors of education, upon discourses of social science, psychometric mea-surement, and the military, that is, discourses that foreclose their own frailties. In this text, and indeed in all of her work, Maxine Greene casts her lot with those who refuse to close down their identifications in the name of social order, effi-ciency, mastery, and yes, even community. The *Bildungsroman* of schooling, then, is also the dialogic of the discontent: the creative artists who offered, through their texts, the future stuff of curriculum—their anxious, celebratory, and transgressive dreams. What they offered, and what Maxine Greene engages, is their refusal to guarantee meaning.

A few years before the publication of Greene's text, James Baldwin addressed an audience of teachers. Baldwin's "A Talk to Teachers" began with the trauma of education: "Let's begin by saying that we are living through a very dangerous time. . . . [Y]ou must understand that in the attempt to correct so many generations of bad faith and cruelty, when it is operating not only in the classroom but in society, you will meet the most fantastic, the most brutal, and the most determined resistance. There is no point in pretending that this won't happen" (325).

Within this room full of teachers, how many could notice that the very resistance to transforming education and the very hope that education might be a site of transformation are an effect of educational design, not of education gone somehow wrong? The trauma of education is its incapacity to respond adequately to its own history of "bad faith and cruelty." And part of this incapacity to respond to an ethical demand has to do with the ways education can deny its own implica-tion in the knowledge it offers. Baldwin could be referencing the historicity of education: the rules that formed its exclusions and inclusions, the structure of intelligibility that oversees what counts and what cannot count as relationships in education, indeed, the education of education. He reminds teachers that education is not the origin but that it does live the effects of how a nation dreams and what a nation must bury in order to sentimentalize its wishes.

These warnings are reminiscent of these of Freud, who, in *Civilization and Its Discontents*, gives a footnote over to education. Like Baldwin, Freud rehearses the effects of disavowal and the pretension that conflict is not a dynamic to study. Freud warns against two denials education is famous for: the conceal-ment of sexuality in the lives of people and the fact that education "does not pre-pare [students] for the aggressiveness of which they are destined to become the objects. In sending the young out into life with such a false psychological orienta-tion, education is behaving as though one were to equip people starting on a Polar expedition with summer clothing and maps of the Italian Lakes" (134 n. 1).

Analyst D. W. Winnicott would continue to explore Freud's insights into the importance of the individual's capacity to acknowledge the dynamics of inter-nal aggression. The beginning of education, for Winnicott, would reside in that strange tension between construction and destruction. The work of recognizing the ambivalence "is an achievement in the emotional development of the individ-ual."[13] The achievement is not possible if destructiveness is only thought to con-cern that which is frustrating and hateful to the self. "When we need to find the things we disapprove of outside of ourselves [we] do so at a price" (82), the diminishment of our capacity to construct something from the destruction. Winnicott relates the capacity to tolerate the vicissitudes of one's own destructive impulses to the question of education: "Toleration of one's destructive impulses results in a new thing: the capacity to enjoy ideas, even with destruction in them, and the bodily excitements that belong to them, or that they belong to. This devel-opment gives elbow-room for the experience of concern, which is the basis for everything constructive" (87).

Baldwin offered teachers some "elbow-room for the experience of con-cern." How many of the readers of the *Saturday Review*, in which Baldwin's talk was published (and Greene must be counted as one of these readers, given how often she cited essays from this magazine in her provocative *Teachers College Journal* columns, "For the Record"), became incited to the free play of critique and imagined themselves as choosing to be unsatisfied and even daring to trans-gress what Foucault would call, a year later, in his archaeology of the human sci-ences, "the order of things"? And yet, within this vast educational design of what might now be called "normalization," an artist addresses teachers.

It is this insistence on the arts as a method for thinking the unthought of education, for exploring what "the schoolmen" could not think precisely because of what they thought, that Greene develops in her 1965 text. Read for its method rather than merely for its content, that is, as a practice for doing something more—indeed, for making education inconsolable—this text can be understood as in dialogue with our present. We might put it in conversation with a question about reading raised by Shoshana Felman. Like Professor Greene, Professor Felman reads the stories of others to say something about her own. And the questions Felman asks about reading might as well apply to education: "If reading has historically been a tool of revolutions and of liberation, is it not . . . because, constitutively, reading is rather risky business whose outcome and full consequences can never be known in advance? Does not reading involve one risk that, precisely, cannot be resisted: that of finding in the text something one does not expect?"[14] How, then, does Professor Greene's method work? What is at stake in "the rather risky business" of reading the *Bildungsroman* of schooling through the concerns of artists?

Maxine Greene narrates a noisy, overpopulated, and haunted history, one that privileges the hesitations, the uncertainties, the detours, and the grand and pitiful operatic gestures made from the dreams of public education. She narrates early stories of a nation built from the stuff of slavery, genocide of First Nations people, and global diaspora. Schooling must bury and repress these traumatic episodes in order to preserve the brutality of its origins. This is, after all, the unconscious of education. But the repressed returns in the form of symptoms. Unsatisfied, yet still in dialogue with the official stories of the schoolmen from Horace Mann to John Dewey, and with the popular news accounts of various moral panics between 1830 and 1914 that imagined the working class, the foreigners, and the rural populations as in need of containment, order, and Christian morality, Maxine Greene juxtaposes these official accounts with fictional worlds of a burgeoning national literature. And she reads this literature symptomatically. It is a world that imagines itself in all the wrong places, sometimes exploring the underside of the lived, sometimes exalting the promise of oneness, sometimes rendering impossible the contradictory humanist dream of transcendence and disinterestedness—of oceanic feelings and confession—and sometimes insisting, in Greene's words, that "knowledge itself may be suspect."[15] The brutality of a nation's origins returns, like the repressed, in its literature.

But this return is not simply a repetition. Rather, it can be read as attempts at working through, what Freud called, "learning." New questions, new interpretations, become possible in literature. Perhaps readers can recall their encounter with Nathaniel Hawthorne's *The Scarlet Letter*. Generations of adolescents have met (and some have even been inflicted with) the abject Hester Prynne and the angelic little Pearl, and maybe the study was of a certain social hypocrisy that could not be so easily tucked elsewhere. If read through the lens of feminist criticism such sentiments would be tied to women's subordination. Freud, of course, would probably have a great deal to say about the Oedipus and castration complexes. Years later, Maxine Greene would speak of this text in terms of the problem of community and freedom.[16] And yet, in the hands of Walter Rico Burrell (in his essay "*The Scarlet Letter*, Revisited: A Very Different AIDS Diary," found in Essex Hemphill and Joseph Beam's anthology, *Brother to*

Brother: New Writings by Black Gay Men) the author himself is placed at stake. Reflecting on his HIV seropositivity and comparing his body to the scarlet letter, Burrell rewrites Hawthorne and returns us to the question of love:

> There is a terrible temptation here to wallow in extreme self-pity, wailing over the lack of love in my life. Some will undoubtedly interpret these lines in exactly that way. I would say to those read-ers that I deserve the right to subscribe to my own definition of love, just as I would allow you yours. . . . [But] who is going to love someone with AIDS? AIDS patients don't even warrant hugs, much less passionate love. And yet, ironically, it was very often a search for love that exposed many of us to AIDS in the first place. (135)

There is then, in all of this life, a fundamental contradiction that makes the project of education inconsolable. It has to do with the question raised earlier by Felman and implied by Walter Rico Burrell. What is actually occurring when education represses uncertainty and trauma if the very project of reading and of love requires risking the self? How could teachers—of any era—teach their national literature if that literature itself broke apart the order, the punishments, the didacticism, the religiosity, the greed, the conformity, indeed, the very struc-ture of disavowal? What would happen to this literature that admits—whether intentionally or not—its own traumas? How could the lid of education be held on if the stuff inside was also taken as the stuff that refuses to be contained?

Well (the reader might think), education has that peculiar talent for ren-dering banal the uncertainties of the lived. We all can remember reading amazing texts in rather unamazing ways, and perhaps even reading unamazing texts in amazement. Maxine Greene anticipates this tension when she repeatedly observes that the schoolmen must "necessarily lag behind the artists."[17] But this belatedness, or perhaps ignorance of the artists' concerns, still leaves its trace in schooling. The imaginative articulations of the artists, even if in fairly selective ways, stumble into the curriculum to become the stuff of canonicity, of the culture wars, and of discourses of multiculture. Education is always lived as an argument, precisely because the repressed must return.

In casting the lot of the early history of compulsory education in with that of the history of early U.S. literature, Greene offers her readers not a content (even though the footnotes of educational history that Greene juxtaposes and crit-ically comments upon are the story neither of romance nor of progress) but rather a method of doing and reading the history of our present. This method seems to take quite seriously Freud's concerns with civilization as the production of unhappiness, and his decision to learn from and listen to the discontents. It is a method that shapes the work of educational theorists such as Bill Pinar, Janet Miller, Deanne Bogdan, Jo Anne Pagano, Madeleine Grumet, Cameron

McCarthy, Warren Crichlow, Roger Simon, Rinaldo Walcott, and Judith Robertson, all of whom, in very different ways, open education with imaginative works.[18] For Maxine Greene, imagination is a method, one that insists that neither the structure and dreams of schooling nor the desires of those who live there can be exhumed from their cultural arguments. In this method, history cannot be rendered as a discrete object, as that great differential alibi for the present. The method structures Maxine Greene's refusal to detach herself with the congratulatory tone implied in claims of how much better it is in her present, how different the present schoolmen are from those who first embraced that name, and how nice education has become. In this 1965 text, one finds a responsibility, something more to do.

Written within the great waves of civil rights in the United States, just eighteen years after the European genocide (the Shoah as Jewish historians now name it), within the great demands for relevancy in education that are the legacy of the student protest movement, during the United States war against Viet Nam, a few years after Hannah Arendt wrote her report on the banality of evil,[19] and written against, perhaps, the contemporary schoolmen of her times—those obsessed with new world orders and with what Maxine Greene calls "the Hegelian need to resolve"[20]—this text of Greene's is oddly a history of her present, perhaps a chronicle of her own library, perhaps the view from the window of her office at Teachers College, Columbia, located "on the edge of the slums in the largest city of all" (160).

We might find ourselves on the edges of Maxine Greene's own contemporary space. An example that stands out is when, in the midst of examining the racism of "the schoolmen" and the National Education Association's refusals between 1870 and 1890 to challenge the structures of educational inequality between white and black children, Greene turns, in a chapter titled "The Predicament of Freedom: The Negro, the Farmer, and Huck Finn," to the words of Ralph Ellison's *The Invisible Man*: "You ache with the need to convince yourself that you do exist in the real world, that you're a part of all the sound and anguish." Then Greene continues: "It was that way in the 1880s; it is that way now. And a variety of re-enactments are taking place, reminiscent of what was happening eighty years ago" (127). In the next sentence, Greene addresses her white readers, who are also living within the movements of civil rights, "to challenge their sense of themselves as persons as well as their conception of democracy." This insistence that history requires answerability, implication—not transcendence—is reminiscent of James Baldwin's "Talk to Teachers." Greene asks educators to witness the self in relation to the other, and hence grapple with who one is becoming when one subordinates another under the name of education. We are asked to imagine who we might become because there is so much to do.

This writing of history, then, is about the presence of a past as a return of the repressed. It is about the study of repetition, but a study that does not gather the ground of repetition. It is *not* a story of certainty or conciliation, nor is it the

mere recovery of tiny social artifacts, occasionally dusted off for the archeologi-
cal museum of educational repression. Still, the social artifacts are there,
described in uncanny ways, like the obscurantist McGuffy *Readers* that "built a
hundred bridges between the Puritan past and the children of the unregenerate
present, who were told they could only be American if they learned what was
True" (56). Such artifacts are not dusted off as examples of what can only be
found in a distant, bad old past. Indeed, I could not help but think of those textual
creatures haunting my own educational baggage, Dick and Jane, running in an
ever orderly fashion into the whiteness of nuclear family value lifestyle. But even
Dick and Jane return in the national literature, this time as grotesque knowledge.
In Toni Morrison's first novel, *The Bluest Eye*, others must be excluded so that
Dick and Jane may live the lives they live. Look at how Pecola's eyes read the
"disinterested violence" of the primer: "Hereisthehouseitisgreenandwhiteithasa-
reddooritsveryprettyhereisthefamilymotherfatherdickandjaneliveinthegreenand-
whitehousetheyareveryhappyseejaneshehasareddressshewantstoplaywhowillpla
ywithjaneseethecatitgoesmeowmeowcomeandplaycomeplaywithjanethekitten-
willnotplayseemothermotherisverynicemotherwillyouplaywithjanemother-
laughs" (8). Then examine the footnotes and tiny social artifacts of education
thought with Maxine Greene.

     Her project is akin to Michel de Certeau's exploration of the function of
history. Here are de Certeau's conditions:

> If, in one respect, the function of history expresses the position of
> one generation in relation to preceding ones by stating, "I can't be
> that," it always affects the statement of a no less dangerous com-
> plement, forcing a society to confess, "I am other than what I wish
> to be, and I am determined by what I deny.". . . In the form of a
> "labor" immanent to human development, [the documents and the
> writing of history] occup[y] the place of the myths by means of
> which a society has represented its ambiguous relations with its
> origins and, through a violent history of Beginnings, its relations
> to itself.[21]

     The myths of history are not so easily subsumed: they, too, can be lived
as an argument and, for the character Lucy in Jamaica Kincaid's novel of that
same name, as homesickness. Lucy, an au pair girl from a Caribbean island,
comes to New York City to work for a white family. She studies them and wonders, "How do you get to be that way?" (20), how does the passion for ignorance
sever the quest for an understanding that exceeds the order of things? These questions come in the form of a memory about her education, pressed into form when
her employer, Mariah, shows Lucy a flower. Lucy remembers the time when she
was forced to memorize Wordsworth's poem "The Daffodils." She evokes her
recitation from the inside out: "I was at the height of my two-facedness, that is

outside I seemed one way, inside I was another; outside false, inside true. And so I made pleasant little noises that showed both modesty and appreciation, but inside I was making a vow to erase from my mind, line by line, every word of the poem" (18). That night, Lucy dreams of being chased by daffodils. A flower that never grew in her country returns, but now as a threat of annihilation, as a representation of colonization and as Lucy's wish to escape. Mariah cannot tolerate the idea that something she finds so beautiful can be spoiled by another's "sorrow and bitterness." Mariah wishes the flower to mean only something beautiful to Lucy and, in this wish, Mariah defends against her own possibility for the "experience of concern." While neither Lucy nor Mariah can get over their respective histories, for history, as it is for us all, is a history of the body, Kincaid's novel still surprises. Sometimes Mariah and Lucy can understand one another. Then we are offered some other dreams, an uncommon sociality that includes the refinding of a difficult "perhaps."

This difficulty is intimated in the conclusion of Maxine Greene's text: "This has been a book about illusions, about green lights and transcendent goals" (165). But the illusions she may be referring to are not merely the misconceptions or even the interminable betrayals of education. Rather, what is at work is something more central than the attempt to survey a particular geography. At once, it has something to do with whether in fact education can be more than colonization, more than the impulse to invent—through its technologies of correction—the needy student, the dangerous individual, the attention deficit, the ignorant parent, the docile body, the dysfunctional gender, and all the other tragic roles that spring forth from the moral panic that stages education. It also has to do with something quite intangible, something to be done. At work in Greene's text, as I mentioned earlier, is a method for interpreting the unconscious of educational life, for puzzling over the strange dream of education, and for imagining education as something different than repression and normalization, something that is capable of surprising itself, something interested in risking itself.

Toward the conclusion of her text, Greene discusses what now might be considered a mere footnote in "that slow moving river of educational theory" (114): a text from 1883 by the self-taught sociologist Lester Ward, called *Dynamic Sociology*. Ward was interested in the problem of freedom and believed that education might be a site where the meanings of freedom could be humanely fashioned. It is significant that Ward engaged some of the same problems confronted by the artists of his day, and this, after all, is the method offered by Maxine Greene. In all of her writing, Greene continually returns to the preoccupations of artists and to what the arts might open in conversation.[22]

Sociologist Ward, according to Greene, worked with two problems—both of which are still a preoccupation, although in ways that were not imaginable, perhaps, to the Ward of 1883 or to the Maxine Greene of 1965. One had to do with the implications of science for people's visions of themselves. The other, with what had become of the hope of progress. And with the close of the twentieth century, these concerns collapse within the pandemic known as AIDS, within worldwide civil wars and their global displacements and genocides of humans, with the incapacity to commemorate Auschwitz and Hiroshima fifty years later, and even within current debates about the human rights of those disenfranchised by identity, by experience, by history. Here, I am thinking of collectivities—and they are not mutually exclusive—of children, women, gays and lesbians, First Nations people, people of color, refugees, and so on. And I am thinking, How is it possible for education as a discourse and as a practice, as an institution and as an experience, to listen to its own exclusions, repressions, and silences? What could education be like if its interest began with Winnicott's notion of "making elbow room for the experience of concern"?

Like Maxine Greene, we can decide to be addressed by the artists of our time and, in doing this, choose to make ourselves into new publics. The artists still worry about this thing called "pedagogy," about what it means to teach and to learn, and about the detours known as history. Eve, the protagonist in Emily Prager's *Eve's Tattoo*, worries about how her New York contemporaries—the artists, the filmmakers, the advertisers, the rock singers, the people waiting, along with their pets, in a veterinarian's office—will think about nazism, the desire for fascism, and the Shoah. On her fortieth birthday, she has tattooed on the inside of her wrist a concentration camp number, first explaining it as something like an MIA bracelet. But it is Eve who is missing in action, and she spends the rest of the novel in a failed pedagogy of educating others about what she herself cannot bear to know.

Tony Kushner's two plays under the banner of "A Gay Fantasia on National Themes"—*Angels in America Part I: Millennium Approaches and Part II: Perestroika*—offer something like a queer diorama of imagined identity performances, all in incomplete acts of community, all trying to solve the problem of love. Characters from different histories confront one another in our time of the AIDS pandemic. They meditate in fits and starts about how to live and love within immense suffering and loss. The plays collect an accidental sociality, in which characters precariously scratch at each other's vulnerabilities. Gracefully and ungracefully, the characters become caught in change and loss. For Tony Kushner, the tension we are asked to bear concerns the possibility of caring for the self in such a way as to care, as well, for another. Like the pandemic known as AIDS, Kushner's plays refuse the old boundaries of inside and outside.

The sheer desire to become somebody, of wanting "to go" anywhere, nowhere preoccupies our protagonist in Patrick Chamoiseau's novella, *School Days*. "My brothers and sisters O!" Chamoiseau begins. "I have something to tell you: the little black boy made the mistake of begging for school."[23] He thought he could "capture pieces of the world" there. But what he found was something more difficult, the mix-up of longing and surival, and a teacher's hatred of his Creole. "The teacher hunted down dreams. . . .That was when he called on you. The dreams took flight" (116). But still these dreams returned, now propped up in the first book where reading could, after all, return the dreams to the boy, even if this return cost the capacity to bother his thoughts.

In Toronto, where I now live, Canadian artist Bruce Eves investigates homosexual desire in an exhibit he calls "Theoretical People." And perhaps in spite, or maybe because, of his edgy and transgressive attempts, this artist made me think about education, stalled in its own attempts to make certain the uncertainties of theory and practice. Elaine Shape's photo exhibit, also in Toronto, elicits a sort of fascination and repugnance toward the traditional roles of women in contemporary Western culture. I think, along with Shoshana Felman, how these women suffer from too many stories, none of which can be their own. Then there is Bianca Nyavingi Brynda's feature-length documentary, that under the title *Roots Daughters* examines Rastawomen in their social, political, and economic contexts, as they fight for equality within Rasta culture and within larger worlds. I am reminded of Jyl Lynn Felman's haunting essay in *Tikkun* titled "If Only I'd Been Born a Kosher Chicken," a sort of kaddish for Jewish lesbians denied membership, forgotten in our own Jewish communities. The film *Go Fish*, offers an "otherwise": it magnifies the minuscule daily anxieties and pleasures of a small lesbian community in the process of making itself. There I study this new generation, marveling over the public accessibility of a film about lesbians doing nothing more than making their lives by figuring the problem of love.

In this all too brief sampling, we see artists unafraid to imagine differences within, to address those who may or may not understand, to fashion communities yet to become, and to engage life at its most incomplete, to return that lost "perhaps." Unlike educators, they seem to proffer only their dreams for interpretation, and then no guarantee. They are interested in the mistakes, the accidents, the detours, and the unintelligibilites of identities. Unlike educators, they gesture to their own constructedness and frailties, troubling the space between representation and the real, between the wish and the need. They explore that twilight of experience in which every reading of the body is a misreading and every search for self leads to the other. They refuse the simple and moralistic romance that we in education call "self-esteem," "role models," and "childhood innocence." The artists are not the invisible hand that centers the child. Theirs are decentered concerns with desire gone awry, with the clash between the desire to represent and the representation of desire, and with the offer of making difference and hence provoking new imagined communities from the limits of experience and history. In so doing, the responsibility for fashioning new meanings, for making new projects, lies elsewhere: in the doing of dialogue, in the arguments over what can constitute authenticity, appropriation, and the limits of culture, in the *Bildungsroman* of schooling. The artists ask us to think the unthought of difference and to imagine that communities are something to do, something to make. And with these insistences, none of which offer any guarantees, perhaps education can begin.

It may be that the problem of bringing these new artists into schools and into schools of education requires a great deal from teachers and students. The artists return to education difficult knowledge. For every story of the arts, we find as well stories of censorship, of the incapacity to engage the difficulties of others, of the refusal to see difference as the grounds of community. In our own time of national reports on the failures of education, the reports must repress the failure of education to engage the difficulties the arts offer. Educators may see these artists as intolerable, too controversial, bothering what they imagine as the normal. After all, how does anyone come to love a knowledge that knows no mastery?

Engagement with the inconsolability that the arts offer, as Maxine Greene's 1965 text reveals, always has been a problem for education. At the same time, learning and teaching require something of us because, as Anna Freud reminds us, education in its widest sense "comprises all types of interference with . . . development."[24] But maybe, precisely because reading is risky business in that selves and cultures are interfered with, there can be made an interest in leaving the notion that knowledge is a settled and affirming space. There can be provoked—and this, after all, is the problem of pedagogy—a decision to listen to stories of another in order to do more with the stories one already holds. If this can be the start, maybe it will begin with an ethical concern for studying what education cannot tolerate knowing, how education can surprise and surpass itself. Maybe then education can engage in that difficult study of its own unconscious, of what it cannot bear to know. At the very least—and this, without her ever saying it directly, is what I learned from Maxine Greene's text—one can respond to what the artists require of us; within the arts, one can find something more to do. It may have something to do with understanding that imagination can exceed what everyday thoughts tolerate as normal.

Still, to return for a moment to the art offerings in the Toronto summer of 1994, we notice that they are crowded with all kinds of publics. Indeed, these exhibits and films make new publics in spite of education. Somewhere, maybe each individual had a feisty fourth grade teacher who affirmed through the cultivation of skepticism. Or maybe someone asked, What is intolerable about your life? Or maybe none of these things happened and still someone became interested in making "something more." But what these artists ask those of us in education, and what Maxine Greene wonders, is whether education can tolerate the arts even as the arts must necessarily exceed the intolerances of education.

Chapter Three

On Becoming a "Little Sex Researcher": Some Comments on a Polymorphously Perverse Curriculum

Eve Sedgwick inaugurates her study *Epistemology of the Closet* with a grand narrative gesture she calls "risking the obvious."[1] The phrasing is deceptive in its simplicity, because when it comes to the language of sex (and the closet, after all, is about that curious referentiality, that "open-secret" of sex) what is obvious for some becomes, for others, something to risk. When speaking about sex, there is that queer contradiction between the ambiguity of language itself and the dominant insistence upon the stability of meaning in sex practices. Cindy Patton wryly observes, "The language of sex is so imprecise, so polyvalent that it is 'hard' to know when we are talking about sex and when we are talking about business or politics or other weighty matters [like education]."[2]

When thinking about the referentiality of sex, one comes up against a curious limit: the dominant insistence upon the stability of bodies, the body as fact, transmitting obvious information. The insistence has to do with more than the fantasy that bodies say what they mean and mean what they say. In our context of education, the normal body must personify a stable meaning even as that meaning must be adjusted through developmental discourse. Now while the problems with this sort of conceptualization are exponential, the little problem this chapter engages is What becomes unthinkable when sexuality is thought to have a proper place? This question is partly inspired by Cindy Patton's *Last Served? Gendering the HIV Pandemic*. Patton challenges the place of sexuality by positing the geopolitics of sexual space, that is, global migrations, global displacements and traveling, and explores how these movements produce sexuality—when bodies move, more than the scenery changes. Patton makes the significant point that travelers perform sexuality differently in different spaces. Her term *sexual land-*

scapes, or the geographies of sex, signals something about the polyvalency of the traveler's body and something about the polyvalency of cultural meanings.

At least three early observations can be made from thinking sexuality as that which is other to boundaries. First, theories of sexuality as movement open very different conceptualizations of safer sex pedagogies, conceptualizations that begin with a dynamic notion of sexuality. Here's what Patton has to say about educating the traveling body: "Truly comprehensive approaches to safer sex will view all sexuality as the mingling of potentially different sexual cultures, requiring each of us to be educated and to educate others about the variety of possibilities for creating sexual identity and sexual practices which can stop the [HIV] epidemic" (48).

In this first practical observation, the sites of safer sex pedagogies are expanded to the travel agent, the barber, the cosmetic counter, the grocery store: all places where bodies travel, meet, and care for the self. They are also sites of desire and of accidental experiences. And if the sites of safer sex pedagogies are brought into the everyday, the actual information to be had at these sites would begin with the consideration of bodies on the move between spaces. The second observation is of a different order and concerns the idea that, if sexuality is on the move, its moves are other to culture. We might insist that sexuality is otherness itself. The third observation concerns a domain of a different order, described by Drucilla Cornell as "the imaginary domain," that psychic space of proliferating design where "our sense of freedom is intimately tied to the renewal of the imagination as we come to terms with who we are and who we wish to be as sexuate beings."[3] This brings the travel back to the body: one does not have to go far away to imagine something otherwise. In fact, all one has to do is imagine.

The movements and minglings of sexualities bear on my discussion because, in the more progressive research on sexuality and adolescents, there is still a preoccupation with fixing the geography of sexuality to the narrowly constructed assignments of culture, gender, age, and neighborhood. These are the preoccupations I wish to disrupt, moving back and forth between the literature of AIDS activists; the theories of sex authored by Freud, Foucault, and Sedgwick; normative versions of sex education in compulsory education; and a few texts on adolescent sexuality.

In bringing such an odd juxtaposition of texts and theories, that is, in becoming curious about the discourses of sex and the discourses of the sexual body, we are left with the questions of what is imagined when sex is imagined and what is imagined when what is euphemistically called "sex education" is imagined. To return to Sedgwick's formulation, what can "risking the obvious" and placing the obvious at risk mean when the labile subject of sex is so conspicuously contested, masked, rated, counted, disavowed, and made synonymous with one's identity?

Our topic becomes even more complicated when one tries to plot the imaginative geography of sex as my beginning remarks might suggest, or when one tries to read sexuality through a favorite theory, instruction manual, or even the views of what can only be called an army of professionals. To muck up matters even more, when inserted into the school curriculum or the university classroom—when, say, education, sociology, or anthropology get their hands on sexuality—the language of sex becomes explication-like and then, well, desexed. Even more, when the topic of sex becomes like a curriculum and is stuck to the under-aged (and here, I mean the legal categories of children and youth), one can barely separate its objectives and fantasies from the historical bundles of anxieties, dangers, and predatory discourses that seem to render some sex intelligible as other sex is relegated to the unthinkable and the morally reprehensible. One might acknowledge the dreariness of even the "thinkable" version that makes sex into a danger and a duty to perform. There, sex becomes something that disturbs innocence and the everyday. It becomes indistinguishable from that strange economy of affects that Jonathan Silin, Eve Sedgwick, and Shoshana Felman term "our passion for ignorance": the paradoxical desire not to know what one already knows, the passionate work of denial and disavowal.[4]

With all of these lacunae in mind, Sedgwick persists in her willingness to place the obviousness of sex at risk. She does this through a series of remarks structured as axioms, the first one of which states: "People are different from each other" (23). She plays with all sorts of differences, while still managing to admit the impossibility of exhausting the possibilities and hence of finally accounting for all the differences between, within, and among individuals. A certain geometric quality is allowed because she begins not with cultural universals but with a curiosity about polymorphous actions, about the capacity of humans to be exponential in their strategies of meaning and passionate attachment, their strategies of sex. Here are a few examples:

- Even identical genital acts mean very different things to different people.
- To some people, the nimbus of "the sexual" seems scarcely to extend beyond the boundaries of discrete genital acts; to others, it enfolds them loosely or floats virtually free of them.
- For some people, it is important that sex be embedded in contexts resonant with meaning, narrative, and connection with other aspects of their life; for other people, it is important that they not be; to others it doesn't occur that they might be.
- Some people's sexual orientation is intensely marked by autoerotic pleasures and histories—sometimes more so than by any aspect of alloerotic object choice. For others the autoerotic possibility seems secondary or fragile, if it exists at all. (25–26)

Sedgwick is interested in the kind of difference that "retains the unaccounted-for potential to disrupt many forms of the available thinking about sexuality" (25). Her project is akin to what Georges Bataille calls "erotism," a certain subjective practice that allows for a question, for the self to be called into the erotic play of the question.[5] Something similar guides the present discussion, where I explore the contest of ambivalent discourses that endeavor to link sex with education. The ambivalence is structured like normative notions of sexuality, described by Anna Freud as "this dual attitude of mankind toward the sexual life—constitutional aversion coupled with passionate desire—[for which] Bleuler coined the term *ambivalence*."[6] But sexuality also is structured by a mode of thought that refuses to secure itself and thus begins with the ascription of sexuality as difference. In this chapter, I am bringing a psychoanalytic curiosity to the conceptualization of sex: neither biology nor anatomy, neither culture nor social role, neither object choice nor aim is at stake. What is at stake is fantasy, Eros, and the vicissitudes of life. Can pedagogy begin with these surprises?

Throughout the chapter, three versions of sex education are discussed: the normal, the critical, and the one not yet tolerated. The last form—the one that is not tolerated—is what I am calling "the polymorphously perverse." The polymorphously perverse conceptualizes sexuality as movement and as otherness and, as such, as a part of the imaginary domain that means to refuse to stabilize sexuality through the consolation of place. In pedagogical literature on sexuality, distinguishing the normal from the critical version becomes difficult because even the critical version cannot exceed the moralism and the eugenic categories of the normal. And yet, in order to examine questions of implication, one must be willing to make an exploration of what it means to link together these two dynamics: sex and education. In thinking about what might constitute such an odd couple, that is, sex and education, we may as well raise difficult questions: Can sex be educated, and can education be sexed? What might sex education be like if it could become indistinguishable from what Foucault, in one of his last works, called "the care of the self" as a practice of freedom?

Could such an exploration be what Freud had in mind when, in his own inaugural study of sexuality, he termed children "little sex researchers"?[7] The idea that a relation might exist between sexuality and curiosity—a relation Freud insisted upon in his study of the Little Hans case—allows us to question both the limits of sexuality, in what is euphemistically termed "sex education," and its beyond: the transgressions, pleasures, and inexhaustible sensualities, or in Foucault's often cited phrasing, the capacity to "produce pleasure with very odd things, very strange parts of our bodies, in very unusual situations."[8] But what precisely is the insistence that there is a relation between curiosity and sexuality? Is the curiosity that Freud engages the same curiosity as the human sciences', that mask power through their knowledge? If we can suggest a difference between little sex researchers and social science, then what can education learn from little sex researchers?

If sex is such a labile subject in its aims, knowledge, pleasures, and practices, then what exactly can be said of sex? Are its labile qualities what has allowed educators to remain so keen on arguing for and against sex, on linking the construct of appropriate sex to the construct of age appropriateness, and on worrying over which knowledge holds in which bodies and in what circumstances? Are its vicissitudes what has allowed many educators to worry about whether sex education causes sexual activity, whether, say, discussions of homosexuality are the first step in the recruitment of sexuality? Does education cause sex? Why have educators been so persistent in their search for the origin of sexuality? And, to borrow an observation from Diana Fuss, if schools were thought to be a site of sexual contagion and prevention, does that mean that early educators already had a sense of sexuality on the move?[9]

These anxieties are not new, and their history in North America seems caught in strange repetitions.[10] As early as 1895, debates over whether sexuality should be placed in the school curriculum occurred in the United States,[11] even as, one might say, sex was already there. In Canada the eugenicists pushed the school doors open to sex education for the normal by bringing sexual life under public scrutiny. By 1910, sex education was linked to the school curricular efforts to produce white racial improvement. Sex education was to become indistinguishable from these efforts, and from the state's concern for white Anglo Saxon racial propagation.[12] In bringing to bear theories of racial degeneracy with those of sexual degeneracy, our eugenic educators could then shift from a preoccupation with defining deviancy to an occupation with constituting normalcy. Teachers were not immune from the effects of the discourse on degeneracy. Under the subheading "Abnormal Teachers," Maurice Bigelow's 1916 *Sex-Education* offers two kinds of warnings: "Certain neurotic and hysterical men or women who lack thorough physiological training and whose own sexual disturbances have led them to devour omnivorously and unscientifically the psychopathological literature of sex by such authors as Havelock Ellis, Krafft-Ebing, and Freud, are probably unsafe teachers of sex-hygiene" (116).[13]

Sex education became the site for working on the bodies of children, adolescents, and teachers. But it also repeated its own ambivalent relation to the workings of sexuality. The shift to a pedagogy for making normalcy, as well as the idea that normalcy was an effect of proper pedagogy and not an a priori state, were essentially the grounds for the social hygiene movement called "sex education." But, as Bigelow perhaps unintentionally reminds us, normalcy is easily disturbed if left on its own, or if given the "wrong" book.

To continue our little chronology of despair, we can go back to what now might be read as one of the first journals (dated around 1863) written by one student teacher, the hermaphrodite Alexina Herculine Barbin. In this *Bildungsroman*—just at the moment when the question "Do we truly need a true sex?" was answered with an emphatic "Yes!"[14]—our student teacher sadly ponders a melancholy chronology that demands life be separated into a "before sex and after sex." Barbin laments what has been lost when what is lost is the freedom of being without a definitive sex, or, in Foucault's phrase, "the happy limbo of a non-identity" (xiii). Perhaps one might learn from Alexina that sexuality is otherness.

Forty years later Freud notes in his first essay on sexuality, published in 1905, that what characterizes the literature of psychological development is the contradiction between the paucity of materials on the sexuality of children and the proliferation of interdictions on their bodies. By paucity of materials, Freud suggests more than that sexuality was not being discussed; the paucity had to do with how discussions of sex were anchored in discourses of pathology and racial eugenics. Against the eugenics of sexuality, Freud produced a counter version and a move against psychology. Sexuality, Freud argues, begins at the beginning of life and therefore is a force indistinguishable from any other bodily experience because the body is all. This is what Michael Balint would call "the career of Eros."[15] Further, Freud insists that sexual instinct is originally polymorphously perverse. It wanders aimlessly and hence is not organized by object choice, true sex, and so on. In answering the question of why so many interdictions are stuck to the child's body, Freud attributes the adult's intolerance of children's sexuality to the adult's forgetting of his/her own infantile sexuality. The dynamic is termed "infantile amnesia," quite a curious category that suggests that infantile memories of eroticism are buried and therefore preserved in repression. Perhaps this might explain the ambivalence Freud noted in his terming the unconscious the "id" or the "it."

Before moving on, shall we accept the psychoanalytic insight that repression does not exactly mean throwing something away? Rather, in psychoanalytic discourse repression is the work of turning away, the work of ignoring and forgetting an idea, or an attempt at undoing the affect from the idea. The movement of repression is dynamic and productive, one of turning and returning. What makes the return of the repressed so uncanny is that new ideas become attached to the old affects. Because of the process of substitution, displacement, and condensation, however, the new content still contains the kernel of the old dynamic or affect. Thus repression is a response to instinctual demand. And, instinctual demand, in analytic terms, inaugurates thought in its most curious form. We can now suggest that repression is a defense against curiosity. I add this little discussion because, of all the discourses offered to education, psychoanalysis is, I believe, one of the most helpful in its theories of learning and in its curiosity toward what is not learned. And given the turns and return of education, one could argue that education as a discourse and as a practice can be seen as staging the return of the repressed.

Education, then, organized as it is by adults, offers tribute to this burial, this forgetting, those "irruptions of the id,"[16] or again this making of the "passion for ignorance." In Freud's view, there is nothing innocent about forgetting, slips of the tongue, jokes, indeed all forms of parapraxes—those bungled actions that point elsewhere even as they can be observed as interfering with daily life. There is nothing arbitrary when one considers the workings of the educational unconscious. In thinking about this first form of forgetting, in which children's sexuality slips between the fault lines of adult recall, Freud locates a second structure of forgetting: education. This allows for the psychoanalytic idea that the very grounds of education requires the disavowal of particular forms of sexual pleasure. But more than this: by imagining that sexuality is akin to normal development, indeed, by insisting that sex be inserted into developmental discourse, the cost of this wish for sex to be a *Bildungsroman* is the necessary forgetting that perversity is the grounds of possibility for sexuality itself. Here my definition of perversity is simply pleasure without utility.[17] But in the insistence that pleasure be confined to utility, the work of the apparatuses of education, law, and medicine becomes preoccupied with normalizing sexuality to the confines of proper object choice and marital reproductive sex. In normative developmental models of education, sex education poses as a problem the specification of the proper object and rewards those subjects who comply with the interdictions of morality and the state apparatus.

Anna Freud would continue the psychoanalytic critique of education.[18] Her lectures to teachers suggest three ways psychoanalysis could be useful to education: by offering criticism of educational methods, by extending teachers' knowledge of human vicissitudes, and, in Anna Freud's words, by "endeavor[ing] to repair the injuries which have been inflicted upon the child during the process of education" (129). Anna Freud is even more specific: "I have to say that psychoanalysis so far has stood for limiting the efforts of education by emphasizing some specific dangers connected with it" (123). Education, in the psychoanalytic sense, harshens the superego by inciting a persecutory guilt that can berate the ego and have enough surplus guilt left over for the ego to berate others.[19] We are left with another queer contradiction: if education demands the renunciation of instinct, how is sex education even possible? Or, what can be the aim of sex education if the object of education is in the renunciation of sex? If, as Michael Balint suggests, the erotic instincts of the ego allow for the subject of education to be educated, can the renunciation of instinct be considered education's own failure to educate itself?[20]

But in a later work Anna Freud presents another kind of advice, one perhaps more modest and urgent.[21] It has to do with her distinction between psychology (a discourse that structures education), and psychoanalysis (a method that works against developmental progression). Remember, for psychoanalysis sexuality does not begin with puberty. And children, forever curious about their own otherness, make their own theories of sexuality. While sexual curiosity is, in psychoanalytic terms, "the clearest manifestation of the child's intellectual activity," the sexual researches of children "hardly ever lead to a knowledge of the true facts of adult sexual life" (165). Something more is required, and it relates to education's capacity for engaging and enlarging the ego's view of the world, its capacity to touch and be touched, and its vision of sexuality. Presently, the struggle between education and sexuality becomes crystallized in the following impossible demand: renounce your instincts and educate your id. And within these coarsened fault lines little sex researchers come to a presumptive knowledge.

The presumptive knowledge of our little sex researchers returns, but now in the form of adult anxiety over the impossibility of separating or even unraveling what Jessica Benjamin calls "the first bond" or the movement of Eros.[22] That humans, from the beginning of their lives, are sexuate beings is, of course, the inaugural speculation of psychoanalysis. The speculation of sexuality, as the grounds both for the elaboration and for the splitting of psychical organization, the social bond, and the potential for crafting libidinal positions from any object, is perhaps one of the key reasons psychoanalysis is so unpopular in education.[23] Indeed, analytic critiques of education begin a double problem. First, educators have yet to take seriously the centrality of sexuality in the making of a life and in the having of ideas. Second, educators continue to ignore the stakes of the demand to renounce instinctual pleasures, specifically as this prohibition may then also work against the capacity to risk love and work. That learning and teaching may also articulate and depend upon sexuality's elaboration and that even the demand to sublimate or redirect sexuality to social ends emerges from the desire both to be and to have the beloved object means, in Michael Balint's terms, "that actual forms of sexual life, of society, and of education are intrinsically interdependent; it is impossible to change one without changing all three."[24]

But if educators are to consider the astounding reach of sexuality, they also might pause to consider, as Foucault considered, the limits of sexuality as historicity. Renunciation is not, for Foucault, the end of the story. Foucault articulates another way to think about sex, one that emphasizes its invention, or what is commonly termed "construction," to oppose the normalizing assertion that sex has a "true nature."[25] Foucault terms the latter wish "the repressive hypothesis": the historical fantasy that there once was a time when sex was repressed and now it is time to discover the secret of sex, to let its true nature speak its truth. The repressive hypothesis structures critical models of sex education, models that link sex with emancipation, liberation, and mastery of one's destiny. Think of the 1960s discourse of sexual liberation or A. S. Neill's school, Summerhill. While the proliferation of talk shows continues to work the fantasy of the truth of sex with great glee—providing, by the way, a stage for our army of professionals to extend the confessional into the living room and the studio audience—Foucault argues that sex is not the liberation of repression: as myth, desire, and representation, sex has a historicity. The historicity is made from sexuality's modern implication in knowledge/power/pleasure.

In fact, for Foucault, if one cares to examine the modern genealogy of sex, one is led not just to education but to the entire academic knowledge-production apparatus, to various eugenic and racist movements, to such seemingly neutral categories of the state as population, demographics, birth certificates, indeed, to bio-power itself. Foucault notes four "great strategic unities" that formed specific mechanisms of knowledge/power/pleasure: a rendering of women's bodies as hysterical, a pedagogization of children's sex, a socialization of procreative behavior, and a psychiatrization of perverse pleasure (105). We will return to these strategies of power and to the cast of characters that spring from them shortly. Foucault's interest is in how the surfaces of bodies have been inscribed by, and therefore have come to take on, new forms of intelligibility through the contradictory workings of modern knowledge, labor, and the state apparatus.

For Foucault, the historicity of sex can be more accurately spoken of as a burgeoning nineteenth-century discourse. Its knowledge targets and invents a series of imagined problem populations: "the masturbating child,"[26] "the hysterical woman," "the pervert," and "the Malthusian couple" (105). These are the great strategic unities of sex.

Now, as a brief aside, the character of the masturbating child—say, an army of little Hans—is a crucial trope in the early discussions over the aims and goals of sex education in the United States. It can be said that the ghost of the masturbating child—that is, the return of the repressed—haunted the "resignation" of Surgeon General Joyce Elders. Remember when she answered "yes" to the question of whether masturbation is a form of safer sex? Even earlier in this century, the development of Kellogg Corn Flakes was originally promoted for their capacity to curb boys from masturbating. I leave it to the reader's imagination as to how the corn flake works even as, to return to the writing of Bigelow, daydreams also can slip too easily into mental masturbation.[27]

But let us return to our strange cast of affected characters. Such a strange cast, made from the stuff of unspecified actions, becomes translated into knowable identities, life-like examples of the value and the strategies of various eugenics movements. One could say that such characters become the poster people for eugenics. More specifically, they become the anchorage points and props for various forms of racism and colonialized orders. How does this work? Again, Foucault considers the strategies of knowledge that produce such a cast: first there must be analysis or the installation of a problem. Then, that problem must be constituted as pathological. Finally, a cure must be offered to normalize the pathology. As with early forms of sex education, what I am calling "normal" forms, children must be constituted as a problem population in need of education or normalization.

But Foucault emphasizes the emergence—at the same time that bodies were becoming the targets of these new forms of knowledge—of yet another dynamic, perhaps the one that leads us to a critical sex education. And here is where renunciation becomes recursive. Because with the making of these new and knowable identities came the demands of those so identified, demands that structure such present social movements as feminism, gay and lesbian civil rights, children's rights, and antiracist education. Essentially, this proliferating geometric design is what Foucault means by power, or "manifold relations of force."[28] What made such identity categories hold good, then as now, were the burgeoning social hygiene movements variously termed as "pedagogy," "criminal justice," "psychology," "anthropology," "medicine," and "sociology" *and* the burgeoning movements that demand civil rights, decolonization, and self-determination. The apparatuses that give sex meaning allow modern knowledge to take hold of the body, and, of course, allow the body to resist and recast modern knowledge. While critical sex education begins with the demands of those identified, more often than not, this mode of education still depends upon the eugenic ideal that certain knowledge be affixed to certain identities.

Foucault gives us another way to think about sexuality, not as development or identity but as historicity and relation:

> Sexuality must not be thought of as a kind of natural given which power tries to hold in check, or as an obscure domain which knowledge tries gradually to uncover. It is the name that can be given to a historical construct: not a furtive reality that is difficult to grasp, but a great surface network in which the stimulation of bodies, the intensification of pleasures, the incitement to discourse, the formation of special knowledge, the strengthening of controls and resistances, are linked to one another, in accordance with a few major strategies of knowledge and power. (105–6)

As historicity, sexuality is on the move. If one cares to tease out a tension glossed in the above quote, sexuality may well be seen as both limiting and exceeding knowledge/power/pleasure. For if sexuality is historicity, it is one that produces the very subject Foucault has in mind, subject to the control of others and subject to one's self-knowledge.[29] We may be closer to Freud than we thought, for Freud too, was concerned with how people suffer from self-knowledge and from helplessness.

To conceptualize sex as that "great surface network," however, allows one to ponder the specific relations made intelligible when sex becomes coupled with education. We might think how sex becomes subjected to larger questions that organize pedagogical efforts and that span relations between children and adults, between home and school, and between identity and its representation. Simon Watney makes similar points in his essay "Schools Out." He offers something different than "the usual question of what children supposedly want or need from education, and [instead] ask[s] what it is that adults want or need of children in the name of education" (398). The question requires adults to implicate themselves in how adult desire also structures educational imperatives and the construct of child development. But something more must be considered in our exploration, and this has to do with the limits of knowledge. We also might consider the possibility that knowledge itself is insufficient because of our time in the pandemic known as AIDS.

It is this possibility—the insufficiency of knowledge—the field of education ignores. But like the return of the repressed, that endless repetition of substitutions that seems so strangely familiar, the insufficiency of knowledge and the incapacity to recognize its limits return in the form of a text. The question I am working with is How does a text on adolescent sexuality get caught in the fault lines of sex education in our time of AIDS? The text is edited by Janice Irvine, *Sexual Cultures and the Construction of Adolescent Identities*. The chapters examine the social effects (in terms of what must be excluded and rendered as deviant) of a sex education that can imagine sex as having a true nature only if it is white, middle class, and heterosexual. The volume is further focused by an emphasis on a prevention model of sex education: prevention of bodily harm (where sex education becomes a protective knowledge against various sexually transmitted infections and to avoid early pregnancy); protection against homophobia, racism, and sexism (where sex education critiques and corrects practices of bodily subordination); and prevention of stereotypes about femininity, disabilities, and perhaps masculinity (where sex education critiques representations of the body). In a certain way this prevention model might be relevant to all parts of the school curriculum, a kind of effective education, borrowing from Foucault's version of effective history, in which the purpose of knowledge is not to affirm the order of things but to work against itself.

The unaccounted problem becomes how to imagine which knowledge will allow for new practices of the self when the dominant knowledge of sexuality is so caught up in, and constituted by, discourses of moral panic, protection of innocent children, the eugenics of normalcy, and the dangers of explicit representations of sexuality. More pointedly, when sex gets into the hands of politicians, social policy makers, religious fundamentalists—all of whom incite the ways education might imagine sexuality, what should a curriculum prevent? If everything causes sexuality, or more interestingly, if anything can make sexuality and therefore makes sexuality perverse, then what should the subject of sex education be?

But alas, the subject is dual. And this is signaled in the title of Irving's volume: "sexual cultures" and "adolescent identities." Most of the contributors, writing within what loosely might be called "poststructuralist theory," maintain the necessity of considering both adolescents and culture as social constructions. They try to hold onto the difficult and slippery argument that constructions or representations, even though imaginary and historical, take hold so well precisely because they are animated by their social affectivity. But in positing a phenomenon as a construction, as opposed to an always-already-there thing, in a field of practice called "education," the notion of construction places at stake both education and its subjects.

In the field of education, the arguments against viewing humans and their efforts as social constructions have been with us for a while. For those who refuse discourse theory, the debate tends to stall between the contradictory assertions that either there are adolescents or there are no adolescents. Either there is culture or there is no culture. A different way of thinking about constructions or discourse might begin with another look at Foucault's deconstruction of the repressive hypothesis, for the repressive hypothesis is a sort of conceptual fortress that preserves the ground for such distinctions as those between innocence and guilt, normality and deviance, and nature and culture.

The repressive hypothesis would say of adolescents that there once was an unencumbered or true adolescence that became subject to all sorts of worries. First adolescents were carefree, and now they are careless. The productive hypothesis would say that such worries produce what we call "the adolescent" or, as Irvine writes, that "recently invented life stage shaped by economic and political influences" (7). In the productive hypothesis, what seems to be at stake is how the body is read (and not whether there is a body) when the body is assumed to stand in for adolescents. In the case of culture, the repressive hypothesis would posit culture as a transhistorical and unitary set of behaviors, customs, modes of address, and so on passed down through generations. The seamless picture becomes distorted only when a culture is interfered with by an outside. In this hypothesis, culture is the sacred object and becomes the sacred ruin through no fault of its own. Moreover, the return to one's culture is a journey back to a priori origins. The productive hypothesis reads suspiciously, positing culture as far more contentious, requiring—as a condition of making and recognizing its members—internal processes of regulation and exclusion. And even these processes of distinction would produce new cultural forms and new demands. From the vantage of the productive hypothesis, culture is never innocent, never without its own arguments.

From these types of assertions one can then question the fault lines of discourses on sex that advocate cultural and age appropriateness. For if both culture and age are constructed terms, then along with the construction comes a target for appropriateness. This, after all, is the limit of appropriateness and where critical models of sex education may become indistinguishable from normative models. Should sex education even be coupled with appropriateness of any kind?[30] What is appropriate for whom if culture has that teleological talent for excluding its members on the basis of cultural appropriateness, or better, on the criteria of authenticity? Can a notion of appropriateness ever be uncoupled from developmental theory? Or, to exceed our present limit and perhaps begin with the perverse: what if sex education became a lifetime study of the vicissitudes of knowledge, power, and pleasure?

Irvine signals some of these tensions when she states this text's problematic:

> Although effective research and education on adolescent sexuality
> can only proceed from a standpoint of strong cultural analysis,
> there is some complexity to this task. . . . In sexuality research . . .
> one must negotiate the tension between simplistic overgeneraliza-
> tion about culture and [in Carol Vance's words] "the anarchy of
> sexual idiosyncrasy." (9)

With Vance's phrasing we are back to Sedgwick's axioms, to the difficulty of pinning down our unruly subjects or even provisionally risking any form of cultural essentialism.

These tensions are significant because the study of sexuality points to the necessity of calling into question three dynamics: research, education, and culture. These dynamics can be seen as comparable to Foucault's operations of knowledge/power/pleasure: analysis, problematization, and cure. Each dynamic or mode of intelligibility has become significantly troubled in our time of AIDS. As AIDS activists continue to teach, the dynamics of research, culture, and education have been constituted by their own passion for ignorance and by their incapacity to theorize beyond the repressive hypothesis. What is at stake when one faces the conditions youth and adults confront as they fashion their lives? What if what is at stake are the limits of our knowledge?

Here, then, are the problems of this text and, more generally, of feminist, antiracist, and gay affirmative educational efforts. They have to do with a reliance on representation in perhaps its most naive and anthropological sense. For in these critical pedagogies there is still an insistence that only certain knowledge be affixed to certain populations and that knowledge itself be wrested from its own otherness to become a provision of anthropological information on cultural attributes. The problem of taking an anthropological approach is that attribution theory is grounded in a eugenics of the body. More often than not, the information models of sex education assume, on the one hand, a stability in language and bodies, and thus cannot think the geopolitics of sexual spaces; on the other hand, they require the mistaken assumption that information will be no problem to the learner or the teacher. What is completely unthought is that every learning is also an unlearning. What is yet to be made is a theory of learning that can tolerate its own implication in the passion for ignorance and in the apparatus Foucault called "knowledge/power/pleasure." Shall we begin to admit that the passion for ignorance structures even critical learning?

This is not to say that youth should not consider cultural relations or be left without access to reliable information. It is to insist, however, that cultural relations and information of any kind be taken as symptomatic rather than curative and final, and as subject to the work of those who engage their myriad meanings. Moreover, in the context of safer sex education, the matching of knowledge to identities cannot admit the crucial understanding that one's sexual conduct is not a window into one's true rational identity but a practice of selves. Indeed, and to return to Foucault again, "We must conceive of sex without the law, and power without the king."[31] At stake here is our conceptualization of the dynamics of cultural relations, specific information, the discourses of sex and what these mean to the potential of our imaginary domain. One might as well engage the problem of how sex can be culturally appropriate; and, if it can be, what of perversity? One might consider culture not as a venerated, sacred object to be protected and preserved but as a highly contentious and contradictory site where discontentment and the discontented are produced, and where the geopolitics of sexuality refuse the stability of cultural, national, gendered, and sexual boundaries.

It may be more useful to consider Jonathan Silin's notion of a socially relevant sex education, that is, curricular endeavors unafraid to consider children and youth as "little sex researchers" interested in the vicissitudes of life and death. Then pedagogical efforts could become unsatisfied with the pinning of knowledge to specific identities and more restless—or better, polymorphous—in what can be imagined when sex is imagined and in what can be acknowledged when the erotics of pedagogy and knowledge are acknowledged. For if we take social theories about the historicity and contentiousness of constructions seriously—as relations of power—then pedagogy might begin with the assumptions that identities are continually being made and not received, and that the work of the curriculum is to incite libidinal identifications, not close them down.

Still, a socially relevant sex education can only offer more questions. To what values, orientations, and ethics should a socially relevant sex education appeal if culture is not a tidy safe house or if culture produces its own set of inequalities along the lines of gender, socio-economic status, sexual practices, age, and conceptions of beauty, power, and the body? If adolescence is a social construction and hence has no universality except for the fact that, in North American contexts, the category takes the form of an extra legal status of citizenship and sexual consent, and is thus subject to the control of parents and school supervision; and if certain other constructions such as HIV, STDs, unplanned pregnancies, and various sexualized forms of violence place adolescent bodies—in whatever ways—at risk, then how are educators and students to engage ethically within a sex education viewed as indistinguishable from a practice of freedom and a care of selves? For these questions to be important, it will not be enough for educators to debate them, make a decision, and then serve up as an easy-bake sex education curriculum. Shall we admit that nothing about sex education is easy and that, if the direction is to make a curriculum that both forgets the difficulty of knowledge and does not incite curiosity, sex education will continue to signify "our passion for ignorance"?

Given such heteroglossic contexts, given the complexity of forces that imagine sexuality, and given our time of AIDS, perhaps part of what is needed are on-going curricular endeavors that begin with antiracist, antisexist, and antihomophobic suppositions. But we must also begin to admit that such suppositions must be forced to cut through the affirmations of cultural appropriateness, age appropriateness, and indeed cultural relevancy itself, for these constructs prohibit the thought that sexuality is movement and bodies travel. I am advocating for a curriculum that can bear to refuse the grounds of eugenics and social hygiene, and for an effort that can come to its own social relevancy because it is fashioned by those participating, because those who make the curriculum are making new interests capable of pushing the limits of critique and pleasure. But in making such a curriculum, can sex education exceed sociological categories and be more than a semester in which bodies are subject to the humanistic constructs of self-esteem and role models and to the endless activities of voting on knowledge and finding stereotypes? More to the point, can sex be thought of as a practice of the self rather than a hypothetical rehearsal, as in preparation for the future? If such questions can be thought about seriously, one might just as well consider *not* how sex can fit into the curriculum but how sex might incite the entire disciplinary enterprise of education to move toward ethical projects of caring for the self.

Such projects are occurring. More often than not, they exist outside public education, beyond the confines of disciplined knowledge and the defensive mechanisms of official school talk. The projects may be known for their contention, for their refusal to tidy categories, for the debates they allow, for the practices that become possible and impossible. And it is precisely these difficulties that education disavows. But one can still think of the poetry of Essex Hemphill and Marilyn Hacker; the dances of Bill T. Jones; the essays of Pat Califia and Joan Nestle; the films of Derek Jarman, Maria Luisa Bemberg, and John Greyson; the novels of Toni Morrison, Samuel Delany, David Feinberg, and Henry Roth, the collection of short essays and stories published by Plume called the *High Risk* series. And just as Sedgwick's list of axioms invites the reader to produce his or her own, so, too, do the artists. For the thing in common begins with the invitation to think, the invitation to imagine, as Foucault imagines, the capacity to "produce pleasure with very odd things, very strange parts of our bodies, in very unusual situations."

For such conversations to even become thinkable in relation to education, educators will be required to get curious about their own conceptualizations of sex, and in so doing become civil libertarians for the explorations and curiosities of others, for the freedom of "the imaginary domain." For when one becomes a little sex researcher, one is interested in the study of pleasures and in the detours taken. When one can study the histories sex provokes, the love it might imagine and perform, then one is likely to engage as well the study of where knowledge breaks down, becomes anxious, is built again. The curriculum moves toward the polymorphously perverse and onto Bataille's notion of "erotism," when the problem becomes the making of questions that can unsettle the docility of education.

The invitation I have in mind has no final place of destination. Rather, the exploration that is on offer can tolerate the study of the vicissitudes of life and death and consider, as a question of ethicality, the surprises of the imaginary domain. Curiosity, or the desire to know within the work of learning, is, after all, a symptom of our sexuality. Our little sex researchers must elaborate themselves, learning the fragile work of loving others while they work through theories of sexuality that do run from the ridiculous to the sublime. In this strange time, as bodies experiment with their capacity for passionate relationality and experience however awkwardly or gracefully their potential to love and to be the beloved, the elusive theories of our little sex researchers meet the elusive theories of our big sex researchers—adults. And while the question such a meeting supposes belongs both to the educator and to the student, the educator has an additional obligation: to learn to place her own thinking at stake in the response. Can the educator listen to the little sex researcher and craft a response that does not diminish the curiosity of either party? Can the educator attempt a dialogue where the little sex researcher begins the work of crafting more generous and complex theories of sexuality and where the material of this dialogue resides in how sexuality is made within life's detours, disappointments, pleasures, and surprises? Can the conversation begin with the educator's interest in the work of crafting a generous sociality that refuses to justify sexuality through the consolation of fixing a proper place?

Chapter Four

Queer Pedagogy and Its Strange Techniques

In an essay that rethinks the historicity of identity politics and the situated question of what is at stake (and for whom) when identities are at stake, Gayatri Chakravorty Spivak worries about education.[1] She asks repeatedly, "What is it to learn and to unlearn?" The call is to think about what institutional education, as a set of discourses and practices, has to do with the self-determination *as well as* the subordination of global subaltern populations. Spivak is not asking that "identity" be restored to a nice ontology, a site of uniqueness or comfort, a fount of self-esteem, or a celebration of individuality. In fact, by centering the question of learning and unlearning, it is precisely the unthought of these regulatory declarations that she takes as a problem. What does learning and unlearning mean when one considers both "cases of exorbitant normality rather than disease [and] cases of confounding the instituted laws" (153)? Can the project of education become the gathering grounds for "deconstructive revolts"? Can pedagogy provoke ethical responses that can bear to refuse the normalizing terms of origin and of fundamentalism, those that refuse subjection?

The concern for "cases of exorbitant normality" and for the production of such "cases" in education is not new.[2] Near the end of *Civilization and Its Discontents*, Freud addresses a footnote to educators. Having already deemed education as one of the impossible professions, he notes one of its faults: "In sending the young out into life with . . . a false psychological orientation, education is behaving as though one were to equip young people starting on a Polar expedition with summer clothing and maps to the Italian Lakes" (134 n. 1). The phrasing "false psychological orientation" can be read as a critique of education's disavowal of the complexities and treacherous conflicts of "civilization": a critique of education's repetitious offer of tidy stories of happiness, resolution, and certainty as if life were something to be overcome and mastered with as little distur-

79

bance as possible. Freud's concern is how education came to conduct itself without a theory of conflict and otherness and how education might think about making selves interested in life as a state of emergency. As with Spivak's call, one might read Freud as saying that there is a problem with narratives that promise the normalcy of life, that presume a life without difference, without a divided self.

What makes normalcy so thinkable in education? How might pedagogy think the unthought of normalcy? To allow such questions, this chapter sets in tension three different forms of practice: queer theory, pedagogy, and psychoanalytic reading practices. Queer theory transgresses the stabilities of the representational; pedagogy situates the problem of normalcy in classroom sites and worries about the social production of the learning self; and psychoanalytic theories of reading work through knowledge as certainty in order to call into question three forms of subjection: the subject-presumed-to-know, the capacity of the subject's response to be unencumbered by that which it cannot tolerate, and the subject's own "passion for ignorance."[3] Taken together, these practices are curious about the means by which normalcy becomes the great unmarked within classroom sites, and the means by which pedagogy itself might intervene to agitate the limits and fault lines of normalcy. Once normalcy is constructed as a historical problem of pedagogy and marked as a production of pedagogy itself, a further question is raised: can the reading of normalcy be a queer reading practice?

Each section of this chapter depends upon the assumption that education is a structure of authority even as it structures the very grounds of authority required for its own recognition. As a practice and as a discourse, education intimately disciplines the conceptual needs of students and teachers. Some of these needs concern a desire for a transparent truth, for stable communities and identities, and for a pedagogy that ignores contradictions. And even those needs that desire an oppositional or critical practice bear the traces of these first demands. At the same time all these contradictions compete with the ways discourses of affectivity and intellect are organized and differentially lived. In bringing into dialogue queer theory, psychoanalytic reading practices, and pedagogy, and by using these three terms to consider the problem of how knowledge of bodies and bodies of knowledge become a site of normalization, this chapter is an attempt to practice the kinds of deconstructive revolts raised earlier by Spivak: to take apart the conceptual orderings that conceal the very difficult question of what difference difference makes. If, then, every learning is an unlearning, "what is it to learn and unlearn"?

My attention to these tensions is part of an attempt to imagine a queer pedagogy (as opposed to a queer pedagogue), a pedagogy that worries about and unsettles normalcy's immanent exclusions or, as many now pose the problem, normalcy's "passions for ignorance."[4] It is a pedagogy that attempts to provoke what Gary Wickham and William Haver term "the very proliferation of alternative sites of identification and critique" necessary if thought is to think the limits of its own dominant conceptual orders and if new desires are to be made.[5] This means thinking a pedagogy whose grounds of possibility require risk, uncertainty, and implication in traumatic times. It means imagining a pedagogy prepared to exceed the doubled Foucauldian subject: "subject to someone else by control and dependence; and tied to his own identity by a conscience or self knowledge."[6] And while it may be difficult to conceive of "self knowledge" as a site of subjection, much of my argument is meant to unsettle old centerings of the self in education: to unsettle the myth of normalcy as an originary state and to unsettle the unitary subject of pedagogy. However, rather than offer a "how to" manual of pedagogy, I am trying to imagine a queer pedagogy along the lines of what Sue Golding calls "technique": "a route, a mapping, an impossible geography— impossible not because it does not exist, but because *it exists and does not exist exactly at the same time.*"[7]

In thinking a queer pedagogy, I wonder if the terms of queerness can exceed and still hold onto its first referent, namely transgression and an economy of affection and practices of desire that, in its hesitations, both speaks and departs from its relational name. And, by holding to this tension, can a queer pedagogy implicate everyone involved to consider the grounds of their own possibility, their own intelligibility, and the work of proliferating their own identifications and critiques that may exceed identity as essence, explanation, causality, or transcendence? The shift, then, of a queer pedagogy is one that becomes curious about identifications and about how identifications constitute desires.[8] The move is meant to pose as a question how it is one decides the desirability and relevancy of representation itself. It is a movement akin to Lee Edelman's curiosity toward "the way in which identity turns out to be a trope of representation."[9] The problem this chapter engages is whether one looks for one's own image in the other, and hence invests in knowledge as self-reflection and affirmation, or whether, in the process of coming to know, one invests in the rethinking of the self as an effect of, and condition for, encountering the other as an equal. In claiming as desirable the proliferation of identifications and critiques necessary to imagine sociality differently, can a queer pedagogy wander, along with Samuel Delany, "the margin[s] between claims of truth and the claims of textuality,"[10] between what is taken to be real and what is constituted as experience, between the immediacies of expectation and the afterthought of (mis)recognition? Can pedagogy move beyond the production of rigid subject positions and ponder the fashioning of the self that occurs when attention is given to the performativity of the subject in queer relationality?

Impertinent Relations

Queer theory proposes to think identities in terms that place as a problem the production of normalcy and that confound the intelligibility of the apparatuses that produce identity as repetition. As deconstructive revolts, queer theories acknowledge the intrusion of exorbitant normalcy and the ways such normalcy ignores the everydayness of queer identifications, pleasures, practices, and bodies. The concern here is in thinking the cost of narrating identities and the cost of identity itself.[11] Queer theory is not an affirmation but an implication. Its bothersome and unapologetic imperatives are explicitly transgressive, perverse, and political: transgressive because they question the regulations and effects of binary categorical conditions such as the public and the private, the inside and the outside, the normal and the queer, and the ordinary and the disruptive; perverse because they turn away from utility even as they claim deviancy as a site of interest;[12] and political because they attempt to confound instituted laws and practices by putting into place queer representations on their own everyday terms.[13]

Queer theory becomes queer when, as Teresa de Lauretis notes, it "conveys a double emphasis on the conceptual and speculative work involved in discourse production, and on the necessary critical work of deconstructing our own discourses and their constructed silences."[14] Queer theory takes up that queer space of simultaneously questioning and asserting representations and outing the unthought of normalcy. The attempt is to provoke yet-to-be-made constructions of subjects interested in confronting what Peggy Phelan terms as "the not all" of representation.[15] As an unruly collection of discursive strategies of reading and of narrating bodies and histories, and as performative street politics that refuse to think straight, queer theory engages what Alexander Duttman terms "a supplement of impertinence"[16] or the dissimilitude within representation: what cannot be recuperated, said, or managed; what becomes undone despite a promise of certainty.

Where queer theory meets pedagogy is in how it conceptualizes normalcy as negation.[17] It constitutes normalcy as a conceptual order that refuses to imagine the very possibility of the other precisely because the production of otherness as an outside is central to its own self-recognition. This orientation to normalcy as the pernicious production of such binaries as the self/other and the inside/outside may be quite significant to the conceptualization and transformation of the education of education.[18] Within contexts of education, the pointing to normalcy as exorbitant production allows one to consider simultaneously the relations between and within those who transgress and undress the normal and those whose labor is to be recognized as normal. When pedagogy meets queer theory and thus becomes concerned with its own structure of intelligibility—with the education of education—and when pedagogy engages its own impertinence, the very project of knowledge and its accompanying subject-presumed-to-know become interminable despite the institutional press for closure, tidiness, and certainty.

And yet, to get to the space where difference and not similitude is the space of pedagogy, a detour into the question of identity is necessary. To notice that "identity" has become what Michel Foucault has termed "an incitement to discourse"[19] perhaps slides too easily over the very problem articulated within the field of queer theories. As an incitement, the concept 'identity' seems to mobilize and regulate whole sets of epistemic anxieties over agitated relations such as identity and politics, narrations and practices, history and representation, identity and identifications. What seems common to queer theory is an insistence on understanding identity both as a social and historical production and as a relational ethic: identity as neither transcendence nor equivalence.

In queer theory, talk about identity has moved well beyond old formulas which accept experience as telling and transparent and suppose that role models are the transitional object to self-esteem. Something far less comforting is being put into place: namely, identity is examined as a discursive effect of the social, constituted through identifications. The self becomes a problem of desiring a self and hence in need of a social. Identification allows the self recognition and misrecognition. And through identification desire is made. But because identification is a partial, contradictory, and ambivalent relation with aspects of objects or dynamics of others, it may be thought of as a means to make and direct desire. Many positionings are possible: identification of, identification with, identification against, over-identification, and so on.[20] Diana Fuss's working definition suggests the tensions of identificatory relations: "Identification inhabits, organizes and instantiates identity. . . . [It can be considered] as the play of difference and similitude in self-other relations [and] does not, strictly speaking, stand against identity but structurally aids and abets it."[21] To shift from an insistence upon identity to an exploration of identifications allows pedagogy to consider the problem of how the self reads itself.

In discussing the debate between identities and politics, Douglas Crimp poses the problem of relationality:

> Identification is, of course, identification with an other, which means that identity is never identical to itself. This alienation from the self it constructs . . . does not mean simply that any proclamation of identity will only be partial, that it will be exceeded by other *aspects* of identity, but rather that identity is always a relation, never simply a positivity. . . . [P]erhaps we can begin to rethink identity politics as politics of relational identities formed through political identifications that constantly remake those identities.[22]

If identity is not identical to itself but only a possibility made in relation to another, and if such a relation is one of difference within as well as difference between identities, what might it mean for pedagogy to think about identity as a problem of making identifications in difference? Such a question does *not* require a naive empathy. For, as Freud reminds educators in *Civilization and Its Discontents*, the project of empathy is actually a projection of the self into the conditions of the other. This projection is forgotten with the hope that it is possible, in Freud's words, "to feel our way into people." And yet, because they are contradictory, historical, ambivalent, and a statement of need, feelings are a response to something and hence are already constitutive of other relations. To feel one's way into someone else cannot be an originary moment, and to act as if it were means one must shut out both the infinite variations and slippages of affect and the fact that feelings are also contradictory and ambivalent forms of thought or structures of intelligibility that depend upon historically specific spheres.[23] In other words, feelings are not capable of transcending history and the relations already supposed. As Freud remarks: "We shall always tend to consider [we can imagine] people's distress objectively—that is, to place ourselves, with our own wants and sensibilities, in their conditions, and then to examine what occasions we should find in them for experiencing happiness or unhappiness."[24] Yet even in this very imagined moment, one can only imagine the self.

If one cannot "feel [one's] way into people" without, in actuality, representing the self as the arbitrator and judge of the other's actions and possibilities, perhaps it is time to question what one wants from empathy and whether the educational insistence that feelings are the royal road to attitudinal change is how identificatory structures actually work. Instead, one might consider feelings as constituting ignorances, ambivalences, and knowledge, and thus as that which cannot exist without narrative conventions and their own structures of intelligibility and unintelligibility. The argument here is not that feelings do not or should not matter or that one should not work with perspectives and conditions that are not one's own. It is to suggest that feelings are symptomatic of more than the individual's intentionality. Precisely because feelings are matters of history, of location, and of bodies, one might consider them as symptomatic of contradictory pushes and pulls of relationality and need. In the context of a queer pedagogy, a more useful way to think about feelings requires attention to what it is that structures the ways in which feelings are imagined and read. This means constituting feelings for another as a curious reading practice, as a problem of ethical conduct, and as a symptom of identificatory engagement. That is, pedagogy might provoke the strange study of where feelings break down, take a detour, reverse their content, betray understanding, and hence study where affective meanings become anxious, ambivalent, and aggressive. Rather than invoking a discourse of empathy that cannot explain itself, pedagogy might become curious about what conceptual orders have to do with affectivity and what reading practices have to do with proliferating one's identificatory possibilities and modes of critique.

Reading Trouble

In questioning the question of reading practices, linking reading practices to forms of sociality and to the very structuring of intelligibility, identifications, modes of address, and civic life, I mean to signal more than just how one comes to recognize, imagine, and contain signs. Rather, in education, the problem becomes how one comes to think, along with others, the very structures of signification in avowing and disavowing forms of sociality and their grounds of possibility: to question, along with others, one's form of thinking, one's form of practice. Reading practices, then, are socially performative. And part of the performance might well be the production of normalcy—itself a hegemonic sociality—if techniques of reading begin from a standpoint of refusing the unassimilability of difference and the otherness of the reader. This case of "exorbitant normality," or passion for ignorance, occurs when "the other" is rendered either as unintelligible or as intelligible only as a special event, never every day. Exorbitant normality is built when the other is situated as a site of deviancy and disease, and hence in need of containment. Such cruel reading practices, all too common, may well be a symptom of what Michael Warner calls "heteronormativity."[25]

Reading practices might well perform something interesting, and this has to do with the production of social selves whose thinking about their own structures of intelligibility recognizes and refuses the confinement of sameness and the seduction of affirmation that has as its cost the expulsion of otherness. Reading practices might be educated to attend to the proliferation of one's own identificatory possibilities and to make allowance for the unruly terms of undecidability and unknowability. One might think about the proliferation of identifications as a means to exceed—as opposed to return to—the self. What if one thought about reading practices as problems of opening identifications, of working the capacity to imagine oneself differently precisely in one's encounters with another and in one's encounters with the self? What if how one reads the world turned upon the interest in thinking against one's thoughts, in creating a queer space where old certainties made no sense?

Having named reading practices as having the capacity to be queered, I am not offering a remedy for the ways reading practices can construct normalcy. The production of normalcy, as Foucault points out, is not "a history of mentalities" or one of meaning, but rather "a history of bodies," and hence of the problem of how sociality can be lived and how politics can be imagined.[26] To focus reading practices as activities central to classroom pedagogics, one might consider reading practices as social effects of something larger than the one who reads, a different order of time than the immediacy reading might suggest. My concern is with constituting reading practices as symptomatic of relations of power, capable both of expressing a desire that exceeds subjectivity and of provoking "deconstructive revolts": reading practices as a technique for exceeding auto-affectivity and the accompanying investment in pinning down meanings, in getting identities "straight." My interest is in thinking of reading practices as possibly unhinging the normal from the self in order to prepare the self to encounter its own conditions of alterity: reading practices as an imaginary site for multiplying alternative forms of identifications and pleasures not so closely affixed to—but nonetheless transforming—what one imagines their identity imperatives to be. Then pedagogy may be conceived within two simultaneous turns: as an imaginative way to

think about and to perform reading practices that still manage, however precariously, to be overconcerned with practices of identification and sociality *and* as a
technique for acknowledging difference *as the only condition of possibility for
community.*

The problem is something different than a plea for inclusion, or merely
for the addition of "marginalized voices" to an overpopulated curriculum.
Inclusion, or the belief that one discourse can make room for those it must
exclude, can only produce, as Judith Butler puts it, "that theoretical gesture of
pathos in which exclusions are simply affirmed as sad necessities of signification."[27] The case of how gay and lesbian studies has been "treated" in a sentimental education that attempts to be "antihomophobic" serves as an example of where
arguments for inclusion produce the very exclusions they are meant to cure. Part
of the tension is that there tend to be only two pedagogical strategies: providing
information and techniques of attitude change.[28] The normal view of inclusion is
that one should attempt to "recover" authentic images of gays and lesbians and
stick them into the curriculum with the hope that representations—in the form of
tidy role models—can serve as a double remedy for the hostility toward social difference (for those who cannot imagine difference) and for the lack of self-esteem
(for those who are imagined as having no self). However, the question that cannot
be uttered is How different can these different folks be and still be recognized as
just like everyone else? Or, put differently, given the tendency of the curriculum
to pass knowledge through discourses of factuality and morality, how can difference be different? And different from what?

The liberal desire for "recovery" and "authenticity" that takes the form
of inclusion in the curriculum, perhaps as an add-on, certainly in the form of a
special event, attempts two contradictory yet similar maneuvers. On the one hand,
the strategy constructs an innocently ignorant "general public." Here I want to
signal how the normal of the normative order produces itself as unmarked sameness and as if synonymous with the everyday even as it must produce otherness as
a condition for its own recognition. For those who cannot imagine what difference difference makes in the field of curriculum, the hope is that the truth of the
excluded might persuade those who do not welcome the diversity of others and
instead "feel [their] way into people" in order to transform, at the level of these
very transferable feelings, their racist, sexist, heterosexist attitudes. But how,
exactly, is it possible to feel one's way into what can only be imagined as difference without producing, in that very act, the same? On the other hand, the
strangely estranged story of difference requires the presence of those already
deemed outsiders. The recovery being referenced is the recovery of what the
norm supposes these different folk lack, namely the "self-esteem" of the same.
The originary myth of self-esteem, or a self-knowledge that assumes the self as
lack, actually works to shut out the very conflictive operations that produce the
self as lack and as incapable of desire.

These liberal hopes, these various narratives of affirmation that are lived, however differently, as conceptual needs—and oddly, as one-way instances of empathy—are, however, really about the production of sameness. Certain excluded individuals might be invited into the curriculum but not because they have anything to say to those already there. Indeed, if these textualized folks began to talk to one another, what would they actually say? Could they even make sense? The problem is that the lived effects of "inclusion" are a more obdurate version of sameness and a more polite version of otherness. David Theo Goldberg puts it this way: "The commitment to tolerance turns only on modernity's 'natural inclination' to *in*tolerance; acceptance of otherness presupposes as it at once necessitates 'delegitimation of the other.' "[29] Pedagogics of inclusion, and the tolerance that supposedly follows, may in actuality produce the grounds of normalization. Lived at the level of conceptual needs, such hopes are able to offer only the stingy subject positions of the tolerant normal and the tolerated subaltern. Put differently, the subject positions of "us" and "them" become recycled as empathy.

Returning to Foucault's double subject, what does this subject know about itself precisely in talk about "the other?" Is there a form of self-knowledge that can untie the self from gender, racial, and sexual centerings? How is it that talk about queerness might refuse such binary oppositions as the public and the private, or refuse to produce a chain of signification like the one Toni Morrison calls "the economy of stereotypes" and instead, in Peggy Phelan's words, make talk that "upset[s] representational economies."[30] How might pedagogy address what Eve Sedgwick terms the "great divide" of homo/hetero, and thus begin to confront the question of everydayness: "In whose lives is homo/heterosexual definition an issue of continuing centrality and difficulty?"[31] Can pedagogy admit, as Judith Butler advises, "the different routes by which the unthinkability of homosexuality is being constituted time and again"?[32] Or, put a bit differently, can pedagogy admit to the unthinkability of normalcy and to how normalcy "is being constituted again and again"?

These questions might provoke a different take on "discourses of information" in terms of its centrality to the intelligibility of educational design and in terms of addressing the trauma it invokes. Along with cultural activists doing AIDS education work, I assume the failure of the old information discourses of education: knowledge of "facts" does *not* provide a direct line to the real, to the truth, and to righteous conduct.[33] As a discourse of knowledge, "information" cannot account for things such as affective investments, recalcitrant and conflictively fashioned within particular narratives. The information model has nothing to say about how "information" produces a hierarchy of addressees and therefore constitutes authority and modes of passions for ignorance. It is not capable of thinking how authorization is imagined and lived in classrooms; nor can reliance upon the evidence of information account for the confusion that results when one's own sense of cohesiveness becomes a site of misrecognition, or for the trauma provoked when the discourses borrowed to work upon and perform the fictions of subjectivity stop making sense. Indeed, the reliance upon facts as the transitional object to attitude change provides no pedagogical theory of negation: the way ideas and facts can become unattached from, and even work against, emotional ties.

At least two regulating fictions about "information" as the direct line to knowledge need to be deconstructed. The first is that "receiving" information, acquiring "just the facts," is no problem for the learner. The myth is that "information" neutralizes ignorance and that learners and their teachers will rationally accept new thoughts without having to grapple with unlearning the old ones. The second fiction is that information is a mirror of the actual and hence work as an antidote for ignorance. The reasoning goes something like this: If people had the real facts, they might rationally decide to act better toward the "victims" of ignorance or view their own ignorance as self-victimization. This view safely positions the "knower" within the normative, as a sort of volunteer who "collects" knowledge not because one's social identity is at stake, or even only made possible through the subjection of others, but rather because such information might protect one from the unintelligibility of others. Thus this discourse called "information" purports to construct "compassion" and "tolerance" as the correct subject position but in actuality performs the originary binary opposition of "us/them" in more elaborate and normalizing terms.

At this point, it is helpful to ask whether discourses of information and the discourse of feelings discussed earlier are actually different from each other. Information models of education assume that "facts" are an objective corrective to ignorant feelings. Feeling models of education attempt a subjective corrective to the distancing mechanisms of objectified knowledge. But as a corrective, what must be ignored is that feelings are not rational techniques of self-adjustment, nor is knowledge uninvolved in its own sets of ignorances. To maintain itself, each discourse depends upon the very inside/outside distinctions that provoke new forms of us/them. These discourses might be best understood as two kinds of social effects that spring from positioning classroom subjects as lack: as either lacking the proper feelings, whether they be those of toleration or self-esteem, or lacking knowledge, the knowledge of the other or the intelligence of information. What cannot be considered is the question of cathexis and negation: where affect meets the idea or becomes the means to refuse ideas one cannot bear to know. The problem here is not to abolish either affectivity or intellect from the classroom; it is where the valorization of either diminishes the very possibility of thinking about what happens when affectivity is imagined as constitutive of conflictive identificatory strategies and when conflictive discourses are imagined as mapping neatly onto desire. The problem is for pedagogy to insist upon affectivity and intellection as dialogic, as desire, and as implication.

Exploring how the experiences of those deemed subaltern are imagined means taking a second look at the status quo and rethinking how its maintenance produces the grounds of estrangement and new forms of ignorance. For some, such a second look means working through the fear that this vantage may well decenter the very terms of their own identity and hence trouble the grounds of intelligibility upon which the self is supposed, coalesced, and recognized. At the same time, when the normative order is already lived as a site of estrangement, as it may be for those always already positioned as an outsider, something different happens when listening to how one's identity gets pinned to estrangement: this has to do with not recognizing oneself in the discourses of otherness, not living one's life as a stereotype and yet having to uncouple oneself from the regulations of stereotypes as the only condition of talk. Can pedagogy make new terms, new subject positions that move beyond voyeurism, social realism, spectatorship, and the metaphysics of presence, and onto ones that take into account the historicity— as opposed to the psychology—of social difference?

Passionate Ignorance

If, as suggested earlier, the only condition of community is difference, which forms of sociality are allowed (and which prohibited) when difference is, however contradictorily, imagined? Consider how two different stories of ignorance are produced when pedagogy stalls within the humanistic faith that representation can deliver what it promises: unmediated access to authenticity. And consider how everyone involved gets caught "in the margin[s] between claims of truth and claims of textuality."[34] The first instance is drawn from the work of Cindy Patton in *Inventing AIDS*. Patton analyzes how U.S. governmental discourses of information both construct and exhaust subjects. The specific crisis of education Patton addresses is the organization of AIDS education when it becomes clear that there is no direct relation between acquiring the facts about viral transmission and fashioning safer sex practices.

Patton examines how purportedly inclusive governmental campaigns of information as a discourse actually work to produce the basis of exclusion, discrimination, and social policing. In early campaigns, the addressees of the "facts" are actually two: the "general public" (who might get the virus) and "risky communities" (who spread the virus). Patton argues that the general public is positioned as having *the right to know*, whereas communities placed at risk have *the obligation to know* so as not to spread the virus. The limits of the campaign stall in the argument over the right to know as opposed to a universalization of safer practices of the body. The general public thus is constructed as innocent bystanders who, with the facts in hand, might be able to protect themselves and this officially inclusive discourse, in and of itself, is antidiscriminatory: if safety can be constituted as if outside the epidemic, then there is nothing to fear. With nothing to fear, the "general public" has no "reason" to discriminate and is safely positioned within the realm of rationality.

This dynamic of subjection becomes even more elaborate in the AIDS information discourse of "No One Is Safe." While ostensibly producing inclusivity, at the level of social effects new forms of exclusivity are being performed. In Cindy Patton's words: "Far from breaking down the sharp dichotomy between "risk groups" and the "general public," the rhetoric of "no one is safe" produced a policing of identity borders as well as community borders: "no one is safe" because you can't tell who is queer" (101).

The campaign No One Is Safe may have provoked the misrecognition identity tries to avoid. Still, what can happen to anyone is that anyone can be queer. In such a campaign Foucault's doubled subject is alive and anxious: tied to self-knowledge and subject to dependence upon others for recognition. But whereas, as Patton suggests, the campaign No One Is Safe works to set in motion a policing of identity borders, something anxious is also produced for the campaign unleashed, in part, the unthinkable: no place of safety, no stable comparisons, and the struggle with the fear of being mistaken, of not knowing or being known. Sometimes, something queer happens when the categories us/them scramble for articulation. Sometimes, they are disrupted.

But the disruption of identity, in its anxious attempts to coalesce, can take a different form. In our second story of the passion for ignorance, even when identities are asserted, however one imagines their emancipatory possibilities, there is no guarantee that representation can instantiate the capacity to know and be known. In *Epistemology of the Closet*, Eve Sedgwick describes the flip side of no one is safe as it is lived in education. In a graduate seminar men and women attempt to read gay and lesbian literature. Sedgwick reports her own discomfort in the course: originally, she and the women of the seminar situated the discomfort in "some obliquity in the classroom relations between [women] and the men. But by the end of the semester it seemed clear that we were in the grip of some much more intimate dissonance" (61). And this had to do with the differences between and within women. In discussing gay and lesbian literature, readers—from whatever position—were confronted with their own self-knowledge. They were, at the same time, subjected to someone else's control even while they scrambled to become tied down to their own identity. In Sedgwick's words:

> Through a process that began, but *only* began, with the perception of some differences among our mostly explicitly, often somewhat uncrystallized sexual self-definition, it appeared that each woman in the class possessed (or might rather feel we were possessed by) an ability to make one or more of the other women radically doubt the authority of her own self-definition as a woman; as a feminist; as a positional subject of a particular sexuality. (61)

Here, the problem is not that no one was safe because, in this case, one could tell who was queer. Rather, telling queerness in the context of identity politics seemed to set up new forms of authority and new hierarchies of knowledge and identity that called into question old forms of authority, namely categories like "woman," "feminist," and "sex." At the same time, newly inverted forms of "us" and "them" emerged from reading gay and lesbian texts, and consequently the boundaries of the inside and the outside were maintained. These positions were neither implicitly pedagogical nor emancipatory in that, in this case, identification remained tied to self-knowledge, to identity. Evidently, and in spite of the curriculum, gay and lesbian literature was read as a special event: perhaps a vicarious means to learn something about the other; perhaps a vicarious means for the other to affirm her otherness and berate those who are imagined as the same. Even when the course material gestured to difference, the question still remained of how difference was to be read and ethically engaged. Because the "facts" of gay and lesbian literature were not telling, acquiring them was a problem for all involved. No one is safe not just because anyone can be called "queer" but because something queer can happen to anyone when one attempts to fix and unfix identity.

As Sedgwick reminds us, this "intimate dissonance" should not be read as a social effect of bad pedagogy but rather as the beginning of pedagogy. If hierarchies first must be inverted, rendered as already estranged, in order to draw attention to themselves, this first move is a tricky beginning. Any inversion, after all, is what should provoke pedagogy to do something more: to engage its own impertinence and imagine what it might mean to be a social subject in a place called "the classroom." But if pedagogy is to do something more than make inverted hierarchies, it must not fall into the cul-de-sac of merely reversing the place of expertise, shutting down identifications with epistemological privilege, and providing a stage for what Foucault calls the "speaker's benefit," or the pleasure that is made from fleeing power.[35] Instead, pedagogy might consider the problem of engaging its own alterity: of staying in that space of difference described by Samuel Delany as lying within "the margin[s] between claims of truth and the claims of textuality."[36] Within these margins, everybody might begin to consider the fact that representations and the identities they assume to serve, however emancipatory, cannot provide access to an unmediated knowledge or even invoke, in and of themselves, thought that can think against itself.

Patton's reading of governmental AIDS information discourses shows how the normal subject-presumed-to-know and the deviant subject-obligated-to-confess are both discursively produced. Both positions require boundary policing even though such policing does not work in the same way and each demands different degrees of subjection. But these networks of power—discursively lived at the level of bodies and disciplined by normative educational practices—depend upon the assumption of stable and hence predictable identities that then can be contained. This, of course, is the authorship of normalization. Then we have Sedgwick's description of her seminar, where differences within, say, the category of "woman" disrupt the impossible promise of sameness, the promise of a community whose very basis depends upon subjects who presume but cannot know the same. In Sedgwick's seminar, the identity hierarchy is reversed and epistemological privilege is still dependent upon the fashioning of bodies into stable identities whose knowledge is thought to spring from an unambivalent identity. In both instances, then, perhaps another version of discourses of information and discourses of feelings, identity disciplines bodies and forecloses its own identificatory possibilities. The cost of "difference" is thus the very acknowledgement necessary for political practices, for what Giorgio Agamben names "the idea of an inessential commonality, a solidarity that in no way concerns an essence."[37]

The two examples, however singular, provoke the same problem, namely a rigid identity when identity claims take on an aura of verisimilitude and hence are taken as if they can exist outside of the very historicity that provokes such claims and their attendant feelings in the first place. What is left unthought, then, is the very reading practices that structure intelligibility and that make identity possible even as these practices perform impossible identities. If a pedagogical project is to move beyond the repetition of identity and the only two subject positions allowed when identity is understood as one of self versus others, then pedagogy itself must become a problem of reading practices, of social relations, and of the means to refuse to think straight.

Reading Practices

Shoshana Felman's exploration of the pedagogical practices of Lacan's return to (and re-reading of) Freud offers a way to rethink reading practices beyond the impulse to instantiate identity as the anxious repetition of sameness. Felman's concern is psychoanalytic: to consider techniques of thinking "beyond one's means," to consider the possibility of exceeding the self by becoming interested in questioning the impulse to normalize. Felman notes three analytic practices of interpretation: those having to do with alterity; those having to do with dialogue; and those having to do with theory. Taken together, these three techniques may allow one to create new strategies for reading. While I will briefly outline Felman's practices, they will be elaborated by re-reading some of the issues raised earlier by Patton and by Sedgwick.

Reading for alterity begins with acknowledgment of difference as the precondition for the self. One does not begin by constructing resemblances with another but "the reading necessarily passes through the Other, and in the Other, reads not identity (other or same), but difference and self difference."[38] As an interpretive practice, reading may then become an imagined means to untie self-knowledge from itself if the self can be encountered as split between recognition and misrecognition. In this way, no category is sufficient, final, or total, nor can any category be mastered or known as sheer positivity.

A second reading practice is provoked in dialogue. Felman borrows Freud's recognition of dialogue as a "structuring condition of possibility." To read is automatically to construct a dialogic relation with a self and with a text to allow for something more. But in making such a dialogue, the reader is asked to consider what she or he wants from the text. Both the text and the self perform differential replies, in the form of perhaps a question, perhaps an argument, perhaps a misunderstanding. Reading thus begins with a supposition of difference, division, and negotiation. When reading practices are privileged over the intentions of the author or reader, the concern becomes one of thinking through the structures of textuality as opposed to the attributes of biography. This makes possible the disruption of the interpreter/interpreted hierarchy. And so the insistence of such a dialogue is implication, not application.

Finally, as a practice, reading provokes a theory of reading, not just a reworking of meaning. How one reads matters. In Felman's words: "There is a constitutive belatedness of the theory over the practice, the theory always trying to catch up with what it was that the practice, or the reading, was really doing" (24). Such belatedness—where the recognition of how one reads in terms of what one wants drags behind the investment in the immediacy of gathering meanings—marks uncertainty as a condition of possibility. In the marking of one's theory of reading, one can begin to study where one's reading breaks down. What might become a problem is the study of one's own theoretical limits.

How then does one get to a place where identity is not the primal scene of reading as a repetition but, instead, a discursive practice, a practice of the self that can exceed the self? In considering Lacan's reading practices, Felman sketches what she terms as "a new mode of reflexivity" (60). For interpretations to be critical and hence to exceed the impulse to normalize and contain meaning, reading must begin with an acknowledgement of difference within identity and not reduce interpretation to a confirmation or negation of identity. This is a question of reading as alterity through the consideration of the failure of translation. The exploration becomes an analysis of the signifier, not the signified, and hence an analysis of where meaning breaks down for the reader. The problem is to think of reading practices as a means for disrupting inside/outside hierarchies—beginning with a self that reads as a means to exceed that very self. And within such excess one might consider the belatedness of theory. In this way, Felman suggests that one might begin to depart from the self in order to think the self as always already divided from itself, as embodying difference and division.

If the problem were posed in terms of how subjection is made from any body and what makes normalcy thinkable in education, then the information campaigns of AIDS education that Patton describes and the hierarchy of identities that Sedgwick worries about might be encountered or produced differently. There might be a decision on the part of those positioned outside the AIDS pandemic to refuse the proffered grounds of innocence and rationality and hence to refuse to identify with the general public. What might become suspect are the categorical imperatives and attendant inequalities produced with this campaign. Then, no one is safe from the governmental campaigns. In the case of Sedgwick's seminar, in which the grounds of identity are still confined to mastery and certitude, there might be a decision to refuse these very grounds. Reading might then be a theorization of reading as being always about risking the self, about confronting one's own theory of reading, and about engaging one's own alterity and desire. Thinking itself, in classroom spaces, might take the risk of refusing to secure thought and of exposing the danger in the curious insistence on positing foundational claims at all costs.[39] No one is safe because the very construct of safety places at risk difference as uncertainty, as indeterminacy, as incompatibility. The problem becomes one of working toward ethical relations.

As Felman suggests, if reading practices could begin to read the social as constructed, as necessarily mediated by a self that is always already divided from itself, identity might be encountered as "never identical to itself" and hence located, however partially and provincially, in that queer space between what is taken as real and the afterthought of (mis)recognition. A queer pedagogy is not concerned with getting identities right or even with having them represented as an end in themselves. The point is to read—in radical ways—the insufficiencies of identity as positivity and to examine and to refuse "cases of exorbitant normality" whether such cases take the form of heteronormativity, racisms, gender centerings, ability hierarchies, and so on. One might read identity as a relation, whether that reading concerns the reader or the read.

These insights into reading practices are impertinent because they begin with an insistence on alterity, the irrevocability of difference within identity, which is to say, the unthought of the thought of identity. As a pedagogical practice, reading becomes a practice of constituting the criteria that make the self and that make another both intelligible and unintelligible, an occasion for thought to think against itself. At the same time, reading practices need to be understood as constituting the dialogic, requiring something more than the self in order to think the self differently. And because reading practices also produce a theory of reading practices, the act of reading might become more complicated. It might return the subject to the problem of one's own subjection, rethinking the way that "self-knowledge" becomes, as Foucault explains it, being subject to someone else's control.

Much of my argument is predicated upon the belief that to recognize difference outside the imperatives of normalcy—that is, beyond the need to render difference through the lens of the same, either through discourses of feelings or through discourses of information—requires attention to how one's reading practices as historically, socially, and psychically configured produce particular conceptual needs. My thinking has been influenced by queer theories that mark the production and valorization of normalcy as a site of subjection and by the psychoanalytic attention to the split and desirous subject. Whether "cases of exorbitant normality" take big forms (such as various racisms, heteronormativities, nationalisms, ethnocentricities, eurocentrism, colonization) or little forms (such as empathy, tolerance, self-esteem, safety, and so on), these cases should become a central problem of educational thought and practice, a central problem of pedagogy. I raise these dynamics as a question of reading practices because, at the level of the everyday, structures of intelligibility are sustained not only by hegemonic and punishing chains of signification but, just as significantly, in the way education closes down how the everyday might be imagined and lived, and hence in how one becomes a social subject in a place called the "classroom."

If reading practices partially structure one's capacity to do something more, to become something otherwise, is there a way for pedagogy to rethink how reading practices are practiced and educated in classroom sites? Are there ways of thinking about proliferating one's identificatory possibilities so that the interest becomes one of theorizing why reading is always about risking oneself, of confronting one's own theory of reading, of signification, and of difference, and of refusing to be "the same"? What if "difference" made a difference in how the self encountered the self and in how one encounters one?

In my work on pedagogy, what I want to call "queer pedagogy," I am attempting to exceed such binary oppositions as the tolerant and the tolerated and the oppressed and the oppressor yet still hold onto an analysis of social difference that can account for how dynamics of subordination and subjection work at the level of the historical, the structural, the epistemological, the conceptual, the social, and the psychic. But such efforts involve thinking through an implication that can tolerate a curiosity toward one's own otherness, one's own unconscious desires and wishes, one's own negations. My interest is to provoke conditions of learning that might allow for an exploration that unsettles the sediments of what one imagines when one imagines normalcy, what one imagines when one images difference. So I wonder whether identity categories will be helpful in this work if identity depends upon the production of sameness and otherness, dynamics that anchor modes of subjection. Maybe, given the desire for knowledge of difference to make a difference in how social subjects conduct themselves and in how sociality might be imagined and lived, the new questions that must be addressed concern what education, knowledge, identity, and desire have to do with the fashioning of structures of intelligibility and unintelligibility, with what education has to do with the possibilities of proliferating identifications and critiques that exceed identity yet still hold onto the understanding of any identity as a state of emergency.

This I take as the beginnings of a queer pedagogy that refuses normal practices and practices of normalcy, that begins with an ethical concern for one's *own* reading practices and their relation to the imagining of sociality as more than an effect of the dominant conceptual order. In the queer pedagogy I am attempting, "the inessentially common" is made from the possibility that reading the world is always already about risking the self, in excess of "cases of exorbitant normality," and with an interest in "confounding instituted law."

Chapter Five

Narcissism of Minor Differences and the Problem of Antiracist Pedagogy

> Like the physical, the psychical is not necessarily
> in reality what it appears to be.
>
> —Freud, *"The Unconscious"*

Freud formulates a rather curious category, in *Civilization and Its Discontents*, to ponder the inclination toward aggressive hatred between social groups. The term *narcissism of minor differences* describes as a problem how individuals imagine themselves as members of a particular collectivity. The tension is not so much that people join together as it is what must be done in the name of group distinction. In Freud's words: "It is always possible to bind together a considerable number of people in love, so long as there are other people left over to receive the manifestations of their aggressiveness" (114). The examples Freud offers are noteworthy in that he rehearses the hostilities among various European people: those who may share the same space of nation and language, those of different nations, and the long history of Christianity's aggressions toward the Jews. At the same time, the dynamics of narcissism of minor differences also extend to aggression within communities: there, they may take the prejudicial form of homophobia, sexism, and abuse. In moving backward and forward—inside communities and between communities—the twists of narcissism of minor differences suggest identity not as explanation but rather as antagonistic and fragile, as history and as relationality. For while narcissism begins in one, to make a narcissism, it takes (at least) two.

97

Freud's naming of this dynamic as "minor" or "small" is not meant to suggest that histories of internal and external subordinations, group hatreds, and nationalist imperialisms are trivial. But he does consider how something so small becomes the material for the epic by examining the social and psychic grounds of these histories as a problem for inquiry and for argument.[1] Freud's approach begins with a curiosity toward what libidinal history has to do with social devaluation in order to argue that affective dynamics proceed and attach to cognitive distinctions. This chapter considers such strange turns of psychic events in the context of antiracist pedagogy, for there, libidinal positions seem indistinguishable from dynamics of social justice. And yet, a theory of love and hate in learning seems obscure, if not beside the point, in most pedagogical attempts to consider inequality and the question of identity.

I have three related purposes in attempting to explore something "besides the point." One has to do with thinking beyond the sociological and psychologistic versions of antiracist pedagogy that shut out, perhaps in the name of group solidarity, the psychic events of ambivalence and Eros. The normal version of antiracist pedagogy, that relies on humanistic constructs of role models and self-esteem building, seems to forget the problem of how group identifications become incited and how communities engage with and disassociate from the question of difference. Why, in pedagogical encounters, is it so difficult to engage Eros and ambivalence, when the material of these encounters center experiences of victimization, inequalities, and the desires for representation? The second purpose concerns rethinking the conceptual grounds of race moving beyond the defensive confines of eugenics and onto what Young-Bruehl terms the "ideological desires" that lend affective force to the contours and wishes of prejudices.[2] The third purpose concerns bringing into tension affective dynamics with cognitive worries over representation. Because the concept of narcissism of minor differences centers questions of love and hate as the basis of identificatory ties and the social bond, bringing this complexity to bear on antiracist pedagogies opens discussion about why antiracist pedagogy historically has dismissed, as a disruption to the sociological fact of racial inequality, sexualities and genders. What is the other to antiracist pedagogies?

When Freud attached the term *minor* or *small* to these differences he offered the possibility that there is no biological ground to the cultural dynamics and hatreds between and within communities. In fact, what is most curious about this concept is the idea that intolerance between and within groups is most strongly articulated precisely because of what is common: sociality such as nation, family, and neighborhood, and experiences such as historical trauma and genocide. The problem raised in the concept is not, I think, with the question of difference, but with the question of love or narcissism. As Freud observes in *Group Psychology and the Analysis of the Ego*, while self-love is necessary for self-preservation, the individual also "behaves as though the occurrence of any divergence from his own particular lines of development involved a criticism of them and a demand for their alteration. . . . Love for oneself knows only one barrier—love for others, love for objects" (102). Where there is love there is the fear of the loss of love. And it is precisely because love can reverse its content, becoming a hatred, that the fluidity and vicissitudes of narcissism are rendered so precarious and fragile. Again, in Freud's terms, love "can turn into an expression of tenderness as easily as into a wish for someone's removal" (105). This point is made more forcefully in Freud's 1915 paper "Instincts and Their Vicissitudes." There Freud maintains that the only time an instinct can change its content (as opposed to its object, aim, or pressure) into its opposite is "the transformation of love and hate" (133).[3]

As if noting the treacheries of love were not enough, Freud also names more problems entangled in the dynamic of narcissism. Narcissism is the first love made from the first love received and the grounds of the ego's possibility. There must be self-regard for there to be a self. But because narcissism is so tied to the ego, whose function is to observe, perceive, project, reality test, and hallucinate, narcissism is also the grounds for sociality. Yet narcissism is easily injured and its strategies of recovery can be cruel and aggressive. This may be because, as a dynamic, narcissism incites questions of value and de-value.[4] More than just self-love, narcissism is, in Grunberger's terms, "an omnipotent feeling of absolute autonomy, of faultless perfection, an overvaluation of the self and a spontaneous tendency toward expansion, a feeling of infinity, of boundlessness, of eternity" (47–48). Such confidence, according to Grundberger, is inspired by the desire for purity, that is, the desire to be unencumbered by the demand of the other, the impossible desire to be one's own author. This desire for purity compels one to project what is impure in the self onto others. The expulsion that is projection, Grunberger argues, psychically frees the subject from his own aggressivity in that the violence against others is accomplished under the larger banners of purity, authenticity, and boundary maintenance such as nation, religion, race, gender-centering, and so on. In this view, the narcissist must hate the body of the other because it cannot be the same body as the ego's. The projection involved is essentially one that returns, but in the form of a threat. Elisabeth Young-Bruehl poses the movement this way: "As a mode of nostalgia [where the wish is for a lost wholeness] narcissistic desire is aimed at a fantasized originary condition—but cannot understand another's way of fantasizing an originary condition."[5]

In Freud's terms, both love and hate are psychic demands elaborated socially, historically, and unconsciously. The narcissism Freud worries about concerns the aggressive intensification and the social and psychic costs of an excessive self-regard. Michael Ignatieff's thoughts about narcissism as prohibiting an acknowledgement of the dignity of the other suggest where its weaknesses may lie: "The facts of difference themselves are neutral. It is narcissism that turns difference into a mirror. In this mirror, a narcissist does not see the others in and for themselves; he sees them only as they reflect upon or judge himself.

What is different is rejected if it fails to confirm the narcissist in his or her own self-opinion."[6]

Part of what the narcissist cannot tolerate is her or his own inner conflict or difference. Some of this difference has to do with the ego's own insufficient mechanisms for perceiving the world and meeting different egos in that world. Paradoxically, the narcissist desires the other to be the same but cannot bear the possibility that there may be commonality because commonality seems to threaten the ego's desire for omnipotence, mastery, and distinction. Young-Bruehl's exploration of narcissism makes this point. She suggests that one of the social forms narcissism takes is the ideology of desire called "sexism." The narcissist who is prejudiced seems to "focus on the realities, signs, or symbols of difference" (236)—for example anatomy, skin color, facial features, and sexual organs—and exaggerates these differences. The tendency to exaggerate mirrors the way the narcissist overvalues the self. This capacity to overvalue is what Freud claims, in his essay "On Narcissism," as the rule of thumb.

Other forms of difference within have to do with the splits of psychic structure and the arguments that play within. What is intolerable is projected elsewhere, onto the other. But in this work of projection a certain obsessiveness is required, for one cannot merely project and then be done with the project. To return to Ignatieff's point, the judgment toward others can return as criticism against the one who judges. And in an odd turn of events, this hostility, now seen as coming back upon the narcissist, confirms the narcissist's need for maintaining her or his defense and excessive self-regard. It is only through the projection that the narcissist can confirm her or his opinion. But this dynamic, best understood by way of a joke, is also discomforting. The analyst Laplanche recounts the old psychiatric joke

> about the man who is a paranoiac and enters the hospital because he is afraid that he is going to be eaten by chickens. He is the grain, and he is going to be pecked up by chickens. He has psychotherapy for a few months, sees a doctor and says, "I know I am not a grain." A few days later, again he criticises the doctor and says, "Well I am not a grain, I am sure of that. Let me leave." The doctor releases him, and just as he goes through the yard of the hospital, the doctor looks out. It is a country hospital, there are some poultry in the yard and the man begins to run. The doctor says to him, "But you know you are not a grain!" and the man replies, "Sure I know—but does the chicken?"

Laplanche then offers the following problem of projection: "At the bottom of projection, there is something that is not projection— that is, a question: what does he want from me . . . a question not about what I am introducing into the other, but that something comes from the other."[7] We are back to Freud's point that the other is imagined as a critic and as a barrier to self-knowledge and self-love.

Freud's concern is with the psychic investments at work in distinguishing the self from the other, in attempting to find out what the other wants, and with the repetitions of psychic conflict in the act of perception when the self has no other strategy to answer this question than to place conflict into the other's identity. He is also interested in how aggression becomes the grounds for bonding within a community. Moreover, in questioning love, and by placing the conflict of love with the demand for social esteem into the realm of the ego—itself an effect of the history of its own perceptions and libidinal ties—Freud can refuse the dominant essentialist discourses that conceptually underpin the intelligibility of race, namely eugenics, biology, and heredity, the European anchorage points or props for various modern racisms.[8]

Such an operatic shift—from the so-called scientific empiricism of race as a biological law to the murky and contradictory interpretations called "history" and "psychic structure"—was, of course, in the Jewish Freud's own interests.[9] By the late nineteenth century, Freud's generation had become the Jewish object that crystallized popular, legal, and scientific racism within Europe. "The Jewish Problem" was a racial problem, and with this racialization came "The Jewish Look." In medical, anthropological, and race science writing, "the Jew" became construed as historical throwback or anachronism in need of explication, containment, and, ultimately, annihilation. As a race, Jews were represented in this literature as capable of tricking (because at first glance they looked like anyone else) and contaminating (because their blood was dirty) Christian Europeans. But Freud was unsatisfied with scientific theories of heredity and degeneration. So he dismissed the eugenic category of "race" as being capable of explaining anything and instead studied the affective and imaginary dynamics of individuals and their dreams and of civilization and its discontents.[10] In its refusal to ground the study of human suffering in the eugenics of science, Freud's psychoanalysis can be considered one of the first antiracist sciences in Europe.[11]

But why begin with Freud when this discussion investigates the ways particular communities form themselves and relate to others? Why pose these dynamics as a problem of love? To bring to bear the psychoanalytic question of narcissism of minor differences on the field of antiracist pedagogy allows us to consider as a problem the conditions for identification and disassociation that divide and trouble the self and the other. This ambivalence is the Freudian sense of love: the romance with domination and mastery, and the problem of what the ego in love must suffer to be socially tamed and named as proper. Throughout this discussion, I will be troubling the sentimental consolation that separates love from aggression and suggest that attention to those narcissisms of minor differences within and between communities permits a different kind of argument for the field of antiracist pedagogy, one that can center on the fashioning of communities, one that admits the fragile relations and fault lines between ethics and cultural memory, and one that figures the geometric conflicts of love. The pedagogical problem is twofold. How might any body come to be called—in the name of community—to the service of the self/other divide? How might the field of antiracist pedagogy rethink the problem of community in ways that allow community to be more than a problem of repudiating others through those narcissisms of minor differences?

To sharpen the above questions, this chapter begins with a focus on the historical constructions of Jewishness as a race and then speculates upon the return of this history when North American Jews and African Americans dialogue between and among each other. I consider how the category of race has been conceptualized in anti-Semitic race writing and how this conceptualization modulates present discussions. But rather than viewing each community as an undifferentiated mass or as mutually exclusive in its experiences, categories, and demands, antagonisms and conflict within communities are theorized as fashioning relations between communities. This strategy, mirroring the psychoanalytic insight that internal conflicts structure what individuals notice in the world, is meant to illustrate a particular dilemma typically ignored when educational efforts focus on questions of race and racism. It has to do with how the category of "race" works to articulate and disarticulate in unconscious ways the alibis of sex and gender. To highlight this complication, I offer the example of race writing by Jewish lesbians.

A short study of selected Jewish lesbian writing challenges the antiracist distinctions that position identity markers such as "race," "sex," and "gender" as capable of being conscious, as separable, and as standing alone. The writing discussed here suggests that the body is neither lived nor imagined in instalments and that, taken together, markers of the body such as race, gender, and sex act upon each other in ways that are unpredictable. To state the obvious, like anyone else, Jewish lesbians do not live in a vacuum: larger historical dynamics shape how Jewish lesbians engage within and between social, cultural, political, and institutional communities. Like anyone else, Jewish lesbians are not reducible to an identity of either this or that, and so considering their discussions might complicate the field of antiracist pedagogy in two important ways. First, their discussions perform what Stuart Hall terms "the new politics of representation [that crosses] questions of racism irrevocably with questions of sexuality."[12] As we will see, the history of Jewish racialization indicates that racist constructions of the body require that the body also be constructed through discourses of gender and sexuality in order for the category of race to be intelligible. What may not be so obvious in this formulation is that even those who write against racism are not immune from excluding large segments of their community from representation, from partaking in the strange dynamic of narcissism of minor differences. The problem, however, in the eschewal of antagonisms within communities is that the underlying reason why prejudice is studied is never considered critically. Indeed, Hall's notion of the new politics of representation can be seen as a critique of the old forms of anti-oppression education. Young-Bruehl makes this same point when she argues: "A theory that holds, in effect, that unfamiliarity between groups breeds contempt—and posits that familiarity will breed respect [cannot] speak to complexes of feelings and images of the 'other' that are unconscious, as resistant to familiarity as the unconscious is to reasoned arguments or progressive social visions."[13] That familiarity also may be a problem returns us to the question of narcissism of minor differences.

While Jewish lesbian writing can open the field of antiracist pedagogy to differences within a community, the second way Jewish lesbian writing complicates antiracist pedagogy relates to how questions of cultural memory are engaged. In this writing, memory is not limited to a template that records one's agreement with past experiences. Rather, following a psychoanalytic model, memory becomes more like a method and a resistance to method, a contradictory dynamic that organizes and produces desire, ignorance, forgetting, and investments. As a method, memory can complicate and contradict itself with events, questions, and histories never directly experienced. As resistance, memory can fixate in repetition and nostalgia for the lost object. One can suffer from one's memory. Perhaps both of these qualities are always at stake if memory can be thought of as a potential space that modulates and elaborates the strange relations between affect and idea. This view of memory should become central to educational efforts, for education is, after all, a means to extend the self with experiences that can be engaged only through the other. To view the elaborated work of memory and its forgetting opens the field of antiracist pedagogy to the argument that bodies are more complicated than the first narcissistic glance can bear to acknowledge, and that first glance is organized by those narcissisms of minor differences.

My concern is to think discursively along with a few conversations within a rather small and often ignored imagined community, Jewish lesbians.[14] Their writing will be juxtaposed with mainstream, mostly male, discussions of Jewishness and race. This rather curious montage may reveal more about the kaleidoscopic fractures of "the new politics of representation" than a traditional explication of the social structures that incite and stabilize the meanings of race relations. The writers I discuss begin with the problematic of social power as it pertains to racial inequalities. But unlike discussions in which the term *white privilege* is treated as if it were monolithic, ahistoric, and unambivalent in experience, debates within Jewish lesbian communities and between Jews and African Americans lend themselves to historical nuance. Taken together, the arguments point to what Ann Pellegrini views as "the crisis of racial definition."[15] They suppose that identity is not the sum of singular and conscious acts but rather a social relation and a psychical event caught up—even as it catches itself—in the unconscious detours of history, memory, and communities.

Many of the arguments between North American Jews and African Americans engage the question of whether expanding cultural memory can allow for the dignity of solidarity between groups of people and hence exceed the narcissisms of minor differences. In mainstream debates between African Americans and Jews, tensions are examined when Jewishness is collapsed into the imperatives of whiteness or when the arguments get stuck in the binary of assimilation and authenticity. Jewish lesbian writing on race takes a different strategy, focusing on conflict between and among Jewish and non-Jewish lesbians. In debates within Jewish lesbian writing, there is an additional refusal to collapse Jewishness into the imperatives of masculinity and heterosexuality.[16] And yet, in making these distinctions, there is still no guarantee of harmonizing community.

To hold onto such dissonance, such differences, remains quite tricky, particularly if one moves both to mainstream literature on Jewish racialization and to the literature that, over the last thirty years, addresses relations between African Americans and Jews in the United States. Part of the problem may be that the category "Jew," like the category "black," cannot signal its own internal differences made from the ambivalent relations among gender, sex, class, and nation. Another part of the problem, as many have pointed out, is that "black" and "Jew" are not mutually exclusive.[17] In a curious detour that renders discussions of racialization even more unwieldy, Paul Gilroy recounts how, while traveling in Eastern Europe during the Dreyfus Affair, W. E. B. Dubois "puzzled over the meaning of being mistaken for a Jew while travelling."[18] Dubois was dropped off at a Jewish inn after he answered "yes" when asked by the carriage driver if he was a Jew. We can complicate matters even further by bringing to bear on this discussion the history of Eastern and Western European Jewish racialization. Given the Shoah, the idea of the Jew as "white" in both North America and Europe is barely fifty years old.[19] In North America, persistent memories of what Joan Nestle calls "a restricted country," the contemporary resurgence of the New Right's militia movement and the movements of Christian fundamentalism to anti-Semitism and racism bother any seamless capacity or desire for many Jews to enmesh Jewishness with whiteness.[20]

If one can begin from the vantage point that the social meanings of race, sex, and gender are cacophonous in their historicity, the noise, in Sander Gilman's study *The Jew's Body*, is made for and by men.[21] The chapters in Gilman's book are organized in terms of how European science imagined the various body parts of male Jews as problematic and in need of explanation, and include "scientific" examination of "the Jewish foot," "the Jewish nose," "the Jewish voice," and "the Jewish psyche." Such features of anti-Semitic writing—cloaked in the authority of scientific discourse—legitimized the mythic but irreversible modern social fact of the Jew as other to white. Thus, as modern white supremacy was distinguishing itself from its other, whiteness required further distinctions like a gender, a sex, and an imagined origin: in this context whiteness became a synecdoche for normality and masculinity. The "[male] Jew" became a metonym for deviancy, illness, and femininity.[22]

The grounds upon which racism is built in this anti-Semitic literature challenges current educational definitions of racism as merely performing the commonly taught formula that racism equals prejudice plus power, and that race is a natural category somehow distorted by racism. Indeed, we are left with the difficult question of something more intractable, namely the fantasy of imagining difference. As well, the modern history of European Jewry challenges commonly taught notions of white privilege as an instant, transparent, and unitary accessory to the body. Such ahistoric conceptualizations are an effect of essentialist discourses of race and perhaps of the educational desire to simplify the complex histories of racism in the name of certainty and correction. These conceptualizations must forget what Foucault termed as "the mechanisms" of power, "ensured [not] by right but by technique, not by law but by normalization, not by punishment but by control."[23] The normalization of race—like the normalization of gender and sex—as an obvious, visible, and predictive feature of the body is thus a discourse that gestures to the problem of the production by mechanisms of power that incite proper and improper bodies.[24]

The problem is that, as a discourse, racism installs a rarefied fantasy of naturalism into the body. Then one's nature—regardless of conduct and actions, and actions in this discourse are read as only confirming nature—can never be altered.[25] It is precisely this fixity—this unchanging, ahistoric nature—that can be read, interpreted, counted, classified, categorized, contained, and rendered visible. Within the Nazi imaginary, Jewishness, as opposed to Judaism, is a problem of blood, not an effect of conscience, desire, practice, or community. The elaboration of racial eugenic sciences and the practices of "racial betterment" fashioned, upon that which could not be seen, a science of visibility organized to imagine the proper body. And in the process of bestowing appearance to what could not be distinguished, race—for the Jew—became a secret to be spoken and a truth to be found. Thus "the Jewish look."

Fifty years later, and referring to North American Ashkenazi Jews, Sander Gilman asks, "Are Jews white? and what does 'white' mean in this context. . . . How has the question of racial identity shaped Jewish identity in the Diaspora?"[26] We can complicate this question with a parenthetical remark pertaining to early twentieth-century discussions about Jews that Gilman inserts in another of his studies: "The very term 'Jew' is as much a category of gender, masculine, as it is a category of race."[27] The problem seems to be twofold: What do race and gender mean in terms of the shaping of difference within Jewish identities, and indeed, in the construction of any identity? And, if the term *Jew* is coded as masculine—and indeed, the mainstream debates between African Americans and Jews are largely debates between middle-class men about middle-class men,[28] and the term *Jew* is also coded historically as "not white"—what are the dynamics of racialization and engenderment for diasporic Jewish lesbians?

Here a disconcerting detour is in order, for Jewish women also may be stereotyped through behavior which in turn constitutes "a look" that becomes "a sound." Being pushy, loud-mouthed, and fussy, the Jewish woman's body is overbearing, bossy, and insatiable. Jewish women are reduced to a noise and a complaint, trapped in "Jewish princess" and "Jewish mother" jokes. In these representations sexuality is foreclosed. The economy of visibility for Jewish men is different: culturally, as Jews, they are obligated to mark—indeed, to cut—their male body. Nothing comparable is demanded of Jewish women, even though, in the first instance, Jewishness is matrilineally bestowed.[29] Religious Jewish males may wear a kippa to identify as Jews whereas religious Jewish females are only obligated to signify their relation to heterosexual marital status.[30] Within, and echoing well beyond, Jewish sociality, the very common complaint about looking (and sounding) too Jewish or not looking (and not sounding) Jewish enough plays differently in terms of gender, sex, race, generation, and geography. These modulations of Jewish difference may signify, as well, questions of assimilation and Jewish self-hatred. Sander Gilman's comment is pertinent, but not without argument: "The desire for invisibility, the desire to become 'white,' lies at the centre of the Jew's flight from his or her own body."[31] The pertinency has to do with the ways in which one's body becomes inconsolable; the argument, with the collapse of the desire for invisibility with the desire to become white. For, at times, the strange desire for invisibility may be a wish to have the body not matter as opposed to have the body become synonymous with that which invokes pain.

James Baldwin recognized this desire for invisibility when, in the late 1960s, he wrote complexly about the narcissisms of minor differences between African Americans and Jews, and about why the incapacity to generalize or transfer sufferings as the claim for intra-group understanding was a misgiving wish: "In the American context, the most ironical thing about Negro anti-Semitism is that the Negro is really condemning the Jew for having become an American white man—for having become, in effect, a Christian. The Jew profits from his status in America, and he must expect Negroes to distrust him for it."[32]

Baldwin engages a double ambivalence: his own refusal of a certain historicity—a particular ethicality—that he wished Jewish (male) difference could reference, and the perception that, in North America, light-skinned Jews can assimilate, or rather, be mistaken for "an American white Christian man." Many Jews have tried to assimilate into an unmarked bodily whiteness that forecloses Jewish difference.[33] But such an escape, if it is indeed possible, raises other questions: For whom is assimilation and passing a preoccupation? How does assimilation work as what Dubois called "double consciousness?" And what does the other want from the one who assimilates, or from the one who might fall into assimilation? We might, however, read Baldwin's passage with irony, for without the trope of masculinity, how would betrayal become registered?

Years later, in what is perhaps now known as one of the most sustained meditations on racism and anti-Semitism by a Jewish lesbian of Eastern European decent, Elly Bulkin holds the tension that one's history of oppression is no guarantee of any kind of social sensitivity or insight into anyone's difference, including one's own.[34] Perhaps reversing Baldwin's equation, Bulkin examines her own contradictory anger in holding to the assumption that people's "gut-level experience of their own oppression will provide them with a ready store of empathy for others. When, for instance, I am dyke-baited on my block by teenagers, white and Black, I am, in total defiance of logic, angrier at the Black kids than at the white ones: *they*, I mutter to myself, should know better!" (150).

But what is being claimed by the claim "they should know better"? Baldwin's essay renders this familiar problem as an uncanny return of narcissism: "If one blames the Jew for not having been ennobled by oppression, one is not indicating the single figure of the Jew but the entire human race, and one is also making a quiet breathtaking claim for oneself."[35]

There is, then, a significant tension within the observations proffered both by Baldwin and by Bulkin, having to do with the question of anyone's cultural memory in the matter of racism, with how a memory becomes a demand and a responsibility, and then, with how one's expectations for the conduct of another turns back upon the self. At stake is the ethicality yet to be made from the flaws of misrecognition and from the difficult acknowledgment that suffering, in and of itself, is not pedagogical. The demand to "know better" is a "breathtaking claim for oneself." This returns us to those narcissisms of minor differences and to the conflicts—indeed, the betrayals—incited when one thinks of the other as "a mirror," or at least as having the obligation to "know better." As Baldwin and Bulkin turn this obligation back to the self, something more significant can be examined, namely the ethical and interminable problem of knowing others and of being known in terms that refuse excessive self-regard and its underside, the subordination and devaluing of the other.

Refusing to be subordinated does not guarantee that one will not subordinate another. Suffering is just the beginning. This tension works differently in one of the first anthologies of Jewish lesbian writing, *Nice Jewish Girls: A Lesbian Anthology*. Today, one might read it as largely testimonial. It offers first-hand accounts of the impossible desire for recognition on one's own terms as one seeks group affinity and affirmation. Many of the contributors sketch the geography of anti-Semitism, homophobia, and racism in North America and Europe and write against the disavowals of these dynamics within feminism, leftist politics, and mainstream Jewish communities. Then we see more clearly how narcissism of minor differences works within groups in which individuals imagine each other as similar but not so much so that their membership is without a question.

The awkwardness of imagining that all Jewish lesbians face the same dilemmas, or even that Jewish lesbianism means something similar to those who claim this identity, is analyzed by Pauline Bart in her essay "How a Nice Jewish Girl Like Me Could." Bart describes a trip to Amsterdam in which, during a heated discussion on lesbian separatism, she meets another Jewish lesbian. Afterwards, Bart asks her how she survived World War II:

> She tells me that she was sent from Christian family to Christian family. I mention that she does not look Jewish. She says, "Of course not. If I looked Jewish I'd be dead." She gets a terrible headache and I feel guilty and stupid. We return to her apartment where I learn of her role in the founding of Israel's gay liberation movement. She left after finding it impossible to live openly as a lesbian. In Israel she was in *galut* because she was a lesbian and in Amsterdam she is in *galut* because she is a Jew. (61)

The economy of guilt and the imperatives of identity are quite complicated here for very different histories of the Jewish diaspora are at stake. Discourses of visibility, assimilation, and authenticity only muddle the stakes of misrecognition. Perhaps Bart remembers the shame of being shut out of one's community but only in retrospect can she consider her own repetitions within needing the mythic "Jewish look." Like Bulkin, Bart might berate herself for not knowing better and for thinking that her own experiences of exclusion are comparable enough to shed a modicum of insight into the exclusions of another. But neither identity nor history is as stable as one's memory remembers. The modulations of historical geographies and genealogies of Jewish racialization and sexualization make both memory and community a question, not an extension of imagined similitude.

In many of these essays there is no tidy agreement on the meanings and effects of racialization, nor even on how Jewishness might be commonly understood. *Nice Jewish Girls* has a section called "Jewish Identity: A Coat of Many Colors," in which differences of geography and generation, and the different meanings of race within and between Jewish communities are discussed. There are questions as to hierarchies within Jewishness in terms of the dominant definition of who can claim Jewishness within religiosity and within secular contexts where light-skinned Jews are seen to assimilate as white and hence not as Jews. These problems cannot be worked through because its authors cannot address something larger: how is it possible to assert difference without asserting a hierarchy of suffering? What is actually being put into place is not so much a coat of many colors as single threads that have the capacity to unravel its seams.

Transposing racial terms to describe differences between Jewish lesbians effects new discussion. Elly Bulkin's essay, published a few years later, argues with some of the racial formulations of *Nice Jewish Girls*. In a rather long footnote, Bulkin reprints a criticism from Rita Arditti, who writes in part: "It seems to me [that *Jews of color* is] a broad term that derives from the North American division between white people in this country and blacks. . . . [*Jews of color*] seems to lump together all the Jews who are not 'white.' And who are 'white Jews'?" (201).

Arditti then asks how Ashkenazi, Sephardic, Ethiopian, and Latin American Jews would be racially categorized and which criteria hold in which places. The rejoinder to the term *Jews of color* raises the question of when racial classification becomes significant to Jews as Jews, particularly given that modern diasporic Jewishness exceeds racial and national boundaries and that, at least since 1492, Jews have been expelled from their country of birth precisely because of their Jewishness.[36]

Still, as Arditti points out, in North America the matter of whiteness matters for those secular Jews with light skin. And, although not acknowledged, part of what matters is the question of how light-skinned Jewish women can be seen as Jews. Bulkin analyzes her recollection of being seen as white and her forgetting that, encountered as a stranger, she may well be seen as white. This concern may mean that other white folks pay her no mind because she is viewed as the same as them. But it also means that if she cannot control how she is seen, she cannot control how she can feel. Bulkin recalls going out for ice cream with a group of women who attended the 1981 National Women's Studies Conference on racism. She happened to be standing alongside a black woman who, upon entering the restaurant, said to herself "Here I come, white folks!" Bulkin poses her own embarrassment at her "unpreparedness for this particular venture into white America. The moment I wandered through the door, *my* skin colour did not grab the attention of the white person sitting over a sundae. ... A few hours after I had been on a panel on racism in the lesbian community, I could imagine going out for an ice cream as a simple and uncomplicated act" (143).

But acts of identity and the ambivalent workings of identification are neither simple nor conscious, and it is not until conflict occurs and is felt that a thought can exceed its own unawareness. Much of the writing by lesbians of any positionality concerns the belatedness of unawareness even as it examines the thousand tiny slights bodies accrue and offer in daily life. While these sorts of sad accountings are made in order to enlarge the accountability of memory and to consider identity as a social relation, there still remains the pedagogical question of how, or even if, otherness can be engaged consciously and why thoughtfulness is always too late. Can (and should) one imagine and predict ostracism and erasure? What would this demand mean in terms both of how the self conducts itself and of how the self imagines what the other wants?

To complicate Bulkin's ice cream memory, consider Leslie Feinberg's *Bildungsroman, Stone Butch Blues*, a novel about the life of a working-class, Jewish, transgendered person.[37] Our protagonist, Jess Goldberg, is a battlefield on two legs. From the cruel gaze of the normative glance that reads the body as a literal confirmation of gender, Jess's body is read as transgressing the intelligibility of both femininity and masculinity. Jess identifies as white, but in the world of strangers this marker does not effect public normalization. Instead, the dominant discourse of the properly gendered body pushes Jess out. Walking into that same ice cream store, Jess would face the hostility that accrues across the small and seemingly insignificant acts of going to the public toilet to the gendered greeting workers are required to make in dealing with customers. The hostility is dual: socially, it has to do with Jess becoming angry at being mistaken and with people's feelings when they get something wrong. Psychically, the hostility accrues within Jess's intimate question of how her own body betrays desires. Jess may wish both to flee and to affirm the body. These turns of dismissal and desire, however, do not grant Jess any immunity from participating in racist discourses. Nor do they allow Jess to imagine how the self becomes diminished by its own passion for ignorance. The Buffalo gay bars of the 1950s and 1960s were, for the most part, segregated by race and class, and this history visits Jess's friendships without an invitation.

For Jess, the possibility of refusing racism before its enactment is troubled by an interracial friendship with Edwin, who gives Jess a copy of W. E. B. Dubois's *The Souls of Black Folk* and forces Jess to consider their differences as lesbians. Jess tells someone: "You know, I always fall back on assuming [that what] Ed and I deal with every day as butches is pretty much the same. . . . Ed reminded me about what she faces everyday that I don't" (129). This acknowledgement occurs the day after the assassination of Martin Luther King Jr., and in the context of the racial tensions within white and black lesbian communities over the meaning of his death. But it was not until years later that Jess would actually read Dubois's text, find the passage Edwin marked on "this double-consciousness, this sense of always looking at one's self through the eyes of others" (178), and begin to think about the psychic ambivalence of living with and without the alibi of gender, race, and sex.

But can the body be without an explanation? In perhaps one of the most provocative attempts by a Jewish lesbian artist to engage this question, Jyl Lynn Felman transgresses the obvious with the imaginary geography of "the erotic," one of the most volatile sites of narcissism of minor differences. Felman thus begins "De Vilde Chayes—The Wild Beasts":

> This is about the erotic. My erotic. About when you see me my erotic. And when you don't. This is about the erotic. My white non-white ethnic white erotic self. And when I'm seen and when I'm not. Seen at all. This is about my erotic. And my sisters erotic. our *sephardic ashkenazic mizrachic* erotic. When you think you are seeing our *sephardic ashknazic mizrachic* white non-white ethnic white erotic selves. And what you don't see. when you think you are seeing me. If you are seeing me. At all. Are you seeing a luscious wild *vilde chaye a zaftig svelt kayn aynhoreh* stunning *vilde chaye*? Or are you seeing loud pushy money lender big nose zionist oppressor that you want . . .? This is about the erotic. My erotic. My white non-white erotic self. About when I'm seen as white and when I'm not. (9)

Such a fantasy refuses to tidy the ambivalence—indeed the vicissitudes—called "love" and "hate." There are no offers of apology and explication, no comfort of experience and identity claims, just the force of desires arguing with the other, becoming other to the pull toward self-mastery and composure. There is no proper body, and the piece demands from its readers something other than moral outrage, the affect that lends quantity and value to narcissism. The concatenation of desire is not within the realm of rationality, representation, or consciousness because it posits the view that multiple and conflictive histories of bodies haunt desire, thereby making the distinction between love and aggression difficult to maintain. Engagement with the phantoms of "De Vilde Chayes" returns us, perhaps more insistently, to Freud's curious category of "narcissism of minor differences," where history as contradiction fashions desire and desire may both dismiss and engage the modulations of its own otherness. This may be the "double consciousness" of Eros. The meeting of the look—the projection that meets the projection—is an erotic and haunted relation and, in this space, racial matters are indivisible from psychic matters of desire and memory.[38]

What, then, might come of an antiracist pedagogy unafraid of examining the question of love and the meaning of social bonding when aggression is admitted as a part of its dynamic? What would actually become a question if the stability of the body as both capable of speaking for itself and capable of even knowing itself were called into question? One possibility resides, I think, in the acknowledgment that the historical constructions of bodies that allow race to be the grounds of racism have both a material and a psychic cost. While antiracist pedagogies have been astute in analyzing the structures of inequality, the reliance upon cognitive content as a corrective to affective dynamics can neither imagine the affective force of narcissism of minor differences nor consider why tolerance of inequality is so pervasive. Examination into the ideologies of desire that render bodies intelligible or disruptive to the mythic norm may complicate any facile gesture to reduce the question of racism to the sole terrain of individual psychology, to ignorance, or to the educational solution of supplying the correct representations. If these problems and repairs are offered as consolations, the writers discussed here would have no place in the classroom or in antiracist pedagogy. But if antiracist pedagogy is to be more than a consolation, it must make itself inconsolable by engaging with what it excludes, namely the complex and contradictory debates within communities over how communities are imagined and made subject to their own persistent questions. This is not a move toward a new inclusivity, even though opening the stakes of identification and learning from the conflicts within communities should trouble what is imagined as a normal race or, more pertinently, as a normal representation of race. The demand that becomes a responsibility is to explore community as a question of love and of antagonisms. Within this space, one might study the ways communities change themselves and center their own movements toward ethicality.

If an ethics can be made of cultural memory, antiracist pedagogy cannot stop with the examination of how the category of race becomes elaborated historically. The sole focus upon the realism of racism does not get at the persistent fantasy structure of racism and the psychical elaboration of the fantasy. Nor does this reliance on cognitive correction reach the more difficult question of how internal conflicts fashion and attach to discourses of hatred. There must be a more intimate exploration of the force of the psychical in attaching to what was named earlier as "ideologies of desire": the contradictory and ambivalent ways the bodily ego imagines its needs and demands for difference and similarity through the paradoxical moves of narcissism. One form of narcissism discussed in this chapter considered the cost of group solidarity when differences within communities are felt as a blow to the community's narcissism. This is the case when differences within, such as homosexuality, become constituted as a failure to adhere to group loyalty, a problem of outside influence or recruitment, or are unacknowledged because such individuals are viewed as spoiling a community's reputation and family values or even as fueling racism itself. Another form of narcissism discussed occupies a different space: the space where the other's failings become the material for excessive self-regard and where even those with experiences in forms of exclusion have something more to learn.

When it comes to examining the history of race—and the writers discussed here render this concern as the beginning—antiracist pedagogies must unapologetically explore the operatic fields of sexualities, of Eros, and of the narcissisms of minor differences, not because suffering ennobles, or because it is comparable, or even because a knowledge of suffering installs the proper guilt. Rather, its appeal must be to incite identifications and enlarge the geography of memory in order for memory to engage the modulations of its own otherness. In studying as a problem that difficult relation called "love"—itself the grounds of community—categories such as race, sex, and gender can be thought as matters that require more than one look; indeed, as social and psychic matters that require an education that can bear an ethical renunciation of representation as mastery and as mirror, as self-aggrandizement and as the grounds for excessive self-regard. When it comes to imagining what problems and relations are at stake in antiracist pedagogy, one might begin with a joke about chickens.

Chapter Six

"That Lonely Discovery":
Anne Frank, Anna Freud,
and the Question of Pedagogy

In the last year of entries to her diary, a fifteen-year-old Anne Frank responded to a London radio broadcast's call for diaries that documented the experiences of war for future generations. "Of course," writes Anne Frank on March 29, 1944, "everyone pounced on my diary. Just imagine how interesting it would be if I were to publish a novel about the Secret Annex. . . . Seriously, though, ten years after the war people would find it very amusing to read how we lived, what we ate, and what we talked about as Jews in hiding. Although I tell you a great deal about our lives, you still know very little about us."[1]

Anne Frank names the pedagogical mystery that is her diary: as a place of secrets, how can it tell us a great deal yet leave us still knowing very little? For pedagogical purposes, this mystery is crystalized in two of its haunting qualities: the painful context of its writing as one document of the European Jewish destruction, and Anne Frank's hopeful knowledge that, while addressing "Kitty," her diary, she was also writing a diary to and for the world.

Versions of the diary have been translated into fifty-five languages.[2] The North American school curriculum largely preserves the 1950s representations of the diary, or what Judith Doneson paradoxically terms "an Americanized universal symbol."[3] Over the course of the postwar years, the diary has been the subject of plays, films, musical compositions, and commemorative sculpture and art. Throughout Europe, streets have been named in memory of Anne Frank, educational foundations and youth organizations have been formed, and, in Amsterdam, the "Secret Annex" has become a historic site.[4] There is even an Anne Frank website on the internet. With the recent publication of a new translation, as well as a more complete diary known as the Definitive Edition, and with

113

the Dutch government's 1986 authorization of the historical authenticity of the diary as an answer to the revisionist attempts to deny the event of the Holocaust, the diary serves both as one proof of the Jewish European genocide and as the document of the particular experience of one Jewish adolescent. In pedagogical efforts, these two purposes seem to collapse into a larger problematic. The diary often is approached as the voice of the one and a half million Jewish children who were murdered in Europe during World War II.[5] But even as it serves the popular imaginary, providing "part of the vernacular of tragedy,"[6] in pedagogy the diary also is used to consolidate an idealized figure for adolescent and adult identification.

Fifty years after the liberation of Auschwitz, educators and students are now faced with a far more complex picture, not just of the daily conditions under which the writing of the diary occurred, but also of the painful death of Anne Frank in the Bergen Belsen Camp. Contemporary writing on the diary and the conflicts within Jewish communities over its capacity to represent something larger than itself also open a fragile understanding of the diary's reception in our own pedagogy. Within our questions of how the diary is represented and the detours of its encounters, of being told too much and knowing too little, three very different senses of time occupy the same space: the time of the writing, the time of finding and publishing the diary, and our own time of pedagogical engagement. These three senses of time coarsen the fault lines of the arguments over the diary's readings and suggest something about the more general stakes of what has become known as "Holocaust education" in public schooling. For if, as Alvin Rosenfeld argues, we know that the Holocaust happened, "what we lack is not an adequate written record but the means to assimilate it to the conceptual norms of interpretation."[7] What is it then to explore the pedagogical limits of "the conceptual norms of interpretation"? How might these competing histories—the history recounted in the diary and the historicity of engaging in a reading of the diary— press into form our pedagogical efforts? And why complicate curricular efforts which seem to strive for preservation?

This chapter begins with the large question of how an acknowledgment of a more contentious history of the diary's reception may focus our pedagogical efforts and hence allow Anne Frank's diary to be and to have both more and less than what Alvin Rosenfeld has called "a posthumous career as a cultural icon" (89). For the young girl called "Anne Frank" does more than haunt the writings about the Jewish European genocide, where one passes through Anne Frank on the way to the consideration of the sheer numbers; her reference appears in the most unexpected places: in book advertisements of adolescent diaries, in television sitcoms, in short stories, and in contemporary films. The figure of Anne Frank has been burdened with, at once, too much history, too much quota of affect. This chapter explores the contentious projections onto the figure of Anne Frank, which often travel under the name of history.

The term *contentious history* is meant to unsettle the idea that the past—whether it goes under the name of *development* or *history*—can be laid to rest through a grasping of the proper order of events. The chronology at stake here in this unsettling inquiry does not respond to linear time but to latent time, to time itself as contradiction. This larger question of confronting a more contentious history—a history that cannot rest even in chronology—is not one that asserts the study of conflict for its own sake. Rather, what is at stake when conflict is at stake is the possibility of working through its repetitious compulsion. And the attempt to bring to awareness and make insight from the contentions we call "history" need not be insensitive to educators' worries that, in highlighting the ambivalent responses to the diary, they may leave their students not only more susceptible to revisionist accounts that deny the Holocaust but also perhaps to decide it is useless to read the diary if adults cannot agree on its meanings. In fact, beginning with these resistances to insight and their attendant strategies to preserve the pedagogical status quo allows for prior questions: why can anyone become susceptible to forces of aggression, hatred and destruction; and why are feelings of ambivalence so difficult to explore and tolerate? One is able to ask, then, what may be at stake for the learner and teacher when the time of learning, and the time of history itself, in the words of Shoshana Felman and Dori Laub, "is *dissonant*, and not just *congruent*, with everything . . . learned beforehand"?[8]

This approach to the historicity of the diary's reception is inspired by what Erik Erikson, in his explorations of the ethics of psychoanalytic inquiry, called "that lonely discovery."[9] Freud's discovery of psychoanalysis seems lonely in at least two regards. One has to do with admitting the stunning singularity and mysterious plays of the psyche. The other has to do with the difficulty of accepting an extraordinary reach of psychoanalytic implication. And with this loneliness doubled, we can extend the reach of its affect of identification to the diary itself. As she sorted through her own conflictive understandings of self and other and grappled with the otherness of the self, Anne Frank was involved in her own lonely discovery. Then the finding of Anne's diary and the making of "the diary" from the documents handed to Otto Frank was a second time of "that lonely discovery." And now, perhaps, that lonely discovery can be made from our present reading. To explore the affective geometry of these psychic events, I bring to the history of the diary both the writing of Anna Freud and my own idiomatic reading practices, which attempt a relation between two kinds of literature that have preoccupied my thinking: literature that questions contemporary diasporic identity and psychoanalytic literature.

Anne Frank and Anna Freud have some things in common: their first language was German, and as Jewish females brought up with the promise of Jewish European enlightenment, both were taught to struggle toward, and to expect, extraordinary lives. Both were preoccupied with education, both deeply respected fantasy and interior exploration, both engaged deeply with their fathers, and both lived in exile.

In 1933, the year that Freud's books were burned publicly in Vienna and the year Hitler was popularly elected as chancellor of Germany, the Frank family fled Frankfurt for Amsterdam. Anne Frank was four years old, and upon the family's arrival in this new country her parents enrolled her in a Montessori school.[10] In 1942, the year Anne Frank received a diary as a thirteenth birthday gift, the Dutch government surrendered to the German Army and the Netherlands came under German law. With all other Jewish children, Anne Frank was forbidden to attend Dutch schools. On July 5, 1942, Anne Frank's sister, Margo, was required to report to the Gestapo for her transport orders. The next day, the Frank family, along with one other family, went into hiding. Later they were joined by an eighth member, Mr. Dussel. Otto Frank had been preparing the attic of his pectin factory for over a year. The factory was located two-and-a-half miles from their Amsterdam home.

The family lived in hiding for about two years. Their connection to the outside world was facilitated by four of Otto Frank's Christian employees and a radio. An anonymous phone caller to the Dutch police reported on the Franks. On August 4, 1944, the Frank family, the Van Damm family, and Mr. Dussel were arrested. Of the 25,000 Jews in hiding in Amsterdam, approximately 9,000 were betrayed. Of the 60,000 Dutch Jews deported and interned in camps between 1942 and 1945, only 6,000 people survived. And of the eight people who lived in the Secret Annex, only Otto Frank survived the war. Miep Gies entered the annex the day after the arrest and gathered from the floor the scattered pages of Anne Frank's diary. She returned the diary to Otto Frank a few months after he was liberated from Auschwitz.[11] The first issue of the Dutch diary's publication, in 1947, was modest, and the publishers worried whether there would be an interested public to receive it.

These are the skeletal facts of the diary's writing. One must pass through the overwhelming numbers to reach the singularity of the event. Still, the skeletal frame is weighed down by stories of implication, what Cathy Caruth calls "history," in which the past as reconstructed "is no longer straight forwardly referential (that is . . . , no longer based on simple models of experience and reference.)"[12] One must take a detour and ponder the failings of an educational system and its teachers, democracy and its public, a publishing industry and its readers, civil law and its exclusions, indeed the social imaginary of pedagogy itself. These failures also preoccupied Anna Freud.

Anna Freud experienced her first analysis during World War I as she studied to work as an elementary teacher. It was in this first war that she began to formulate her lifelong interest in children living through the traumatic times of war. In 1933, the year her father's books were publicly burned (and the Franks left Frankfurt for Amsterdam), Anna Freud was thirty-eight, a practicing lay psychoanalyst and a lecturer at the Vienna Psychoanalytic Institute. In 1938, three years after Hitler annexed Austria, Anna Freud and her immediate family fled from Vienna to London. The Freud family went into exile a few days after the Gestapo picked up Anna Freud for questioning. In 1939, an ailing Sigmund Freud died in exile.[13]

A comparison of these two lives also must consider the significant differences between them. Anna Frank's writing was crafted in the vulnerable context of hiding and fear. Much of Anna Freud's writing examines an archeology of fears, loss, aggression, and the ego's mechanisms of defense. Anna Freud, as we know, survived the war to live and to write, well into her eighties. In 1945, Anne Frank, along with 50,000 other Jews that last year, died a difficult and lonely death in the Bergen Belsen camp. Two large questions can be raised from the juxtaposition of these two figures. What project has the diary of Anne Frank been attached to in school curriculum? And how does the work of Anna Freud, and of psychoanalysis generally, open our thinking to the more difficult possibilities of our hopes for both the diary's and our students' places in the school curriculum?

The Curious Time of Learning

In our own time, which, after all, is never just our own time, how can we grapple with the stakes of the learning when the learning is made from attempts at identification with what can only be called *difficult knowledge*? The term of learning acknowledges that studying the experiences and the traumatic residuals of genocide, ethnic hatred, aggression, and forms of state-sanctioned—and hence legal—social violence requires educators to think carefully about their own theories of learning and how the stuff of such difficult knowledge becomes pedagogical. This exploration needs to do more than confront the difficulties of learning from another's painful encounter with victimization, aggression, and the desire to live on one's own terms. It also must be willing to risk approaching the internal conflicts which the learner brings to the learning. Internal conflicts may be coarsened, denied, and defended against the time when the learner cannot make sense of violence, aggression, or even the desire for what Melanie Klein calls the "making of reparation."[14]

But in claiming that difficult knowledge may work at the level of psychic trauma, it is useful to consider two dynamics of learning noted by Sigmund Freud: learning about and learning from.[15] Whereas learning about an event or experience focuses upon the acquisition of qualities, attributes, and facts, so that it presupposes a distance (or, one might even say, a detachment) between the learner and what is to be learned, learning from an event or experience is of a different order, that of insight. Both of these learning moves are made more fragile in difficult knowledge. But precisely because insight concerns the acknowledgment of discontinuity from the persistence of the status quo, and hence asks something intimate from the learner, learning from requires the learner's attachment to, and implication in, knowledge. While initially the learner attaches to the experience of the other by way of wondering what she or he would have done had such an event occurred in her or his own life, this is not yet an implication. For this experiment in empathy actually may provoke defenses and resistance to insight. This is so because what tends to be projected is the learner's undisturbed present and not the way the learner's life has become her present. But just as significantly, the learner's strategy of projection impedes an understanding of the differences between the learner's knowledge and the knowledge of the other. It is precisely this merging that is encouraged when the diary's readers are offered the famous and empty declaration: "We are all Anne Frank."[16]

The kind of implication in knowledge that Freud is after begins when one moves toward the question of what difference can mean for one's present life. The learner must be willing both to confront outside knowledge as a mode of address that demands the learner's transformation of memory and to tolerate psychic or existential time, the time of the belatedness of understanding. Learning from demands both a patience with the incommensurability of understanding and an interest in tolerating the ways meaning becomes, for the learner, fractured, broken, and lost, exceeding the affirmations of rationality, consciousness, and consolation.

To consider the vicissitudes of learning from difficult knowledge, educators must begin by acknowledging learning as a psychic event, charged with resistance to knowledge. The resistance is a precondition for learning from knowledge and the grounds of knowledge itself. And yet this insight—that difficult knowledge may be refused—is painful to tolerate when the subjects studied are genocide, ethnic hatred, and the experiences of despair and helplessness. The reach of this refusal touches the educator's desire for the learner to just accept and understand the tyranny of hatred in all of its guises. Such a wish, however, also can be a symptom of the educator's own struggle to master her or his own difficulties. Shoshana Felman and Jonathan Silin, following Lacan, suggest the term *passion for ignorance* to evoke the affective pressures that urge the work of the refusal to learn from the resistance to learning. Such passion is made when the knowledge offered provokes a crisis within the self and when the knowledge is felt as interference or as a critique of the self's coherence or view of itself in the world. These confrontations, according to Felman and Laub, partly provoke "the crisis of witnessing," in which the learner is incapable of an adequate response because the knowledge offered is dissonant in the order of trauma, so that the response can be only a working through—a mourning—of belated knowledge. This insight into what such knowledge "does" to the learner and what the learner "does" to knowledge has been central to psychoanalytically inflected discussions on the Holocaust[17] and to recent analytically oriented discussions on pedagogies of social difference.[18]

Perhaps this time of belatedness, when learning is made from loss, makes learning from difficult knowledge so difficult. Freud's second order of learning—learning from difficult knowledge—suggests the psychic time of learning as one in which the confronted self vacillates, sometimes violently and sometimes passively, sometimes imperceptibly and sometimes shockingly, between resistance as symptom and the working through of resistance. When the movements of affect and idea are in conflict, as they are in the time of resistance, and when, as Freud points out in his *Interpretation of Dreams*, the "word representation" is other to the thing it represents, varying forms of aggression also can be staged as the self struggles for elusive mastery through strategies such as the discounting of an experience as having anything to do with the self and the freezing of events in a history that has no present. These mechanisms of defense—undoing what has already happened and isolating the event in a time that has long past—are key ways the ego attempts to console itself. But the cost of consolation is severe.[19]

What becomes crucial for educators to consider are theories of libido and aggression in relation to the acknowledgment that learning is a psychic event. For if such painful and ongoing histories as those offered by the diary are to affect our actions, advocacies, and thoughts, and if teachers and students are to commit themselves to the interminable work of social justice and ethical understanding, it is still necessary to explore how the learner comes to identify and dis-identify with difficult knowledge.[20] If educators are to do more than hope that one learns from—as opposed to about   history (including one's own history), then the pedagogical staging of experiences of social violence must attend carefully to what the study of aggression might open. Moreover, how does the very tangled engagement with experiences of victimhood and the aggressor become difficult for educators themselves? What happens when that other war, the war within, meets the conflicts and aggressions enacted in the world outside?

Significantly, educators are aware of the idea that knowledge of human cruelty can be depressing, debilitating, and defensively engaged. Indeed, this very worry is an implicit tension in discussions of Holocaust education and in the teaching of the diary.[21] Can the study of genocide avoid a painful encounter? Is the amount of pain the thing that provokes disengagement? But paradoxically, these anxieties may be an effect of the educator's disavowal of her or his own difficulties of engagement. Then, the educator's worries transfer into an ambivalent pedagogy that wishes to protect adolescents from—even as it introduces adolescents to—these representations. The disavowal, or the refusal to engage a traumatic perception of helplessness and loss, often pushes educators to the opposite spectrum of affect: the focus on hope and courage as the adequate lesson to be made from difficult knowledge. However, hope is a very complex affect that may actually take the form of a defense. Michael Silberfeld argues that hope is neither a static concept nor "a token that can be given or taken away. . . . The dynamic concept of hope is related to the feelings of loss and in turn, to the sense of entitlement."[22] This is so because hope may be seen as a bridge to continuity and expectation. Precisely because hope speaks to the wish for attachment, it is also quite vulnerable to the very conditions that constitute its founding moments: times when one must also come to terms with discontinuity and loss.[23]

In a pedagogy that insists upon hope as a strategy to slide over the pain of loss, in which hope's dynamic qualities are ignored, hope works as idealization in two ways: hope works to idealize, and hope is the idealized part of reading the diary. Both moves involve the effort "to place some aspect of oneself or the group on a pedestal to then derive faith, hope and sustenance from this idealized part."[24] Yet the force of idealization has an underside. For idealization is a projection of an ideal situation onto an object and, as a projection, it disguises its own wish to both be and have the desired object—"an object," in the words of analyst Andre Green, "which is never the cause of any frustration and, consequently, of any projection. The subject has no project (to use the word in its most ordinary sense), because the object has anticipated it. There is also nothing to project, in the more restricted sense of the word, because there is no frustration; therefore there is no aggression, since aggression arises from the need to release tension, and without frustration there is no tension."[25]

And yet the diary does give rise to frustration, to ambivalence, and to some measure of anger, fear, and depression. Idealization is a wish for this tension to disappear and, paradoxically, it may well be a symptom of the "crisis in witnessing" and of the ambivalence in distinguishing between learning about and learning from. How is this so?

The problem with the reader's desire to idealize is that the strategy is an attempt to find an ultimate truth in a context that, to return to Alvin Rosenfeld's point, defies any of our personal means "to assimilate [the event with] the conceptual norms of interpretation." When the vicissitudes of life and death cannot conform to the idealization of a life that should surmount the difficulties, it becomes very difficult to live with, or in, loss. While the recourse to hope and courage may serve as the learner's ego-ideal, the ego-ideal has the potential to become a means to berate either the self or those who cannot be perceived as courageous. The injunction for hope and courage can be felt as tyrannical to the ego and hence may inhibit any understanding or allowance for experiences where hope and courage cannot be mustered or where these desires can be considered only in the belated time of mourning. Moreover, if the learner shuts out altogether the conditions of helplessness, loss, and conflict, the vicissitudes and profundity of even making the smallest amounts of hope and courage cannot be worked through. As we will see, however, the placing of the diary on various pedestals of affirmation in efforts to dissipate the dissonance and loss of its traumatic context is not peripheral, but integral, to the traumatic histories of the diary's reception. Indeed, the histories of the diary's reception may well mark our pedagogical unconscious.

The Times of the Finding

In pedagogical efforts that refuse the more troubling possibilities of the text, the *Diary of a Young Girl* is isolated from its own contentious historicity. The time of

Anne Frank becomes static, as if there were only the ethnographic present of Anne endlessly making her entries. And while this quality may be implicit in the genre of diary and be sustained by the 1950s play and Hollywood film, the figure of Anne Frank placed only at her desk seems to preserve the wish to keep her safe in hiding. This is not to suggest that the Holocaust is somehow left unmentioned either in the diary or in pedagogy. Indeed, while the wish to keep Anne Frank safe from harm may well be a rescue fantasy provoked by the knowledge of what happened at the end of this time of writing, it is also impossible to read this diary and not consider the painful conditions of its writing and its finding. The ambivalence of the ethnographic present, however, serves this wish for preservation, defending its reader against loss.

But the diary's history no more ends with its writing than it begins with its finding. It begins with postwar Jewish ambivalence over our status in European and North American societies after World War II. And this history is tangled in an exponential Jewish sense of loss and an ongoing mourning marked partly by an anxiety about the general public's anti-semitism, partly by this public's despondency toward the magnitude and traumatic residues of the destruction, and partly by the interminable question within Jewish communities of the meanings of the loss to Jewishness.[26] When Anne Frank's diary was first considered for publication, the question raised— albeit differently—by Otto Frank and the Dutch publisher was, how could postwar Christians read the diary as relevant to them? This question, still with us today, haunted the diary's promotion and returned to structure its rewriting for the 1955 play and 1959 film.

Otto Frank believed the reception would best be facilitated by publicity which presented the diary as having universal appeal. Otto Frank wanted his daughter's diary to be a story of adolescence, not a Jewish story. Before the war, the Franks had been a highly assimilated middle-class Jewish family of enlightenment. Indeed, Otto Frank served in the German army in World War I; the family considered themselves German citizens and, in the prevailing anti-semitic definitions of their time, racially Jewish.[27] By 1947, Otto Frank and the Dutch publishers understood that Jewish particularity would not sell well to a general public that had grown weary of the sheer magnitude of the Jewish genocide. Otto Frank was not certain that a Jewish child could or even should be a universal figure capable of standing in for every child; at the same time, he hoped that the publication of the diary could be a means of introducing Christian readers to the humanity of the loss.[28] This, too, is our present preoccupation.

Both the Dutch and the English versions of the diary originally were marketed as an extraordinary statement about a young girl's hope for humanity in spite of war. Recall one of the most famous extrapolated sentences from one of the last entries to the diary that now works as synecdoche: "I still believe, in spite of everything, that people are truly good at heart" (332).[29] In expressing Anne's wish for a normal life and for a magical healing (a time when "people would find it very amusing"), parts of the diary do wonder about the capacity of humans to exceed hatred and despair. But what tends to be lost in this idealization of her belief is that Anne Frank's hope for, and expectation of, continuity were betrayed. And much of the diary is a meditation on Jewish suffering and on the melancholic condition of being, for the simple fact of Jewishness, an outcast.

Here is what Anne Frank wrote near the end of her April 11, 1944, entry, after a break-in and police examination of the first floor of the pectin factory:

> We've been strongly reminded of the fact that we're Jews in chains, chained to one spot, without any rights, but with a thousand obligations. We must put our feelings aside; we must be brave and strong, bear discomfort without complaint. . . . The time will come when we'll be people again and not just Jews!
>
> Who has inflicted this on us? Who has set us apart from all the rest? Who has put us through such suffering? . . . In the eyes of the world, we're doomed, but if, after all this suffering, there are still Jews left, the Jewish people will be held up as an example. . . . We can never be just Dutch, or just English, or whatever, we will always be Jews as well. And we'll have to keep on being Jews, but then, we'll want to be. (261)

Unlike the Hollywood film that rewrites this entry into a universal declaration that all people and nations have suffered, the passage in the first English version is complex, ambivalent, and conditional. It sets in conflict Anne's experience of the world's need for Jewish denial with the Jewish demand to choose Jewishness. One of "the thousand obligations" that emerged from this antagonism was the injunction to idealize bravery in a context where bravery could not surmount, repair, or even make sense of Anne's knowledge of deportation, or her thoughts on impending death. Paradoxically, the only proof of bravery becomes silence, the prohibition against narrating one's doom. Within this prohibition lies still another obligation: the forced confrontation with an anti-semitic definition of Jewishness that renders irrelevant the ambivalent longing both to belong without distinction and to be seen as distinct. The diary becomes a space for working through such obligations. In her reflection on the persistent struggle against claustrophobia, Anne Frank can also refuse these impositions by inventing a fantasy of life in the past, present, and future. Then the diary defies any obligation, specifically in those entries that examine her inner world and craft small pleasures from listening to Mozart on a radio broadcast, commenting on her collection of pictures of Hollywood film stars, and exploring the mysteries of love and sexuality. But even these passions are haunted by her terror of, and incredulity toward, the cruel actions of those who complied with the Nazi occupation.

With the publication of the Definitive Edition, there is now a larger awareness that in the original 1947 diary Otto Frank edited entries where Anne candidly discusses sexuality and her stormy relationship with her mother. This might be the second finding in Otto Frank's ambivalence about publishing his daughter's diary and his worries over how those depicted in the diary would be remembered.[30] But there is a parallel history of the diary's reception, in its crafting by postwar Jewish communities in North America, Europe, and Israel.[31] This other history crystallizes in author Meyer Levin's epic battle with Otto Frank; despite a bitter thirty-year struggle for the rights to publish his play about the diary, Levin was finally unsuccessful.[32] For Levin, while the diary could come to represent a story of Jewish suffering, which only a Jew could tell, there would always be the question of those who would not listen to and acknowledge—even within Jewish communities—the particularities of Jewish suffering. Whereas Otto Frank desired Anne Frank to be universalized as adolescent in her capacity to hope, Meyer Levin's desire was for Anne Frank to be a monument, indeed what Vamik Volkan, in his work on complicated mourning, terms "a linking object" to the memory of six million.[33] While both responses may have in common the desire to memorialize, neither is outside the traumas of loss and the ways the vulnerable work of mourning is interrupted, even as it must proceed bit by bit with the knowledge that comes too late.

Meyer Levin first came to the French version of the diary in 1950 while living in Europe. Prior to the war, Levin had published many novels of Jewish life but always felt fame had eluded him because the publishing industry viewed his work as "too ethnic" and "too Jewish" for mass appeal. In 1945, he was an eyewitness reporter to the liberation of Buchenwald. When Levin first encountered the diary, he became convinced that this document, *along with his efforts to make it known*, would radically reshape how the Holocaust could be understood. When the diary was published in English, carrying a preface signed by Eleanor Roosevelt, its popularization and reprinting was largely due to Levin's 1952 essay review, first published in the *New York Times*. In that review, one sentence continues to stand out in terms of contemporary pedagogical efforts: "Anne Frank's voice becomes the voice of six million Jewish souls."[34]

Meyer Levin then wanted to write a play based on the diary. Otto Frank agreed that he should try. But while, for Levin, only a Jew was capable of identifying with and writing about the suffering of Anne Frank, Otto Frank desired a play that would focus on the indelibility of the human spirit and would have the power to dramatize just that. The identity of the author was thus irrelevant to Otto Frank, who eventually selected the play by the Christian team of Frances Goodrich and Albert Hackett over Levin's own play.[35] Levin saw this choice as an affront to Jewish memory and would come to see it as "the second death" of Anne Frank. This betrayal, from Levin's perspective, inspired his thirty-year public struggle against Otto Frank.

By 1974, still hoping for vindication and sympathetic acceptance, Levin had published his own story of what he felt had gone terribly wrong. After all, Levin had sued Otto Frank for the rights to publish a play based on the diary, and this legal action was scandalous. Running over three hundred pages, Levin's near-epic account is aptly titled *The Obsession*. Much of this text is a struggle to understand his three engagements in psychoanalysis where he tried to confront his own compulsion to control the reception of the diary. His second analyst asked, "The enemies you tell of are undoubtedly real. The question is, are they worth all the trouble you give yourself over them?" (19). The question cannot be answered, for a larger struggle preoccupies him. Levin cannot decide whether some obsessions are worthy, even as the cost in his life is misery.

The first paragraph of *The Obsession* tells the whole story in miniature:

> In the middle of life I fell into a trouble that was to grip, occupy, haunt, and all but devour me these twenty years. I've used the word "fall." It implies something accidental, a stumbling, but we also use the word in speaking of "falling in love" in which there is a sense of elevation, and where a fatedness is implied, a feeling of being inevitably bound in through all the mysterious components of character to this expression of the life process, whether in the end beautifully gratifying or predominantly painful. (7)

Levin's fall into trouble repeated and reversed the mystery of the diary. Anne Frank wrote: "Although I tell you a great deal about our lives, you still know very little about us." For Meyer Levin, the sentence might read: "Although I tell myself all, I understand little." For pedagogy, the sentence might repeat Levin's poetic insight into the fall, for educators cannot know whether in the end their *own* efforts with the diary will be "beautifully gratifying or predominantly painful." In each of these sentences we might read the ambivalence of learning, the difficulties of knowledge.

Both Otto Frank and Meyer Levin desired Anne Frank's diary to be an inspiration and an education. This is also the present pedagogical hope. But we are unable to decide, any more than Levin could, whether engaging with the diary should be "beautifully gratifying or predominantly painful." Nor is there agreement, as Otto Frank worried, on whether the diary should represent the particularities of Jewish suffering or the universal condition of adolescents. This is a further pedagogical dilemma if we think of adolescents as in need of protection from suffering or incapable of encountering the suffering of another. In both indecisions, the strained hope for the diary is symptomatic of significant anxieties that begin with how it should be encountered and what it might take for readers to identify with it. This too is part of its pedagogical history, in which the time of Anne Frank persists as an ethnographic present that both works to preserve her status as a cultural icon and responds to the wish to rescue and so not betray again the family in hiding.

History leaves us with difficult pedagogical questions. How do the contentious receptions of the diary unconsciously live in our pedagogy? How is it possible that histories of which we have no knowledge return as symptoms of education? Can the diary serve both as a universal coming of age story and as a voice for the vast numbers of murdered Jewish children? Does the appeal to universalism actually work as a disavowal of the psychic event of learning from the diary? How do those not directly affected by the Holocaust encounter its meanings? And how do these unresolvable tensions structure the fault lines of our own unconscious pedagogical efforts? These haunting questions require a return to that first "lonely discovery": psychoanalytic investigation.

The Psychic Time of Aggression

What is learning in times of war and what is learning from war in times of relative peace? These preoccupations organize the text *War and Children: A Message to American Parents*. There, Anna Freud and Dorothy Burlingham begin with the assumption that, for children, "inner conflicts form the basis of interests in world affairs" (181). It is the children's own internal conflict between good and bad that structures how they notice and explain to themselves, and to others, the good and bad in the world. Our authors describe this curious order of attention in a short section titled "Children's Reactions to Hitler." For older children, Hitler represents not so much a powerful enemy but "the incarnation of evil, i.e., a new edition of the devil" (181). The "devil," Freud and Burlingham insist, is an object/figure of uncanny fascination. The movement of making sense of evil is a curious one in which, along the way to learning, the learner passes through and projects onto new situations something of the conflicted self. Psychoanalysis names this dynamic transference: new editions of old conflicts. Anna Freud observed a child commenting on this doubled and recursive dynamic. Near the end of this short section, a small girl is quoted: "Whenever I think, I think with my head, isn't it funny" (184).

If we return for a moment to the struggle between Meyer Levin and Otto Frank over the import of the diary, we can extend the observation that inner conflicts form the basis for children's interests in world affairs to the basis of interests adults hold. By implicating adults in this observation we are left with more than a statement of developmental stages, as if internal conflict somehow dissolves and then there is nothing really funny about thinking with one's head. Psychoanalytic thought poses the curious time of development as one of tentative and ambivalent transformations, into new editions of the old self. Internal conflict does not just vanish. And the placement of it elsewhere—outside the self—only exacerbates the trouble for then, it seems, what is put outside threatens to turn against, and *even* come aggressively toward, the self.

Still, it is difficult to accept the view that inner conflicts form the basis of interest in the world, particularly if this claim is taken as a dismissal of the pain of the outside world. Our analysts are not so naive. What they are after is an understanding of how the startling and even traumatic ways the world is made meaningful, irrelevant, or awesome may say something about the individual's own internal conflicts and her or his interest in, or need for, relations and boundaries. The observation that inner conflicts form the basis of individual interest in the world provokes the question of how attention, investment, and identification— the psyche if you will—structure the argument over what becomes important or irrelevant to the learner.[36] The interminable questions are those of shifting boundaries and relations and of learning about and learning from. Attention to and interest in the world is also a working through of the self. What becomes the ego and what becomes the object? What belongs to me and what belongs to the other? These questions often dissipate into the angry gesture of us and them, where it is they who are making my life miserable, not me. Psychoanalysis resides within these difficult tangles of implication: how *the me lives in that and the that lives in me*. Like the children who use the devil to recognize Hitler, adults work on themselves as they perceive and work on the world.

The text *War and Children* is not only about children and their responses to living in times of war, for to speak of children one must also speak of the adults who surround them. A large section of this study analyzes how mothers, fathers, and teachers think with their heads and convey to other adults and to children their affective response to separation, loss, and the profound disruptions which war has worked in their lives. The analysts consider how children respond to adult needs. But in analyzing the children's responses, the founders of this nursery are not focusing upon the explanations and myths that adults offer children to show them what war means and how it goes away. To focus on explanation or on the literal content of a statement forgets the sort of work children, and indeed adults, do to translate what they are told into meaningful accounts of how they feel.

We are back to the question of how students respond to the teacher's affect that is pedagogy and of how the teacher responds to the students' affect that is learning. It is this sort of transferential relation, one that suggests the ambivalence of learning from and learning about, that education must engage. For what the children "pick up" and think with their own heads about are the grown ups' affective response to the difficulties of war and their precarious attempt to make from aggression and social breakdown a moral lesson. Children notice and learn from the nervousness, anxiety, restlessness, and ambivalence of parents and adults, the symptoms of our own pedagogy. Essentially children are engaging not with the adult's rational explanations but with their failures, in the very places where the adult strategies break down. Children attend to what the analysts term "that other war," the war within, where "destructive and aggressive impulses are still at work" (22).

While the analysts' immediate concern is the relation between "the other war" and the world war, ours moves outward to the relation between aggression and love and how education might engage these instincts and their vicissitudes. Two directions are at stake here. One concerns the history of the teacher's own instinctual conflicts. The other, how these conflicts are rearranged, repeated, or worked through in pedagogy and curriculum.

The analysts become more explicit in their message:

> The danger lies in the fact that the destruction raging in the outer world may meet the very real aggressiveness which ranges inside the child. . . . It must be very difficult for them to accomplish [a reaction against destruction and] this task of fighting their own death wishes when, at the same time, people are killed and hurt every day around them. Children have to be safeguarded against the primitive horrors of the war, not because horrors and atrocities are so strange to them, but because we want them at this decisive stage of their development to overcome and estrange themselves from the primitive and atrocious wishes of their own infantile nature. (23–24)

Now we are squarely confronting the psychoanalytic theory of the instincts—the pleasure principle and its beyond—which is quite other to the adult myth of childhood innocence and the adult desire to protect children from the harsh world. In analytic terms, the very flawed foundation of the self begins in the fault lines of conflict. Sigmund Freud described the psyche as a crystal formation, made from the fragments, the flaws, of those first others. The psyche is patchwork, made possible through the suturing of its flaws.[37] Freud extends this metaphor to consider how the psyche shatters: "If we throw a crystal to the floor . . . [i]t comes apart along its lines of cleavage into fragments whose boundaries, though they were invisible, were predetermined by the crystal's structure."[38] A psychoanalysis resides in, and attempts to read within and learn from, these fault lines, considering the psyche's fragility, coarseness, and capacity to coexist "along its lines of cleavage."

What precisely are the cleavages noted in the text *War and Children*? And why should education continue to attend to its message? One sort of cleavage has to do with the psychoanalytic acceptance of internal aggression as a condition provoked by the libidinal desires for social engagement. The war within has to do with how the demand for love reverses its content; the reversal is necessary because, where there is love, there is the fear of the loss of love. When the demand for love, which is a demand for self, meets those first others, the parents, this doubled and fantastic demand—*that others* love the ego as it loves itself—quickly exceeds need and suddenly becomes want. Sigmund Freud observed that while self-love is necessary for self-preservation, it also "behaves as though the occurrence of any divergence from its own particular lines of development involved a criticism of them and a demand for their alteration. . . . Love for oneself knows only one barrier—love for others, love for objects."[39] And it may well be this barrier that Freud had in mind when he wrote: "Love can turn into an expression of tenderness as easily as into a wish for someone's removal" (105). The internal aggression begins along the lines of cleavage in love.

We can extend this difficult observation to learning and perhaps say: "Learning for oneself only knows one barrier—a learning from others." After all, learning demands alteration in that the self must interfere with itself and reconsider its previous investments. New knowledge is first confronted as a criticism toward and loss of the learner's present knowledge if the knowledge offered is felt as discontinuous with the self, if it seems to threaten the ways the world has been perceived. But both love and learning, because they are relations, are quite susceptible to what makes them possible in the first place, namely to reversal. The desire to learn can reverse its course, transforming itself into a wish for the removal of knowledge (or a removal of the teacher). Teachers themselves are not immune to these dynamics. Indeed, the wish to remove knowledge, what was earlier termed as "the passion for ignorance," also structures curricular decisions. We might consider this form of censorship in psychic time and ask What is the teacher worried about when the teacher removes knowledge? If learning itself is dependent upon transferential love, the condition of its own possibility is an acknowledgment of the curious conflict between the inside and the outside, between the self's otherness and the other's otherness.

While the first cleavage in the psyche concerns the dynamic of internal aggression, the second begins with what conflict means in development. In psychoanalytic terms development is a metaphor for new editions of the old self. The conflict is between the new and the old selves. Like the time of learning, the time of development is other to the linear chronology of progress and dialectic resolution. The psyche is not characterized by synthesis but by contradiction. In this curious geography, two or more experiences occupy the same place at the same time. And even the accommodation of such a crowd can never be grasped fully, for consciousness has its own other: the unconscious wishes that consciousness cannot tolerate knowing. Conflict between the new and the old is what allows the self its movement and, of course, its interminable suffering. What seems to be funny about thinking with one's head is the contest and coexistence of wishes, prohibitions, and ideas: the volatile combinations of love and hate that render actions paradoxical. It is the doubleness of feelings and the symptom of action—the split between unconscious wishes and conscious attitudes—that is at stake in attending to the cleavages known as "psychic topology." The doubleness of feelings—the idea that feelings can represent two divergent forms of thought at the same time and become embodied in one puzzling action—is what compels the educational efforts of our analysts and their excursion into the ambivalence of development. But if education, in any analytic sense, is to become a permanent influence, the stakes of its own learning must be reconceptualized.

The difficulty of living in times of war is that war confirms the aggressive instincts of the human. The difficulty in ignoring aggressive instincts in times of peace is that insight into the split between one's own actions and feelings cannot be made. The analysts' message to parents and teachers is that war is all too familiar, and the preoccupation in times of war with fighting, with overpowering, indeed, the will to dominate and destroy others, resembles that other war, the war within. Thus the message these analysts offer to parents and teachers is one that makes education a significant intervention to assist the sublimation of aggression. But if education is to be an intervention, it must also admit its own preoccupation with an unadmitted violence that is cushioned under the names of *nation, law, order,* and *exploration,* a preoccupation Freud notes in his essay, "Thoughts for the Times on War and Death." There, Freud glances at the school curriculum: "Even today, the history of the world which our children learn at school is essentially a series of murders of people" (292).

The point, however, is not to disavow the history of social violence and the attendant conditions of helplessness and loss for those who are afflicted. Nor is it to reduce history to a set of unfolding events caught in the ethnographic present and hence occupying a time that is always out of reach. These strategies, as we have seen in the struggles to control how readers might engage the diary of Anne Frank, are defensive and the coping mechanisms they invoke only confuse the very possibilities the diary offers, in Anne Frank's attempt to work though her own experiences of aggression and violence and grapple with her own ambivalent consolations. It seems as though, in our rush to make Anne Frank an object of adulation that can then serve as a means for identification, we have ignored the complex conditions of hope. These conditions are what Freud called "the work of mourning." For remember, if hope is to be complex and dynamic, one must be willing to acknowledge the difficult conditions that invoke hope in the first place, namely the vicissitudes of loss.

If education indeed can be a cure, it can be a cure only in the psychoanalytic sense: in creating new conditions for the capacity to love, to work, and to learn without invoking more harm and suffering. Conflict, in this story, will not go away. But what might be altered is our capacity to respond. Such work requires, I think, a very different orientation to how such dynamics as life and death can be encountered and rendered through curriculum. What might one learn from the study of life in times of war and death? And how is this study marked by the very trauma it attempts to work through? Can the study of aggression consider "that other war," internal conflict?[40]

The Belated Time of Losing and Being Lost

We can now return to Anna Freud. Her work with war evacuees began shortly after her own exile from Vienna to London in 1938, although even in Vienna Anna Freud had worked with children and adolescents living in difficulties.[41] We already know that in 1938, a few days after she had been released from arrest for questioning by the Gestapo in Vienna, the immediate Freud family escaped to

London. A crucial detail in that story is missing. Sigmund Freud's four sisters remained in Vienna, in the mistaken hope that they would be in no danger because they were elderly and apolitical. That Jewishness itself would put the aunts at risk was, at the time, unthinkable to the Freuds. But it was not until 1946 that Anna Freud would learn the fate of the aunts who had remained in Vienna. They were killed in 1942 by the Nazis; the Red Cross originally reported that "Marie [died] in the Theresienstadt camp, and Dolfi, Rosa, and Pauline in the camps to which they had been shipped after Theresienstadt. (Only years later did records surface indicating that Rosa had died in Auschwitz, her two sisters in Treblinka.)"[42]

Miss Freud's engagement with this terrible knowledge of the aftermath of war and all that was lost can be read in a short essay, "About Losing and Being Lost," which was written soon after the war, during her recovery from collapse into illness in 1946. The essay is a working through, what Sigmund Freud would also call "learning from," and it follows a similar dynamic sketched in A. Freud and D. Burlingham's text of how that inner conflict—the war within—structures what one attends to in the outside world. For Anna Freud, the inner conflict concerns how she imagines her family and the burden of her aunts' murders. The belated and perhaps intolerable question was why she and her family could not understand that all Jews—regardless of political actions, class privilege, age, and affective relations to Jewishness—were the subjects of Nazi-organized genocide. The terrible question Anna Freud grapples with is whether the aunts were discarded by the family.[43] How could the Freud family believe the aunts would be safe in Vienna when they themselves fled? How does one move from ambivalence and guilt to the ethical responsibility necessary to the work of mourning? How does one understand the implication that is loss?

But the implication that is loss is a belated knowledge, a knowledge that arrives too late, a knowledge that must enlarge the scope of pain and loss. These questions persist in our own time, when the Holocaust continues to be inconceivable, frustrating not just "the conceptual norms of interpretation" but also the very possibility of thinking what it means to acknowledge a society driven to its own destruction. And yet, if we can now look back and consider that those who lived through, and were murdered in, the Holocaust could not comprehend their own devastations, how can we expect from those who now look back the capacity to order and to rationalize the chaos and infinitesimal details of such destruction? How does anyone live with a knowledge that comes too late?

These are also the questions Sigmund Freud raises in three earlier essays, "Mourning and Melancholia," "Thoughts for the Times on War and Death," and "On Transience." Freud seems to be struggling with two kinds of experiences: lifework and deathwork and the essential ethicality noted in the end of his "Thoughts" essay: "To tolerate life remains, after all, the first duty of all living beings" (299). But what is it to tolerate life? It is to tolerate not just the myriad disappointments, failures, broken meanings and missed opportunities but also the vicissitudes of its chances, the detours of suffering—indeed, life and death.

Freud's last impossible sentence says as much: "If you want to endure life, pre-
pare for death" (300).

Freud's interest is in how individuals work through and live with both
the death of a love (be it a beloved person or an ideal) and their own aggressive
impulses, that is, their own death drives. In "Mourning and Melancholia," Freud
names both of these responses to a death as "work," but whereas in mourning the
individual comes to terms with what she or he has lost in herself and still, after
some time, finds a way to return to the world to risk life and both love and work
again, in "the crushed state of melancholia" (248) the psyche's cleavages become
coarser and exaggerated in its splitting; the melancholic cannot rejoin the world.
In melancholia, the love for the object becomes agitated and ambivalent in loss.
Love reverses its content, becoming a hatred of the world and of the self. Both
mourning and melancholia engage the contradiction between reality's demand
that the lost object be given up and the ego's desire or libidinal wish to keep and
be kept by the beloved object; this is the contradiction which the melancholic is
unable to work through. The fragile distinction between these categories can be
made only within the ego's possibility to risk love again and resume the work of
attaching to life. And so, in Freud's words, "The complex of melancholia behaves
like an open wound . . . emptying the ego until it is totally impoverished" (253). In
a sense, the melancholic suffers two deaths: death of the object and death of the
ego. In this other death, the death of the ego, the melancholic intensifies his or her
own psychic pain. One might say that, in answer to the question of where misery
originates, the melancholic makes her or his own misery in an effort to preserve
something.[44] This is why Freud also characterizes melancholia as work, but a
work that concerns "a regression of libido into the ego" (258).

Anna Freud's essay "About Losing and Being Lost" is both a rejoinder
to her father's work and itself a work of mourning for the losses of friends, family,
and strangers.[45] In this essay Miss Freud explores the paradoxical wish both to
keep and to lose something of value, pursuing the geometric traces of the sorrow
of loss, remorse, and ambivalence that seems to haunt the loser. Like all her writing, the essay is deceptively simple and modest in tonality. The writer's own
experiences are couched in the third person, deflecting attention from the messen-
ger to the message.

The essay is divided into four sections. It begins with a discussion of the
economics of the libido's attachment to things and the ease with which the libido
is overtaken by aggression. This curious stress on economics is characteristic of
psychoanalytic writing. There is an attempt to sketch the workings of the geography of pain in terms of quantity, transfer, and displacement from one site to
another. Anna Freud moves in the second section to some reactions to losing
things, how losing possessions reminds one of that originary childhood dejection
of being alone and the ways one displaces this feeling through the personification
of the object: "It got lost," and not, "I am lost without it." We return then to a
slight alteration of "that lonely discovery," as the discovery makes one lonely. In

fact, Miss Freud considers this existential loneliness when she introduces into her essay the character of "the chronic loser," who has difficulties holding onto her or his possessions.

In considering the drama of "chronic losers," the topic of the essay's third section, Anna Freud offers an example of the doubleness of identification: that the making of attachments is always troubled by ambivalence born of the anticipated possibility of the loss of love. This is the trouble expressed in the desolate sentence "Why should I hold onto it when it will only leave me?" The chronic loser is one who has lost love and who, in losing her or his possessions, enacts a double identification: both with the passivity of the lost object and with the aggression of the actor who seemed to discard it. Note the complexity: the loser's identifications are split between the object of loss and the subject who loses it. This is the structure of ambivalence. Anna Freud already defined this dynamic of identification in her work on the ego and its mechanisms of defense. This early double identification—what she called, building upon the work of Sandor Ferenczi,[46] "identification with the aggressor" accompanied by identification with the discarded object—pinpoints the dynamic qualities of identification as contradictory, partial, and highly ambivalent.

The essay closes with some questions of mourning, but rather than presenting specific clinical case studies, Miss Freud moves to the realm of literature and myth, tracing cultural preoccupations with ghosts, hauntings, and wandering lost souls, *nebishes* in Yiddish. These beings represent ways for the living to maintain identification with the dead. But as figures, they are marked with the ambivalence of the living to the dead, with the ambivalent desire both to remain loyal to the dead and, at the same time, to rejoin the world of the living. The figures function to displace "the survivor's desolation" (314), the loneliness of being left behind. And it is from this desolation that the work of mourning and melancholia begins. This interminable work is dependent upon the desire to rejoin the world, as one "detach[es] one's] hopes, demands, and expectations from the image of the dead" (316) and reattaches them to the world. This, of course, is the work of mourning, and it proceeds bit by bit, memory by memory.

We move then from the vicissitudes of loss to the work of mourning, the work through which, as one stops demanding things from the dead, one can begin to demand something from life. Anna Freud offers that reading literature may well be a way of working through loss and the experiences of being lost if the reader can make from the reading a work of the self. In a sense we have come full circle, from the writing to the finding of Anne Frank's diary to "that (other) lonely discovery," the reading of the diary. For if reading the diary can be a work of mourning, and can provide a space for exploring experiences of losing and being lost then to exceed a melancholy idealization the reader must move from the desolation of the survivor to the position of analyzing her own attachments in and to the world. Just as Anna Freud has moved to the world of literature to study its hauntings, we move back to the world of the diary, itself a crystal formation.

The haunting historicity of Anne Frank's diary suggests some of the cleavages which structure our pedagogical unconscious. My sense is that our pedagogy still resides in the ambivalent fault lines of mourning and melancholia, in our desire to remain loyal to the dead (by keeping Anne Frank at her desk and ignoring the conflicts made from the last fifty years of the diary's reception) and in our desire to make from the diary an insight into our selves (by offering young readers Anne Frank's difficult observations). Perhaps these contradictory desires—learning about and learning from—however differently lived, were also those of Meyer Levin, Otto Frank, and Anna Freud. But what seems to be in need of attention is how this demand to remain loyal shuts out insight into the conflicts, ambivalences, and desolations that are part of the work of mourning.[47] Loyalty is not the same thing as identification with the fate and positions of another. Nor is loyalty synonomous with practices of remembrance. Indeed, the demand to be loyal actually may work as a disavowal of the conflicts that provoke the reasons why we must demand something of each other. So too with the demand to have hope, a compromise formation, an idealization, that in an attempt to bury actually preserves the pain of loss. What seems most crucial is a way to consider what the risk of learning has to do with the work of mourning. And perhaps the greatest risk of learning is that lonely recognition that knowledge of loss and our own insufficient response can be made only in a belated time.

The Time of Pedagogy

At the heart of psychoanalytic work is an ethical call to consider the complexity, conflicts, and plays of psyche and history. These are the conflicts—Eros and Thanatos, love and aggression—that education seems to place elsewhere. And then these forces seem to come back at education as interruptions, as unruly students, as irrelevant questions, and as controversial knowledge in need of containment. These are felt as aggressive returns when education conducts itself as if the separation of good and bad were not a dilemma for the learner and the teacher and as if stories and their conflicts somehow end on the last page and do not reach elsewhere. Yet, as Sigmund Freud observed, these conflicts return: their symptoms are the difficult knowledge held in curriculum, where we ask students to engage with difficult knowledge of life and death without acknowledging the war within and without thinking about how pedagogical idealizations might coarsen the psyche's capacity to respond. The problem is that these conflicts seem to be placed outside of the very individuals who also live them. It is this splitting—putting good inside and bad outside—that renders any engagement with ambivalence intolerable and that makes it impossible for educators to notice transferential love in learning. How might educators begin to complicate not just the response to difficult knowledge on the outside but also the response to the difficult knowledge within—that other war?

Part of the consideration is being able to tolerate the study of the difficult reception of the diary and the ways this reception inadvertently repeats in the form of pedagogy. For perhaps what the historicity of the diary offers is not the voices of millions but the ways millions have tried to engage the voice of one. We cannot predict whether this engagement "falls into trouble" like Meyer Levin's, or whether, as Anna Freud suggests, the engagement can be an exploration of the vicissitudes of loss and attachment and the woeful insufficiency of the belated response. This, after all, is part of the message to parents and teachers offered by Anna Freud and Dorothy Burlingham. In the study of difficult knowledge, we are given too little and too much, too early and too late. To tolerate this time of otherness is, I think, the challenge of pedagogy.

This challenge of pedagogy is also the challenge to the pedagogue. Recall Anna Freud and Dorothy Burlingham's concern with how children learn from adults. They suggest that children learn from the adult's affect toward, and dynamics in, knowledge. Learning, it turns out, is crafted from a curious set of relations: the self's relation to its own otherness and the self's relation to the other's otherness. This is forgotten when the adult's desire for a stable truth, in its insistence upon courage and hope, shuts out the reverberations of losing and being lost. But if what individuals notice in the world is simultaneously what is also in the individual, then prior to offering a resolution it behooves educators to engage in the making of reparation that begins in the acknowledgment of their own psychic conflict in learning and how this conflict is transferred to pedagogy.

Now we reach our last lonely discovery: teaching, it turns out, is also a psychic event for the teacher. If the pedagogy of the diary enacts the educator's desire for a rescue fantasy, stable truth, and the splitting of good and evil through the idealization of the good object, such strategies preclude the possibility of the learner and the teacher working through the ambivalences of their own conflict. For just as resistance to learning must be made into a curiosity to learn from resistance, the study of ambivalence—in which love and hate co-exist and are directed at the same object—also must be tolerated, not encrypted.

A few years ago, a group of analysts met in Israel for an international conference titled, Persistent Shadows of the Holocaust: The Meaning to Those Not Directly Affected. In a curious way, this conference lived the tensions that come from engagement with, and hopes for, Anne Frank's diary. The learning in this conference, like any learning, could be approached only by way of an obstacle made from the conference's title. The conference participants could not agree on what being not directly affected meant, partly because they were so interested in the reverberations and haunting of history and the ways people learn from and ignore the magnitude of the Holocaust. While they could acknowledge that the Holocaust does not affect everyone the same way and that those who identify as affected do so very differently, there was still the problem of conveying difference and even tolerating a conversation between a Jewish analyst and a Christian German analyst. Even the most neutral definition of not being directly affected was insufficient, for most of the analysts could acknowledge that the self is susceptible to known and unknown forces of history.[48] Also, they worried over the ways the Holocaust has entered "the vernacular of tragedy"[49] as they transformed the question of who is affected into one of what affects exist for whom.

The analysts could not come to a common definition of mourning. One suggested that, when it came to the event known as the "Holocaust," the work of mourning is interminable because the loss is inconceivable even as it demands an addressee. Curiously, what brought them together was the particular hesitation which is the question that returns us to education. If one can say that individuals do the work of mourning, can we say also that such work can be attempted by nations? How does a nation come to terms with its internal violences, and how do these internal violences return in the form of curriculum? How does a nation mourn its history? And what place does education have in such a project?

The figure of Anne Frank also haunted this conference. She returned in the form of a symptom known as "the Anne Frank syndrome." The term is given over to children of survivors who try to rescue their parents from what the parents have already been through. The child or adult wishes to preserve a happiness that could not have occurred.[50] This designation raises the question of how the Anne Frank syndrome might haunt our own pedagogical attempts, our own crises of witnessing.

If education is to become a working through, a learning from, then we might work within the words of Anne Frank when she began reformulating her diary for others: "Although I tell you a great deal about our lives, you still know very little about us." And so, "although we say a great deal about the diary, we still know little about how we read it through ourselves." The curious time of pedagogy is the time of knowing too much and learning too little, of being too early and too late. But what can allow this time to be meaningful is the interest in provoking new conditions of learning that can tolerate times of losing and being lost, when the contentious history of the diary meets *those other contentions, our selves.*

Notes

Introduction. Toward a Psychoanalytic Inquiry of Learning

1. A. Freud, *Four Lectures on Psychoanalysis for Teachers and Parents*, 101.

2. Williams, *Keywords*, 95.

3. The phrasing "what every educated person should know" has become an industry in both compulsory and in higher education and in the new press for "educational relevance" in children's programming. See, for example, Diane Ravitch, *The Schools We Deserve*; Allan Bloom, *The Closing of the American Mind*; and William Bennett, *Our Children and Our Country*.

4. See Donald Morton and Mas'ud Zavarzadeh, eds., *Theory/Pedagogy/Politics*; Gerald Graff, *Beyond the Culture Wars*; Jane Gallop, ed., *Pedagogy: The Question of Impersonation*; William Spanos, *The End of Education*; Cary Nelson, ed., *Theory in the Classroom*; Henry Giroux, *Border Crossings*; Gayatri Chakravorty Spivak, *Outside in the Teaching Machine*; Bill Readings, *The University in Ruins*.
   There also exists a different kind of writing on pedagogy, in which pedagogy becomes a frontier concept made from the meeting of two unconscious. In this literature, knowledge itself is suspect, not because it cannot matter but rather because of the ways knowledge transforms into structures of authority and love and becomes synonymous with the subject presumed to know. The metaphors pose the time of pedagogy as a symptom of interpretation: pedagogy as interminable; as dreamy and uncanny; and as transference. See, for example, Shoshana Felman, "Psychoanalysis and Education: Teaching Terminable and Interminable," in *Jacques Lacan and the Adventure of Insight*, ch. 4; Constance Penley, "Teaching in Your Sleep: Feminism and Psychoanalysis," in *The Future of an Illusion*, ch. 9; and Deborah P. Britzman and Alice J. Pitt, "Pedagogy and Transference."

5. The concept of 'psychic event' is at the heart of psychoanalytic inquiry. The term begins in Freud's insistence that perception is dynamic, as opposed to a passive record and in Anna Freud's view that the ego's capacity to observe the world passes through and constitutes its mechanisms of defense. Perception, then, does not reside solely in consciousness. Rather, it is a border line concept that wanders between the wish and

the need. This curious speculation has to do with Freud's view of the instincts and the ego's work of mediating and distinguishing inside and outside pressures. The instinctual pressures must become attached to an idea for the instinct to be considered at all. But given the fluidity of the instinct to become attached, to substitute ideas, misconstrual is also a possibility, as is repression of the instinct's representative ("The Unconscious," 177). Thus perception is woven with cathexis or libido and by repression and misconstrual.

Freud suggests that a psychical act is not equivalent to consciousness. The psychical act, in Freud's view, is a two-phase dynamic of pressure and "a kind of testing (censorship)" (173). In the first phase, a psychical act is unconscious, and if, when attached to an idea, it is rejected by censorship, it resides in this first phase. Freud remarks that even if this act passes censorship, "it is not yet conscious, but it is *certainly capable of becoming conscious . . . that is, it can now, given certain conditions, become an object of consciousness without any special resistance" (173). At the same time, Freud offers the hypothesis that "an idea may exist simultaneously in two places in the mental apparatus—indeed, that if it is not inhibited by the censorship, it regularly advances from the one position to the other, possibly without losing its first location or registration" (175).

Given the fluidity and dynamic moves of the psychical act, we might then speculate on the vicissitudes of learning as psychic event, or as the libidinal working out or working over libidinality in learning. It is primarily through the individual's capacity to feel learning as a pressure that requires education to grapple with how love, hate, and ambivalence constitute the psychical working over (or working out) of learning. This work, as Laplanche and Pontalis suggest, "consists in integrating the excitations into the psyche and establishing associate links between them" (*The Language of Psychoanalysis*, 365). Laplanche and Pontalis also term Freud's notion of working out or working through as a "frontier concept between the economic and symbolic dimensions of Freudianism" (366).

6. In educational studies, Elizabeth Ellsworth's 1989 article "Why Doesn't This Feel Empowering?" unleashed a veritable industry of educational critique within critical pedagogy, although the debates still have difficulty acknowledging the interminability of the pedagogic relation and the "what else" of dialogue across differences. See, for example, Carmen Luke and Jennifer Gore, eds., *Feminisms and Critical Pedagogy*; Audrey Thompson and Andrew Gitlin, "Creating Spaces for Reconstructing Knowledge in Feminist Pedagogy"; and Nicholas Burbules, *Dialogue in Teaching*.

Many of the criticisms of critical pedagogy focused on the masculinist and Eurocentric bias of the educator and the assumption that the educator is capable of transcending his/her positionality for pedagogical purposes. Earlier, and from a different vantage, Stuart Hall's discussion in "Teaching Race" suggested that, when considering questions of racism, teachers must be prepared to listen to racist discourse in their classrooms. Whereas Ellsworth is interested in working through the repressions, Hall suggests that the repressions work in any learning, specifically in learning how social structures live in individuals and how individuals live in history. While both directions, it seems to me, are central to a complex discussion of learning, more intimate experiences of ambivalence, loving and being loved, and love and hate must be made more central to our discussions.

7. *Problems of Human Pleasure and Behavior*, 26.

8. "Observations on Transference-Love," 160.

9. *On Private Madness*, 101.

10. "The Unconscious." For a discussion of Freud's shaky reasonings, see Jacqueline Rose, *States of Fantasy*. Rose offers the thorny question: "So which is it? Do we find it virtually impossible to believe in the mental existence of others, or do we automatically and without reflection assume they are a version of ourselves?" (34).

11. One of the most difficult insights psychoanalysis offers concerns how it imagines questions of boundaries and directionality, or the strange relations between the inside and the outside. Freud's discussion of the term *instinct* in "Instincts and Their Vicissitudes" suggests this dilemma, when he attempts to discuss its "pressure," "aim," "object," and "source." He speculates that instinct is a constant relation elaborated over the course of a life. The instinct "impinges not from without but from within the organism, no flight can avail against it" (118).

    Oddly, the instinct requires a representative in the form of an idea. And then, the instinct becomes a problem of meaning and satisfaction. This postulate leads Freud to view the instinct "as a concept on the frontier between the mental and the somatic, as the psychical representative of the stimuli originating from within the organism and reaching the mind, as a measure of the demand made upon the mind for work in consequence of its connection to the body" (121–22). Thus even in the inside, the demand for a working through of the instinct requires dynamic relations of attachments.

    Andre Green, in his essay "Instinct in the Late Works of Freud" suggests the instinct can be considered as a mode of address: "If we call this an object relation, we are emphasizing the fact that the bodily demand presupposes not only a "something" but also a "someone" with whom it wants to be connected. . . . The concept of instinct relates to a reality that is unknown but can be described as a wandering force that searches without knowing exactly why what it is searching for" (136). This I take as the interminability of conflict and the inauguration of both the psychical and the social.

12. Jacqueline Rose, *Why War?*

13. "Some Elementary Lessons in Psychoanalysis," 282.

14. *Four Lectures*, 121.

15. *New Introductory Lectures on Psycho-Analysis*, 149.

16. *Why War?* 36. The argument Rose makes for an ethics of failure emerges from her meditation on the common question Why war? Rose argues that war is the limit of absolute knowledge, a time when cause and effect collapse and when projection and reality cannot be separated. If war signifies the failure of knowledge, the violent attempt to reunify knowledge through war exacerbates the hatred. Rose posits the following ethic: "Knowledge will be possible only if we are willing to suspend the final purpose and ends of knowledge in advance" (37). This ethic of failure as opposed to mastery works against the entire enterprise of education and its founding insistence upon the linear relation between teaching and learning and between knowledge and

conduct. The ethics of failure, then, points to the question of how to do less harm in social, ontological, and epistemological breakdown.

17. Elisabeth Young-Bruehl, *The Anatomy of Prejudices.*

18. *New Introductory Lectures*, 149.

19. While mechanisms of defense emanate from the ego, they also may be expressing what Michael Balint calls "faulty reality testing" (*Thrills and Regressions*, 49). Whereas reality testing signifies the work of deciding the relevance of one's perceptions in the world, Balint revises this in his view that what actually is tested is the reality of one's affective response to the world. Balint suggests a series of moves in the "mix up" of reality testing: deciding whether a sensation comes from the inside or the outside; figuring out the cause of the sensation; finding its significance; and deciding on a reaction. These also might be the movements of learning to attach to a new idea. But the first three "decisions," Balint points out, are independent of outside reality. The relation between the inside and the outside is made from interpretation, yet one that cannot be settled or stable. Balint, then, offers a view of reality testing that cannot be separated from the vicissitudes of affect and suggests that at the heart of reality testing is the subject's attempt to craft a relation rather than assert an absolute boundary between the inside and the outside. The interminable issue Balint offers is one that could be asked of learning: "whether or not our feelings, affects, and emotions are justified by external events and are appropriate reactions to them" (52). This view suggests reality testing is indistinguishable from the question of making ethical relations.

20. *Four Lectures*, 81–82.

21. *The Ego and the Mechanisms of Defense.*

22. Green, *On Private Madness*, 174.

23. For a stunning discussion of the desires and fantasy frames that prop up both defenses and their inscription in the social, see Eric L. Santer, *My Own Private Germany.*

24. *The Ego and the Id*, 56.

25. *Heterologies*, 27.

26. "Instincts and Their Vicissitudes."

27. M. Balint, *Primary Love*, 149.

28. *The Ego and the Mechanisms of Defense*, 125.

29. *Final Lectures*, 37.

30. *Terrors and Experts.*

Chapter 1. The Arts of Getting By

1. *The Anatomy of Prejudices*, 14.

2. *Sisyphus or the Limits of Education*, 3.

3. "On the Genealogy of Ethics," 231.

4. *Anatomy*, 328.

5. *Kant's Dove*, 39.

6. "Identification."

7. *The Early Years of Life*, 12.

8. Otto Rank offered educators a different scenario to think through the emotional and pedagogical relation of the educator to the student: the Prometheus complex. The Prometheus complex poses as a problem the adult's desire to mould the student in her or his own image. In this relationship, organized through projection, the student becomes the teacher's ego ideal. However, this imaginary creation of the educator is bound to fail. In Rank's words:

> The attainment or realization of one's own ego-ideal is *always* bound up with disappointment, no matter whether we see this idea realized in ourselves or another. . . . The reason for this disappointment in the ego ideal is that . . . only striving for it is pleasurable insofar as it unburdens the ego projectively. The attainment of one's ego-ideal disappoints because it *inhibits* the projection, that is, inhibits a form of self expression. ("The Prometheus Complex," 204)

In the Prometheus complex we have a story of education as desire, which returns us to the governess's story discussed in the Introduction. Whereas in Bernfeld's account both educator and student seem to push each other ("two justified wills"), in Rank's view it is the educator who, at least in the beginning, suffers from the Prometheus complex and the punishment of Prometheus.

9. *Early Years*, 119.

10. "Community of Daydreams," 300.

11. Edith Kurzweil's chapter "Education," in *The Freudians*, her comparative study of how psychoanalysis is shaped by national history, makes similar points. The chapter begins with Sandor Ferenczi's denouncement of teaching methods, described as "hothouses fostering neurosis" (127). Ferenczi's paper, first read in 1908 to the First Psycho-Analytic Congress in Salzburg, is a startling condemnation of cruelty in pedagogical method and a plea for "an education to be worked out in the future" ("Psycho-Analysis and Education," 224). Ferenczi argues that education's forgetting of the pleasure principle (a forgetting that is itself a symptom of the educator's own infantile amnesia), both in pedagogical methods and in relations with children, serves the work of repression. Given that adults organize education, Ferenczi advises educators to begin working on their own enlightenment rather than reforming the system. Part of this enlightenment has to do with the educator's confrontation with dogma and moralism in education, a symptom of what Ferenczi calls an "education to *introspective blindness*" (223). His critique of the educator's lack of insight into the vicissitudes of the instincts and hence of the capacity of educational methods to provoke unhappiness,

suffering, and neurosis, is one of the central interferences psychoanalytic accounts offer to education.

But at issue is also the ambivalence of applying psychoanalysis to education. This ambivalence begins with Freud's repeated claim that he did not know much about education. In his foreword to August Aichhorn's *Wayward Youth* Freud draws what he calls a "conservative conclusion": "that educational work is *sui generis*, not to be confused with nor exchanged for psychoanalytic means of influence. Psychoanalysis of the child may be drawn upon as a contributory help, but it is not a substitute for education" (vi). Freud ends his introduction with the suggestion that psychoanalysis may be most useful for the educator's own analysis.

12. In my explorations of the relation between psychoanalysis and education, what became obvious was that both fields offer common terms, such as *conflict, perception, interpretation,* and *anxiety,* but each one thinks of these terms differently. There are plenty of histories that narrate the development of each field, but, as of yet, there is no psychoanalytic history of either one.

While there have been attempts to put Freud's work into psychoanalysis (see, for instance, Nicolas Abraham and Maria Torok, *The Wolf Man's Magic Word*), to consider the symptoms between Freud and the keeping of the archive (see Jacques Derrida, "Archive Fever"), and to compile an analytically inflected dictionary of Freudian terminology (see J. Laplanche and J. B. Pontalis, *The Language of Psychoanalysis*), a psychoanalytic history of psychoanalysis may well be an impossible demand as pointed out in J. Laplanche, *Life and Death in Psychoanalysis*; Michel de Certeau, *Heterologies*; and J. B. Pontalis, *Frontiers in Psychoanalysis*.

13. *Primary Love*, 209.

14. For example, Elisabeth Young-Bruehl, *Anna Freud*; Lisa Appignanesi and John Forrester, *Freud's Women*; Nina Sutton, *Bruno Bettelheim*.

15. For example, Jacqueline Rose, *Why War?*; Young-Bruehl, *Anatomy*.

16. For example, Carolyn Steedman, *Strange Dislocations*; Denise Riley, *War in the Nursery*.

17. For example, Bruno Bettelheim, "Psychoanalysis and Education"; Anna Freud, *The Ego and the Mechanisms of Defense*; Maud Mannoni, *The Child, His "Illness," and the Others*; Otto Rank, *Modern Education*.

18. For example, Rudolf Ekstein and Rocco Motto, "Psychoanalysis and Education"; Shoshana Felman, *Jacques Lacan and the Adventure of Insight*; Kate Field et al., *Learning and Education*.

19. For critiques of mainstream psychology in education, see Arthur Jersild, *When Teachers Face Themselves*; William Pinar et al., *Understanding Curriculum*; Julian Henriques et al., *Changing the Subject*.

20. There are of course educators who deeply grapple with analytic insight and who insist on the psychic dimensions of learning. But even when taking into account their attempts to consider the relations between psychoanalysis and education, most must

comment upon their field's resistance to the difficulties analytic views of the subject pose, and many must work through education's woeful disregard of the psychological field of instinctual play. See, for example, Arthur Jersild, *When Teachers Face Themselves*; William Pinar, *Autobiography, Politics and Sexuality*; Steven Appel, "The Unconscious Subject of Education" and *Positioning Subjects*; Joe Kincheloe and William Pinar, eds., *Curriculum as Social Psychoanalysis*; Victoria Muñoz, *Where "Something Catches"*; Jeffrey Berman, *Diaries to an English Professor;* and a range of discussion in Pinar et al., *Understanding Curriculum.*

However, a revision of the the above scenario can be found in Stephen Appel's *Positioning Subjects.* His study brings to the attention of the discipline of critical sociology of education the psychoanalytic debate on the inauguration and failings of subjectivity. Much of the text is explicative of the debates within social psychoanalytic views (and detours are taken through Althusser and arguments on ideology), even though throughout it Appel insists on the difficulties of changing the subject and critiques educators' manic insistence on the possible triumphalism of consciousness. This work can be situated in the tradition, initiated by Siegfried Bernfeld, of attempting to bring into dialogue "the crowded street" and the Freudian couch. Appel is correct in stressing that educational sociology has repressed the Freudian notion of the unconscious in its resistance to a philosophy that "promises nothing." His work suggests the need for working through the symptoms of repression in the actual production of sociological knowledge and for an exploration of how unconscious desire works within critical sociology of education. What would be at stake if sociology could admit its resistance to transforming itself? Can the critical sociology of education be read as a symptom of the return of the repressed? And, if the repressed could be analyzed, would one still need the discipline of the critical sociology of education?

21. Editor's note in Nicolas Abraham and Maria Torok, *The Shell and the Kernel*, 76.

22. *Terrors and Experts*, 3.

23. See, for example, Wilfred Bion, *Learning from Experience*; Abraham and Torok, *The Shell and the Kernel*, vol. I; V. D. Volkan, *The Need to Have Enemies and Allies*; Adam Phillips, *On Kissing, Tickling and Being Bored.* What such a divergent list of analytical writing has in common is the assertion of the psychical work of disengagement.

24. Melanie Klein makes this point quite explicitly: "The extremely important role played by the school is in general based upon the fact that school and learning are from the first *libidinally* determined for everyone, since by its demands school compels a child to sublimate his [or her] libidinal instinctual energies" ("The Role of the School in the Libidinal Development of the Child," 59). This difficult exchange is the topic of chapter 3.

25. "Identification," 318.

26. *The Ego.*

27. *The Inhuman*, 18.

28. *Cracking Up*, 103.

29. "Psychoanalysis and Education—An Historical Account."

30. Christopher Bollas, *Being a Character*.

31. "The Means of Education," 327.

32. In analytic literature, what seems to distinguish transference from transference neurosis is not the nature of their content but whether what is carried over to the new learning is the neurotic compulsion to repeat old conflicts in new situations or the working through of one's history of learning to love. See for example Stephen Mitchell and Margaret Black, *Freud and Beyond*; Gail Reed, *Transference Neurosis and Psychoanalytic Experience*; and Aaron Esman, ed., *Essential Papers on Transference*.

33. Horney, *Final Lectures*, 96.

34. *Jacques Lacan and the Adventure of Insight*.

35. Editha Sterba, "Interpretation and Education."

36. *Four Lectures on Psychoanalysis for Teachers and Parents*, 125.

37. *Self-Analysis*.

38. *Anatomy*, 174.

39. *Being a Character*, 180.

40. See Willard Waller, *The Sociology of Teaching*; Louise Rosenblatt, *Literature as Exploration*; Maxine Greene, *The Teacher as Stranger*.

41. *When Teachers*, 27.

42. Rose, *Why War?*

43. *Early Years*, 93.

44. Winnicott, *Playing and Reality*, 100.

45. *The Child, His "Illness" and the Others*.

46. Young-Bruehl, *Anatomy*.

47. Laplanche and Pontalis, *Language*.

48. Muñoz, *Where "Something Catches"*; Alice Pitt, "Subjects in Tension"; Sharon Todd, "Pedagogical Imaginary and the Politics of Identity"; Judith Robertson, "Cinema and the Politics of Desire in Teacher Education."

49. Edith Buxbaum, "Three Great Psychoanalytic Educators."

50. "Means," 327.

51. "Observations on Transference-Love."

52. *An Outline of Psychoanalysis*, 174.

53. *Wayward Youth*.

54. *Frontiers*, 170.

55. "Education and the Reality Principle."

56. D. W. Winnicott, *Playing and Reality*, 10.

57. Young-Bruehl characterizes this rescue fantasy of saving children as a recognition of the social's larger disavowal of children's sexuality. Within her formula, one could insert the construct of the heroic teacher for education:

> There is a kind of historical rule of thumb that can be applied to the adolescent institutions of the early twentieth century: the greater the felt danger of puberty (the more explosive sexuality is expected), the more education is called to the rescue—specifically, education for self-control or, if self-control is beyond reach, submission to authority. To put the matter badly, by reinforcing the idea that puberty is explosive, education of this period promoted hysteria and then got progressively better at promoting obsessionality. (*Anatomy*, 332)

58. Bettelheim, "Education and the Reality Principle," 76.

59. Since Bettelheim's death in 1990, two biographies have been published, those by Sutton and by Pollack. Both studies reside in the controversy of Bettelheim's work and are organized by considering the charges against Bettelheim after his death. Pollack's study is an accounting of Bettelheim's failings. The history of how Pollack came to consider Dr. Bettelheim is itself traumatic. On a larger scale, this biography seems to bear witness to Laplanche's discussion of *Nachtraglichkeit* or deferred action, for Pollack's younger brother was a student in Bettelheim's Orthogenic School in Chicago. During a home visit, the boy was killed in an accident Pollack himself barely escaped. As an adult Pollack attempted to learn more about his brother and Bettelheim's work with disturbed children.

> Deferred action is a two-stage mechanism, and neither of its stages can be detected on its own. . . . If it is true to say that *it always takes two traumas to make a trauma*, or two distinct events to produce repression, then it is also true to say that primary repression, or trauma, is not something that can be pinpointed thanks to observation, even if the observer is a psychoanalyst. Analytic observers are fated to being either too early or too late, not because some ill-defined metaphysical curse has been laid upon them, but because their object itself is constructed in two stages. (Laplanche, *New Foundations for Psychoanalysis*, 88)

We might read these biographies as a symptom of deferred action where the trauma cannot be pinpointed.

60. "Means," 328.

61. Steven Luel, "Bettelheim on Education," 573.

62. Sigmund Freud, *The Ego and the Id*, 35.

63. Freud, *The Ego and the Id*, 56.

64. *Identity, Youth, and Crisis*, 224.

65. "Education and the Reality Principle," 133.

66. *New Introductory Lectures on Psycho-Analysis*, 80.

67. *The Ego and the Id.*

68. *New Introductory Lectures*, 80.

69. *Wayward Youth.*

70. "August Aichhorn," 352, 349.

71. This ethic of doing less harm is a key theme in the text dedicated to Aichhorn on his seventieth birthday and edited by K. R. Eissler, *Searchlights on Delinquency.* While the collection varies widely in terms of analytic perspective, each essay begins with a thoughtful regard of Aichhorn's legacy and his insistence upon the dignity of the individual.

72. *The University in Ruins*, 128.

73. *Self-Analysis.*

74. *Final Lectures*, 18.

Chapter 2. On Making Education Inconsolable

1. Eric K. Washington, "Sculpture in Flight," 191.

2. "Revolutionary Action," 218.

3. *On Private Madness*, 43.

4. *The Interpretation of Dreams*, 507.

5. *Playing in the Dark.*

6. *Interpretation*, 434.

7. Here, I am borrowing Sigmund Freud's formulation that the condition for membership in civilization is the renunciation of instincts, or at the very least their sublimation. (See *Civilization and Its Discontents.*) In addition, I am juxtaposing Anna Freud's writing on defense mechanisms. (See *The Ego and the Mechanisms of Defense.*)

8. See Anna Freud, "About Losing and Being Lost," and Sigmund Freud, "Mourning and Melancholia."

9. *Playing in the Dark*, 35.

10. *Heterologies*, 27.

11. *Jacques Lacan and the Adventure of Insight*, 92.

12. *The Public School*, 45.

13. "Aggression, Guilt, and Reparation," 81.

14. *What Does A Woman Want?* 5–6.

15. *The Public School*, 65.

16. *The Dialectic of Freedom*, 36–37.

17. *The Public School*, 157.

18. See, for example, William Pinar, *Autobiography, Politics, and Sexuality*; Janet Miller, *Creating Spaces and Finding Voices*; Deanne Bogdan, *Re-Educating the Imagination*; Jo Anne Pagano, *Exiles and Communities*; Madeleine Grumet, "The Beauty Full Curriculum"; Cameron McCarthy and Warren Crichlow, eds., "Toni Morrison and the Curriculum"; Roger Simon, *Teaching against the Grain*; Judith Robertson, "Cinema and the Politics of Desire in Teacher Education"; Rinaldo Walcott, *Black Like Who?*

19. *Eichmann in Jerusalem.*

20. *The Public School*, 160.

21. *The Writing of History*, 46.

22. See the following books by Maxine Greene: *The Teacher as Stranger*; *Landscapes of Learning*; *The Dialectic of Freedom*.

23. *School Days*, 11

24. "Psychoanalysis and Education," 317.

Chapter 3. On Becoming a "Little Sex Researcher": Some Comments on a Polymorphously Perverse Curriculum

1. *Epistemology of the Closet*, 22.

2. "Visualizing Safe Sex," 374.

3. *The Imaginary Domain*, 8.

4. Jonathan Silin, *Sex, Death, and the Education of Children*; Eve Sedgwick, *Epistemology*; Shoshana Felman, *Jacques Lacan and the Adventure of Insight*.

5. *Erotism.*

6. *The Ego and the Mechanisms of Defense*, 157.

7. *Three Essays on the Theory of Sexuality*, 194.

8. Cited in David Halperin, *Saint Foucault*, 88.

9. *Identification Papers.*

10. In *Identification Papers*, Diana Fuss offers a stunning literary exploration of "the highly-charged erotic climate of the single-sex school" in terms of its fears and desires for lesbian subjects (108). In positing the fault lines of a discourse on sexuality that worries about contagion, she gives insight into the more normative fear of sexuality as contagion. While this direction has been significant in tracing the persistent phobic discourse against gay and lesbian civil rights, my chapter takes movement in a centrifugal (as in fugitive) direction.

11. Nathan Hale, *Freud and the Americans*.

12. Angus McLaren, *Our Own Master Race*.

13. I thank Kate Kaul for pointing this text out to me.

14. Foucault's introduction to Herculine Barbin, *Herculine Barbin*, vii. Herculine, it must be remembered, elaborated sexuality in school as a student and then while student teaching.

15. *Primary Love*, 11.

16. Anna Freud, *The Ego*, 17.

17. In its common usage, the term *perversion* connotes a moralistic judgement on the transgression of social convention, nature, and what is accepted as "normal." This chapter works with the term *perversity* in the psychoanalytic sense. There perversity invokes any sexual activity that deviates from coitus with a person of the opposite sex for the purpose of reproduction. Essentially, and regardless of object choice, perversity refers to every other practice of bodily pleasure that has no other reason than pleasure. Laplanche and Pontalis offer the following observation:

> So-called normal sexuality cannot be seen as an *a priori* aspect of human nature [and citing Freud]: ". . . the exclusive sexual interest felt by men for women is also a problem that needs elucidating and is not a self-evident fact.". . . One could . . . define human sexuality itself as essentially "perverse" inasmuch as it never fully detaches itself from its [infantile] origins, where satisfaction was sought not in a specific activity but in the "pleasure gain" associated with functions or activities depending on other instincts. Even in the performance of the genital act itself, it suffices that the subject should develop an excessive attachment to forepleasure for him [or her] to slip toward perversion. (*The Language of Psychoanalysis*, 307–8)

Throughout this chapter, my use of perversity is meant to signify erotic actions without utility, in opposition to the unfortunate moralistic usage that structures homophobic discourse.

18. *Four Lectures on Psychoanalysis for Teachers and Parents*.

19. The sense of guilt that inaugurates the superego is, as Freud suggests in *Civilization and Its Discontents*, the beginning of the subject's conscience. This guilt arises from two opposing dynamics: the parent's prohibitions and the parent's love. That is, the

child accepts the parent's prohibitions in exchange for the parent's love. A sense of guilt, in these terms, is a compromise formation between the child's desire both to have and to be the parent. In Melanie Klein's terms, the working through of prohibition and love is tied to the subject's capacity for destruction and construction. Klein argues that the desire to destroy and to repair are necessary to the subject (*Love, Guilt and Reparation*).

But if, as Donald Winnicott argues, guilt can become entangled in the desire to destroy, then ethical action cannot be formulated from guilt. Then guilt becomes persecution. Winnicott suggests: "The difficult thing is for each individual to take full responsibility for the destructiveness that is personal, and that inherently belongs to a relationship that is related to loving" ("Aggression, Guilt and Reparation," 82). The problem a sex education must consider is that if it only offers prohibitions to the potential of sexuality, then what is foreclosed is a sense of guilt capable of transforming into constructive attachments. Winnicott's notion of a sense of guilt, then, "comes from toleration of one's destructive impulses in primitive loving. Toleration of one's destructive impulses results in a new thing: the capacity to enjoy ideas, even destruction in them, and the bodily excitements that belong to them, or that they belong to. This development gives elbow-room for the experience of concern, which is the basis for everything constructive" (87).

Thus we are back to the relationship between curiosity and sexuality offered by Freud, a relation that must be considered in elaborating a sex education that can exceed prohibition and that is interested in allowing for the space where the learners can elaborate "elbow-room for the experience of concern."

20. Balint argues that the erotic component of the ego instinct, "makes the ego-instincts educable. It is this component that makes attachment to the educator possible. The satisfaction of the erotic component in the transference love compensates the individual under education for the frustration of the original instinctual urge, thereby enables him [or her] to endure education" (*Primary Love*, 43).

21. *The Ego.*

22. *The Bonds of Love*, 11.

23. Those analysts that consider the clash between the demands of education and the demands of psychical life begin with a critique of education's woeful disregard and even hatred of sexuality, which takes the form of authoritarianism in education. See, for example, Melanie Klein, "The Role of the School in the Libidinal Development of the Child"; Otto Fenichel, "The Means of Education"; Sandor Ferenczi, "Psycho-Analysis and Education"; Alice Balint, *The Early Years.*

24. *Problems of Human Pleasure and Behavior*, 20.

25. *The History of Sexuality.*

26. For a discussion of the relation between social hygiene movements and sex education, see Hale, *Freud and the Americans.*

27. *Sex-Education*, 144.

28. *History of Sexuality*, 94.

29. "The Subject and Power," 212.

30. For discussions of how the construct of age appropriateness and the discourses of development deny the sexuality of children and produce the exclusion of gay and lesbian bodies, see Silin's critique of developmental psychology in *Sex, Death*, ch. 4, and Watney's "Schools Out." For a study of conceptions of the term "adolescence" see Nancy Lesko's "Denaturalizing adolescence."

31. *History of Sexuality*, 89.

Chapter 4. Queer Pedagogy and Its Strange Techniques

1. "Acting Bits/Identity Talk."

2. McLaren's study of the eugenic movement in Canada details the historical shift from defining and containing "deviancy" to the movement leaders' preoccupation with the fashioning of normalcy through progressive measures such as the introduction of school nursing, hygiene, sex education, and pedagogies directed at white racial improvement. From a different vantage, Foucault's first volume on sexuality traces this shift whereby constituting normalcy becomes the central strategy of knowledge/power/pleasure.

3. The notion of "the-subject-presumed-to know" and "a passion for ignorance" is discussed in the work of analyst Jacques Lacan. In Lacan's view the subject-presumed-to-know is the other who is assumed to already possess omnipotent knowledge. Paradoxically, such a subject is propped up by the other's passion for ignorance. Lacan theorizes ignorance as a residue of knowledge, not its constitutive outside. Statements of dismissal and disimplication such as "I don't want to know about it," or "That has nothing to do with me" support the work of ignorance. This view depends upon Freud's notion of negation, discussed in chapter 1.

    But the work of ignorance also takes a different turn. Jessica Benjamin discusses the traces ignorance bears in the following observation: "One is in theory more likely to be determined by a prior body of thought precisely when one thinks it can be overcome simply by rejecting its postulates. The act of rejection shapes one's starting point, and one adopts an oppositional stance that unconsciously reverses the original coordinates of thought" (*Like Subjects, Love Objects*, 5).

4. See Shoshana Felman, *Jacques Lacan and the Adventure of Insight*; Jonathan Silin, *Sex, Death, and the Education of Children*; Eve Kosofsky Sedgwick, *Epistemology of the Closet*.

5. "Come Out, Come Out, Wherever You Are."

6. Foucault, "The Subject and Power."

7. "Sexual Manners," original 166.

8. Mikkel Borch-Jacobsen, *The Freudian Subject*.

9. *Homographesis*, 16.

10. "Street Talk/Straight Talk," 28.

11. The cost of narrating identities is not, in queer theory, a problem of getting identities right. Rather, there is a significant moment in queer theory that agonizes the conceptualization of identity: how it "works" as history, how it is narrated as synecdoche (a part capable of standing in for the whole), and how its exclusions permit its categorical claims. (See, for example, Sedgwick, *Epistemology*). This mode of questioning owes much to the work of Michel Foucault.

   Judith Butler raises a significant tension in considering Foucault's work: "The political challenge Foucault poses . . . is whether a resistance to the diagnostic category of identity can be effected that does not reduplicate the very mechanism of subjection, this time—painfully, paradoxically—under the sign of liberation" ("Sexual Inversions" 355). The last sentence in Foucault's introductory volume on sexuality says as much: "The irony of [the deployment of sexuality] is having us believe that our 'liberation' is in the balance" (*History of Sexuality*, 159).

12. The claim of "perversity" as a marker of identification is quite contradictory in queer theories. Foundationally, the claim draws from the Freudian notion of all sexuality as perverse, as in polymorphous perversity. (See Jean Laplanche, *Life and Death in Psychoanalysis*). But two kinds of claims about perversity are made in queer theories. On the one hand, perversity works as a means to dispute dominant chains of signification, or what D. A. Miller names as "not a name but the continual elision of one [that disrupts] a system of connotation" (*Bringing Out Roland Barthes*, 24–25). On the other hand, Mandy Merck (in *perversions*) and Eve Sedgwick (in "White Glasses") take up perverse reading practices meant to disassemble the temples of gay and lesbian mythology. Both challenge the essentialist feminist and gay and lesbian claims of identification as issuing from identity. For a debate on the question of whether claims of perversity are political claims, see "Perversity, a special issue," in *New Formations*.

13. My use of the term *everyday* has been influenced by the work of Gary Wickham and William Haver. Specifically, I am tying to theorize along with their insight that "violence against queers is installed not merely in a legal apparatus, but in 'daily life' itself, as well as in the objectification, thematization and valorization of everydayness (as in 'family values,' for example)" (5). Their formulation opens the question of how it becomes conceivable for some folks to have an everyday while other folks become either a special event or a disruption of the everyday.

14. "Queer Theory," iv.

   The use of the term *queer* works quite differently in community/street politics. In a discussion of the discursive deployment of this term in AIDS activist groups and in gay, lesbian, and bisexual forms of militancy, Michael Warner argues that the term *queer* is "thoroughly embedded in modern Anglo American culture and does not translate easily. . . . As a politically unstable term . . . queer dates from the Bush-Thatcher-Mulroney era" ("Something Queer about the Nation State," 14). This historical conservatism and the refusal of the state to redress civil rights produced a performative politics meant to disturb the seemingly seamless construct of the normal from its modes of materiality.

15. *Unmarked*, 32.

16. "What Will Have Been Said about AIDS," 112.

17. The concept of 'negation' is discussed in chapter 1.

18. The paradoxical phrasing—the education of education—is meant to signal that education is not simply an originary network of institutions, policies, learning theories, curricular moves, and a social network of subjects. Rather, such a phrasing approaches education as an effect of knowledge/power/pleasure, thus caught in larger historical apparatuses to which education responds.

19. *The History of Sexuality.*

20. E. Sedgwick, "White Glasses."

21. *Identification Papers*, 2.

22. "Hey, Girlfriend!" 12.

23. In Joan Copjec's terms, happiness is both objective and subjective. She clarifies Freud's views of empathy with the following observation: "If we cannot judge immediately what measure of pain or pleasure belonged to a historical individual, this is not because happiness is subjective and we cannot project ourselves into her private mental sphere, but rather because we cannot so easily project ourselves into her objective *social* sphere in order to disarm the categories of thought that constructed her expectations, narcotized her against disappointment, made her obtuse to her own suffering" ("Cutting Up," 228).

24. *Civilization*, 89.

25. "Introduction," xxi. I find the term *heteronormativity* more interesting than the familiar and often misused *homophobia* because debates about gay and lesbian oppression and desire must move beyond the humanist psychological discourse of individual fear of homosexuality as contagion (and not, coincidentally, the centering of heterosexuality as the normal). The term *homophobia* rarely ventures into political critiques of how normalcy becomes produced and sexualized as heterosexuality. That is, how sex becomes inserted into normalcy and how normalcy becomes inserted into sex is not an area accessible to the naming of homophobia because the term is centrally given over to the correction of individuated attitude. The term *heteronormativity* begins to get at how the production of deviancy is intimately tied to the very possibility of normalcy. Normalcy can be intelligible only through the construction of its other: the deviant. In such a relation, normalcy must always make itself normal, must always normalize itself. Recent writing in queer theory suggests the problem is not fear of queerness but obsession with normalizing and containing queerness and, not coincidently, otherness. The odd story is that such mechanisms are, in actuality, about the production of normalcy. (See, for example, Judith Butler, *Bodies That Matter*; Jonathan Dollimore, *Sexual Dissidence*; Fuss, *Identification Papers*; Sedgwick, *Epistemology*; and Warner, "Introduction.")

26. *History of Sexuality*, 152.

27. *Bodies That Matter*, 53.

28. Deborah Britzman, "The Ordeal of Knowledge"; Cindy Patton, *Inventing AIDS.*

29. *Racist Culture*, 7.

30. T. Morrison, *Playing in the Dark*; P. Phelan, *Unmarked*, 26.

31. *Epistemology*, 40.

32. "Imitation and Gender Insubordination," 20.

33. Cindy Patton's groundbreaking study *Inventing AIDS* traces how discourses of information produce the grounds of estrangement since one may "know" the facts but not how to relate "facts" as relevant to the self. In Patton's words: "Several studies suggest that teenagers and young adults believe that other people acquire HIV infection or develop AIDS through specific and known sets of acts while they perceive their *own* susceptibility to HIV or AIDS to be a matter of chance" (109). Such a formulation crystallizes two subject positions discussed throughout this chapter: the subject-presumed-to-know and the passion for ignorance. Moreover, if every learning is an unlearning, discourses of information negate this complexity with a naive theory of ignorance as a lack to be filled by information.

34. Delany, "Street Talk."

35. *History of Sexuality.*

36. "Street Talk."

37. *The Coming Community*, 189.

38. Felman, *Jacques Lacan*, 23.

39. William Haver, "Thinking the Thought of That Which Is Strictly Speaking Unthinkable."

Chapter 5. Narcissism of Minor Differences and the Problem of Antiracist Pedagogy

1. Dominick LaCapra, *Representing the Holocaust*; Elisabeth Young-Bruehl, "Discriminations" and *The Anatomy of Prejudices.*

2. Young-Bruehl's epic study of prejudices begins with the claim that prejudices, or types of hatred projected onto others, are social symptoms of desire or need. Further, she claims that the history of the social sciences' attempts to characterize prejudice as a generalized attitude shuts out the psychical question of what unconscious desires are being fulfilled. In Young-Bruehl's words: "When victim groups and their representatives get caught up on the designation of prejudices according to their targets, they lose focus on the perpetrators and the circumstances, the social and political contexts, of the perpetration. They fail to perceive prejudices as fulfilments of needs or desires and to ask what needs or desires are being fulfilled. Classifying prejudices according to target groups obscures the fact that the same need or desire can be fulfilled by directing prejudice at a victim group defined by colour or at one defined by sexual preference" (20).

She suggests that one might consider what is being projected and acted out in ideologies of desire.

3. Freud notes three dynamic movements of love: loving-hating; loving-being loved; and loving/hating-ambivalence. With these movements, Freud speculates upon the Eros of hatred. Because love and hate are the only instincts that can change their content into their opposite, and because love can be transformed into hate, "hate acquires an erotic character and the continuity of a love relation is ensured" ("Instincts and Their Vicissitudes," 139).

4. Bela Grunberger, *New Essays on Narcissism*.

5. *Anatomy*, 136.

6. "Nationalism and the Narcissism of Minor Differences," 19.

7. J. Fletcher and M. Stanton, eds., *Jean Laplanche: Seduction, Translation, Drives*, 37.

8. Michel Foucault, *The History of Sexuality*; Sander Gilman, *The Jew's Body* and *Freud, Race and Gender*.

9. The present chapter can be seen as in dialogue with a larger discussion of the relations between psychoanalysis and Freud's Jewishness. While it is influenced by Sander Gilman's work, other views also have been important in my thinking. See for example Estelle Roith, *The Riddle of Freud*; Dennis Klein, *Jewish Origins of the Psychoanalytic Movement*; Daniel Boyarin, *Unheroic Conduct* and "Freud's Baby, Fliess's Maybe"; Elaine Marks, "Juifemme," in *Marrano as Metaphor*; and Yosef Hayim Yerushalmi, *Freud's Moses*.

10. Michel de Certeau, *The Writing of History*; Foucault, *History of Sexuality*; Gilman, *Freud, Race, and Gender*.

11. It must be noted that in the fin-de-siècle Jewish professionals were quite divided over how to think about the category of Jewish racialization. For a study of the contradictions on Jewish scientists' resistance to nineteenth- and twentieth-century racism, in which the category of race is maintained but in some ways re-inflected with a positivity for Jewish definitions of Jewishness, see John M. Efron, *Defenders of the Race*.

12. "New Ethnicities," 29.

13. *Anatomy*, 96.

14. While this chapter engages the work of writers who claim the identity of Jewish lesbians, the strategy of centering Eros and ambivalence as the grounds of sociality is also at stake in the consideration of the costs of any identity, including those historically disparaged within communities. For stunning examples of this method, perhaps a method of the discontent, see Hinton Al's inversion of the familiar trope of "the Negress" in *The Women*; Louise Kaplan's retelling of Madame Bovary from her child's point of view, "Berthe's Dead Mother," in *No Voice Is Ever Wholly Lost*; and Phillip Brian Harper's analysis of the "crisis" of black masculinity in culture production in *Are We Not Men?*

15. *Performance Anxieties*, 21.

16. Writing by Jewish lesbians on questions of identity and social difference is quite extensive. See, for instance, Jyl Lynn Felman, "If Only I'd Been Born a Kosher Chicken"; *Fireweed's* "Special Issue on Jewish Women"; Marilyn Hacker, *Winter Numbers*; Judith Katz, *Running Fiercely toward a High Thin Sound*; Melanie Kay/Kantrowitz, *The Issue Is Power*; Melanie Kay/Kantrowitz and Irena Klepfisz, eds., *The Tribe of Dina*; Irena Klepfisz, *Dreams of an Insomniac*; Andrea Freud Lowenstein, *This Place*; Joan Nestle, *Restricted Country*; Sara Schulman, *My American History*; Muriel Rukeyser, *Breaking Open*; Jo Sinclair, *Wasteland*.

17. In the context of North America, see for example, bell hooks, "Keeping a Legacy of Shared Struggle"; Abraham Lavender, ed., *A Coat of Many Colors*; Julius Lester, *Lovesong*; and Josylyn Segal, "Interracial Plus." But while these very different (and taken together, antagonistic) discussions begin with the fact that Jews constitute many races, see also Ellen Willis, "The Myth of the Powerful Jew." Willis argues that *Jew* is not a racial term. And, from a very different vantage, two of the most interesting discussions on the interrelations between "blacks" and "Jews" that address the inessential commonalities can be found in Paul Gilroy, *The Black Atlantic*, and Joe Wood, "The Problem Negro and Other Tales."

    These disputes are further complicated by James McBride's memoir, *The Color of Water*, that tells of his white mother's conversion from Judaism to Christianity, her marriage to his African American father, and McBride's own sense of evolving racial identity as a black man. This memoir testifies to McBride's ambivalent struggle to consider how Jewish ethics unconsciously have contributed to his own views of race, identity, and education. Throughout the memoir, McBride also examines those narcissisms of minor differences both within and between Jewish and African American sociality, coming to an acceptance of good and bad within each community.

    But perhaps the complications noted above, mixed as they are in history and in its ambivalent retellings, are more forcefully engaged in fiction. For example, see Caryl Phillips, *The Nature of Blood*.

18. *The Black Atlantic*, 212.

19. The concept of 'race' that I am drawing upon is not couched in the eugenic terms of "phenotype" but in terms of what David Theo Goldberg calls "racialized discourse," which he defines as "not consist[ing] simply in descriptive representations of others. It includes a set of hypothetical premises about human kinds (e.g. the 'great chain of being,' classificatory hierarchies, etc.) and about the differences between them (both mental and physical). It involves a class of ethical choices (e.g. domination and subjugation, entitlement and restriction, disrespect and abuse)." (*Racist Culture*, 47).

20. But within North American Jewish communities this desire is fraught with ambivalence. There is a contradictory Jewish desire for gentiles to acknowledge Jewish difference (as in Jewish uniqueness) but at the same time not to draw attention to desiring difference, for in drawing attention to difference one may suggest a certain empathetic similitude. This, of course, is the narcissistic tension. One example of its complications can be observed in the 1995 Los Angeles trial of O. J. Simpson. During closing arguments, Lawyer Johnny Cochrane termed former police detective Mark Furhman as "worse than Hitler." The father of the late Ron Goldman viewed such a statement as

a double disavowal of the uniqueness of the Shoah and of his murdered Jewish son. And while, ostensibly, for Mr. Goldman there could be no one worse than Hitler, his angry response to Mr. Cochrane implied that what is worse than Hitler is someone who tries to find someone worse than Hitler. Here, we have the painful positions of narcissism fighting narcissism.

21. Ann Pellegrini makes this same point when she considers the history of Jewishness as gender and raises the stakes by asking "what such 'articulations' (to borrow Judith Butler's formulation) of gender and race have meant for Jewish women," specifically when Jewish women were so prominent in the imagination of fin-de-siècle Europe (*Performance Anxieties*, 17).

    Naomi Seidman, while acknowledging the new turn in Jewish studies toward constructions of "masculinity," notes that much of this new work on the feminization of Jewish masculinity seems to preclude analysis of gender inequality within Jewishness and tends to valorize the Jewish male body ("Theorizing Jewish Patriarchy *in extremis*"). She concludes: "The Jewish man-woman . . . is not *necessarily* a culture subversive, a sexual outlaw, or a woman's dream come true: to put it differently, the feminized Jewish man may as easily feed patriarchical power as qualify or negate it" (46). Here we note the tension in how narcissism of minor differences within Jewish studies structures scholarly interest.

22. Hans Mayer, *Outsiders*. Also see Sander Gilman, *Franz Kafka*.

23. *History of Sexuality*, 89.

24. To constitute discourses of "the visible" as an imagined category is not to deny the material effects of racism and the racist's obsessional reliance upon categorization and identification of the victim. Indeed, in North America, the view of race as phenotype is quite central to the operation and maintenance of everyday racism. See, for example, Regina Austin, "'A Nation of Thieves.'" Franz Fanon made this point as well but for the purposes of distinguishing anti-Semitism from racism. See Young-Bruehl, *Anatomy*, 446–516.

25. Zygmut Bauman, *Modernity and the Holocaust*.

26. *The Jew's Body*, 170.

27. *Freud, Race and Gender*, 8.

    Earlier in this chapter, I described how, in anti-Semitic writing, the "Jew" is coded as feminine. Femininity becomes a code for a failed masculinity, or, in slightly different terms, an effeminate/homo masculinity. But two problems emerge in these constructions, having to do with what happens to both femininity and masculinity. It may be that the term *Jew* was masculinized in the form of a hysterical hypermasculinization by heterosexual Jewish men in order to renounce anti-Semitic representations of themselves. This is essentially Sander Gilman's reading of Freud's transposition of masculine hysteria onto femininity, a reading that may well ignore the questions of what precisely masculinity and femininity are in psychoanalytic discourse. But in masculinizing the term *Jew* and in generalizing heterosexual Jewish male experience onto an entire people, much of the contemporary writing by mainstream Jewish male spokespeople is structured by a disavowal of sexual and gender difference within

Jewish communities. This form of narcissistic identification (and its reliance upon visibility as the only marker that matters) is, I think, part of the problematic dynamic between communities.

28. Jeffrey Melnic, "Black and Jew Blues."

29. In writing about her own identity, about what she calls "the personal," "the political," and the "poetic," Elaine Marks observes her own Jewish sights and sounds:

> First of all, my awareness as a child that only boys and men were really Jews: boys were circumcised, some boys wore yarmulkes, some boys had bar mitzvahs. You could see, if you looked at their penises, that boys and men were Jews. I could hear that my maternal grandmother was Jewish because every morning and every evening she recited prayers in Hebrew and Yiddish. But hearing is not seeing. . . . If my imaginary Jews were men, goyim were women. (*Marrano as Metaphor*, 144)

In these strange twists of visibility and invisibility, being heard and not seen takes on new meanings. However, in her discussion of the poetics of identity Marks refuses the terms of these binaries: "In all honesty I must conclude that the *Je suis* (I am) that we understand but neither hear nor see matters more to me now, and always has, than what we hear and see in *Juifemme*" (153).

30. To complicate the matter a bit more, Art Spiegelman, the author of the graphic comic *Maus: A Survivor's Tale*, drew for the cover of the February 14, 1993, Valentine issue of *The New Yorker* a passionate kiss between what appeared to be a Hasidic man and an African American woman. In the illustration, while the man could be coded as "Jew," the main marker available to the woman was "race." This illustration provoked significant debate across and within communities and appeared again on the cover of Berman's anthology.

31. *The Jew's Body*, 235.

32. "Negroes are Anti-Semitic Because They're Anti-White," 37.

33. Hannah Arendt wrote complexly as well on the question of the ambivalence of assimilation in her essay "Part I: The Pariah as Rebel": "That the status of the Jews in Europe has been not only that of an oppressed people but also what Max Weber has called a 'pariah people' is a fact most clearly appreciated by those who have had practical experience of just how ambiguous is the freedom which emancipation has ensured, and how treacherous the promise of equality which assimilation has held out" (*The Jew as Pariah*, 68). Part of that treachery, according to Arendt is a story of traumatic implication that has yet to be learned: "For the first time [Arendt writes in 1944] Jewish history is not separate but tied up with that of all other nations. The comity of European peoples went to pieces when, and because, it allowed its weakest members to be excluded and persecuted" (67). We might imagine all peoples who have been marginalized as a symptom of the shattering of the social.

But from another vantage, Elaine Marks chapter "Marrano as Metaphor" considers the question of what is beyond normal discourses of assimilation when questions of Jewish secularism are centered. Marks turns to literature to engage the space between the private and the public, usually shut out of debates when discourses of assimilation are confined to accusations. Marks refuses the binary of assimilation/authentic roots to explore the ambivalence of being both progeny and other. In that chapter, Marks maintains the tensions among "multiple languages, countries, cultural traditions, a refusal of separatism, a going beyond the discourses of history . . . neither stereotypes nor identity politics" (*Marrano as Metaphor*, 141–24).

34. *Yours in Struggle.*

35. "Negroes Are Anti-Semitic," 41.

36. For a very different discussion of the historical shifts of racialization among Jews of different nations, see Alain Finkielkraut, *The Imaginary Jew*, particularly section II, "The Visible and the Invisible."

37. In Feinberg's novel, our protagonist, Jess, runs away from an abusive Jewish family and into the ambivalent arms of gay and lesbian communities and labor union struggles. One may argue that categorizing this novel does not settle much: outside of noting the protagonist's parents' religion, it makes no further mention of Jewishness.

   If Feinberg's novel can be placed within North American traditions of secular Jewish proletarian novels such as Michel Gold's *Jews without Money*, Henry Roth's *Call It Sleep*, and Jo Sinclair's *The Changeling*, in another example of how narcissism of minor differences plays out within communities, writings by Jewish gays and lesbians are not claimed by mainstream Jewish scholars as contributing to, and indeed being capable of, revitalizing the field of Jewish secular literature. But at the same time, as Elaine Marks points out in her study of Jewish French writing and anti-Semitism, the categorization of literature according to the author's identity is more a political gesture than a grappling with the unintended effects of absolute category and the essentializing of race, class, ethnicity, or gender.

38. The racialization of sexuality and the ambivalence of the erotic tie have been explored quite explicitly by gay writers of color such as Melvin Dixon, *Vanishing Rooms*; Phillip Brian Harper, *Are We Not Men*; Kobena Mercer, "Skin Head Sex Thing"; Richard Fung, "Looking for My Penis"; Darieck Scott, "Jungle Fever"; and in the video and film work of Marlon Riggs and Isaac Julian. For a discussion of the difficulty faced by teachers and students in considering these texts as relevant to antiracist pedagogy, see Dan Yon's ethnographic study *Elusive Culture* and his "Pedagogy and the 'Problem' of Difference."

Chapter 6. "That Lonely Discovery": Anne Frank, Anna Freud, and the Question of Pedagogy

1. *The Diary of a Young Girl*, 243–44.

2. For a thorough discussion of the different translations of the diary, see Alvin Rosenfeld, "Popularization and Memory: The Case of Anne Frank." While translation always means a transfiguration of meaning from one language to another, Rosenfeld's study shows how Schultz's German translation of the diary went further, actively changing Anne Frank's consideration of German responsibility for the Jewish geno-

cide into a vague condemnation of war. The Schultz translation drops whole sentences, deleting specific references to German responsibility. Rosenfeld argues that two contradictory understandings result from this "softening" of the diary. On the one hand, Anne Frank, who was born in Frankfurt, is not presented as a German who lost her citizenship. On the other hand, the fact that Germans persecuted German Jews also can be forgotten. Rosenfeld notes that, in the censorship of the postwar German issue of the diary, "some of the most telling features of Anne Frank's story have never been told to German readers, who for some four decades now have been reading a bowdlerized version of the diary" (268).

3. "The American History of Anne Frank's Diary," 150.

4. On February 1, 1997, the Toronto *Globe and Mail* reprinted Daniel Pearl's report on a legal dispute over the protection of the Anne Frank name from commercial exploitation. The dispute is between the Anne Frank House in Amsterdam and the Anne Frank Fund in Basel, Switzerland, both established by Otto Frank. Prior to the publication of the Definitive Edition of the diary and the resurgence of Anne Frank's popularity in school curricula by the mideighties, the organizations were cooperative: "The Anne Frank Fund and the Anne Frank House have rejected overtures from American companies proposing Anne Frank coins, persuaded Singapore investors to shut down an Anne Frank import-export company, and shamed a Spanish Company into dropping plans for Anne Frank jeans" (C 16). By 1994, however, The Anne Frank Fund officials attempted to register the name Anne Frank as an official trademark. But they learned that the Anne Frank House had already done so. Over the years the Dutch and Swiss groups disputed each other over the use of the name, the relationship between the fund and the restoration of the annex, and, according to the fund's view, the house's downplaying of Anne Frank's Jewishness and the place of Jewish board members on the house's board of directors.

   This litigation is taking place in the Swiss courts at the same time that the Swiss banking industry is in dispute with Holocaust survivors over the release of Jewish funds in the Swiss bank and over the Swiss bank's relations to national socialism. The survivors have charged that the secrecy of the Swiss bank operations veils the fact that the gold Swiss banks received from the Nazis during World War II was stolen from Jewish communities throughout Europe. More horribly, the gold bars currently stored in Swiss banks and in the banks in the United States are now thought to be made from the dental work of victims. This charge, unresolved at the time of this writing, challenges not just the official history of Swiss neutrality during the war but the Allies' implication in this gold. It seems as though the traumatic knowledge of history returns, scandal by scandal.

5. Deborah Dwork's *Children with a Star* discusses the difficulties of studying the experiences of Jewish European children under the Nazi regime. Dwork notes that, in many areas, Jewish children under the age of ten were not required to wear a Jewish star sewn on their clothing. Deported to camps, children were murdered quickly with their mothers; Dwork notes that only 11 percent of Jewish children alive before the war survived it. Those who were able to go into hiding kept few administrative records due to the danger of these documents being found. Except for the documents preserved from the Theresienstadt ghetto, the paucity of surviving records suggests that the vast

majority of children could not engage in documenting their lives. The documents that exist in spite of state-sanctioned efforts to erase the genocide are, as Dwork argues, threads of specific lives woven in devistating conditions. In Dwork's words:

> At a much younger age than their elders, and with far less maturity and a less developed sense of identity, children also had to cope with the Nazi (and their Fascist allies') process of differentiation (wearing a star), separation (segregation from their erstwhile "Aryan" companions), isolation (banishment from their former physical world of school, park, playground, library, cinema, ice cream parlor), and, finally, deportation and extermination. (xxxii)

While these were also the conditions endured by Anne Frank, her situation was unusual in that her family stayed together in hiding and attempted to live life normally despite their state of emergency; as well, Anne Frank had, for the two years in hiding, conditions in which she was able to write her diary entries. Dwork notes that the diary written by Anne Frank is exceptional in this regard.

Three recently published memories of childhood also suggest the utter singularity of accounting for life during the Jewish European destruction: Binjamin Wilkomirski, *Fragments: Memories of a Wartime Childhood*; Sarah Kaufman; *Rue Ordener Rue Labat*; and, Magda Denes, *Castles Burning*.

6. Doneson, "The American History," 151.

7. "Anne Frank—And Us," 80.

8. *Testimony*, 53.

9. *Insight and Responsibility.*

10. Jon Blair's documentary, *Anne Frank Remembered*, includes a short excerpt of a 1979 interview with Otto Frank, in which Mr. Frank states his reason for leaving Vienna: "I didn't want to raise my children in German education."

11. Miep Gies was an employee of Otto Frank and became one of the key links to the outside world for the families. See Miep Gies and Alison Leslie Gold, *Anne Frank Remembered.*

12. *Unclaimed Experience*, 11.

13. Ilse Grumbrich-Simitis's study of Freud's manuscripts points out the near devastating consequences to psychoanalytic thought wrought by the Nazi government: "Today, a half century after the end of the war, it is almost impossible to imagine the extent to which the Nazi regime succeeded in causing Freud's writings to disappear from the German book market and in banishing from the public consciousness the universe of thought he had brought into the world in his magnificent prose" (*Back to Freud's Texts*, 48).

14. Melanie Klein's complex concept of the making of reparation begins with the acknowledgment that love and hate are in constant interaction. Thus even the desire to make reparation "develops in connection with aggressive impulses and in spite of

them" (*Love. Guilt, and Reparation*, 306). Klein viewed the making of reparation as fundamental to the capacity to love and as the means for exceeding aggression, guilt, and intense greed. In her view, precisely because each of us has the capacity to destroy, the making of reparation is at once a relation to the self and to the other.

15. "On the Teaching of Psycho-Analysis in Universities," 173.

16. For problems associated with the oceanic sentiment, "We are all Anne Frank " see Rosenfeld, "Anne Frank—And Us"; and Julius Lester, "The Stone That Weeps."

17. Felman and Laub, *Testimony*; Ernst Federn, *Witnessing Psychoanalysis*; Saul Friedlander, ed., *Probing the Limits of Representation*; Dominick LaCapra, *Representing the Holocaust*; Rafael Moses, ed., *Persistent Shadows of the Holocaust*; Anne-Lise Stern, " 'Mending' Auschwitz, Through Psychoanalysis?"

18. Elizabeth Ellsworth, *Teaching Positions*; Alice Pitt, "Fantasizing Women in the Women's Studies Classroom"; Silin, *Sex, Death, and the Education of Children*.

In working through the pedagogical issues raised by Anne Frank's diary, readers might consider a few parallels between these specific dilemmas and those encountered by other forms of pedagogy that attempt to grapple with difficult knowledge, namely pedagogies structured by antiracist, feminist, and gay and lesbian civil rights movements and present formulations of "Identity politics." Some of the dilemmas include questions of how identity politics structures a berated community's responses to contradictions within communities, how the demand to hold in abeyance one's own discontentment with community shuts out difference within communities, and how the insistence upon ego ideals may produce effects of increased hatred. And, while there exists a growing body of educational literature that documents student and teacher resistance to the demands of these civil rights movements, much of this research shuts out consideration of the dynamics of learning that might be made from the study of social violence, exclusion, and marginalization within and between communities.

19. Freud calls "undoing" a negative magic, for it is not just the consequences that must be ignored but the event itself is "blown away." A person decides that the event did not happen. Isolation is when the event is acknowledged but it is nonetheless "deprived of its affect, and its associative connections are suppressed or interrupted so that it remains as though isolated and is not reproduced in the ordinary process of thought" ("Inhibitions, Symptoms and Anxiety," 120).

20. Roger Simon and Cynthia Eppert, "Remembering Obligation."

21. Felman and Laub, *Testimony*; Edward Linenthal, *Preserving Memory*; Doneson, "The American History."

The anxiety over the ways the diary may be dismissed by students is the subject of a recent play by Cherie Bennet, "Anne Frank and Me," reviewed in the *New York Times* by Lawrence Van Gelder (December 11, 1996: B3). The play begins in our own time, when a group of high school students cannot understand the diary's relevance. A Christian high school girl is transported in time to Paris during the German occupation, where she re-encounters the people she already knows: her high school principal (who is now her father) and her English teacher (who is now her mother). The girl is now "Jewish" as well, and she meets Anne Frank aboard a train bound for Auschwitz. This experiment in empathy allows for the student's identification with Anne Frank and ostensibly with the force of the diary. But the play repeats the dilemmas discussed throughout this chapter, for what is stressed is the slogan We are all Anne Frank rather than the conditions that provoke the view of the diary's irrelevancy.

22. "The Psychology of Hope and the Modification of Entitlement Near the End of Life," 47.

23. The breach between hope and loss is, of course, the founding condition of Anne's own writing of the diary. She received the diary at the age of thirteen and begins writing with the hope that it will become a friend. The diary is an imaginary other. This hope seems to spring from her view, prior to the time of the family's hiding, that she does not yet have good friends. In a sensitive discussion of Anne Frank's diary as a document of female adolescence, Katherine Dalsimer attempts to hold this tension of hope and loss: hope for the question of both becoming an adult and mourning the loss of childhood. In Dalsimer's words:

> I suggested earlier that keeping a diary is a way of staving off the full affect associated with loss: the diary was therefore the first of her "most vital belongings" that Anne brought with her into hiding. I believe that the diary serves this function not only in relation to the overwhelming loss which history forced upon Anne Frank, but also in relation to that sense of loss which is at the heart of normal adolescence, inherent in the painful process of disengagement from the original objects. It is for this reason that diaries are more often kept during adolescence than at any other period of life—and why they are finally abandoned. (*Female Adolescence*, 72–73)

24. Moses, *Persistent Shadows*, 193.

25. *On Private Madness*, 87.

26. It is well beyond this chapter to consider in depth the question of the different forms of Jewish responses (and of course the differences in generation, geography, and diasporic location in Jewishness) toward the meanings of the events known as the "Holocaust" and its aftermath of loss and the work of mourning. Anne Karpf's self-study of second generation trauma, *The War After*, is one attempt to work through the unstable relations among social and psychic disavowal within Jewish communities and in the larger Christian community, as well as her own view of the insufficiency of literature that attempts to trace the experience of postwar life for Jews in England. Art Spiegelman's two-volume graphic novel, *Maus*, grapples with the costs of representations and the interminable difficulties of understanding the present through the hauntings of an irretrievable past. So, too, with Isaac Bashevis Singer's novel, *Meshugah*, where suddenly a survivor, thought to be dead, appears in New York City to the shock of his friends. And with the recently translated novel of a German ghetto's daily life in World War II, Jurek Becker's *Jacob the Liar*, we have a novel about the problem of hope. That novel is distinguished in terms of its unreliable narrator, who addresses the reader directly in his ruminations over the hopeful lie told by one man. Becker offers readers two different endings. Says our narrator:

> No matter how often Jacob rediscovers, repeats, invents battles and circu-
> lates them, there is one thing he cannot prevent: inexorably the story
> approaches its infamous ending. Or, rather, it has two endings; actually, of
> course, only one, the one experienced by Jacob and the rest of us, but for
> me it also has another ending. . . . I devised it over the years. . . . Besides,
> they all deserved a better ending, not only Jacob, and that will be your jus-
> tification, in case you need one. (222)

This short sampling of novels and reflections does not, as the Revisionist accounts
argue, engage the question of whether the Holocaust happened. Rather, beginning with
Hannah Arendt's report on the Eichmann trial in Jerusalem, the question is one that
engages what happened in the Holocaust for the Holocaust to have happened. We are
back to Rosenfeld's insistence on the insufficiency of "assimilating the event to the
conceptual norms of interpretation," perhaps the movement where learning about and
learning from resist each other. (Also see Dominick LaCapra's ambivalent argument
with the effects of Lanzmann's *Shoah*.)

27. Lawrence Graver, *An Obssesion with Anne Frank*.

28. Otto Frank expressed his ambivalence in a letter to Meyer Levin: "I always said, that
    Anne's book is not a warbook. War is the background. It is not a Jewish book either,
    though Jewish sphere, sentiment and surrounding is the background. I never wanted a
    Jew writing an introduction for it. It is (at least here) read and understood more by gen-
    tiles than in Jewish circles" (cited in Graver, *An Obssesion*, 54).

29. The next, less-quoted sentence goes on to situate this belief in the traumatic context of
    hiding:

    > It's utterly impossible for me to build my life on a foundation of chaos,
    > suffering and death. I see the world being slowly transformed into a
    > wilderness, I hear the approaching thunder that, one day, will destroy us
    > too, I feel the suffering of millions. And yet, when I look up at the sky, I
    > somehow feel that everything will change for the better, that this cruelty
    > too shall end, that peace and tranquility will return once more. In the
    > meantime, I must hold on to my ideals. (332)

30. Otto Frank's anxiety over how those people would be remembered is reversed in what
    might be thought of as the third finding, when the Dutch authorities' authorization of
    the diary's authenticity became written into the Definitive Edition, reminding readers
    of the necessary confrontation they must have with revisionist accounts that deny the
    event of the Holocaust.

31. Sander Gilman, *Jewish Self-Hatred*; Graver, *An Obssesion*; Rosenfeld, "Populariza-
    tion and Memory."

32. Lawrence Graver's *An Obsession with Anne Frank: Meyer Levin and the Diary* is a
    richly detailed account of Meyer Levin's thirty year struggle for the right to craft the
    meaning and reception of the diary. In documenting the very contentious Jewish
    response to the staging of the diary, Graver makes the insightful argument that, rather

than a footnote in the history of Jewish secular arts, the episode of Meyer Levin's "obsession" with the diary is emblematic of the trauma of the Shoah, of Jewish response to North American anti-Semitism, and of how these experiences of the Shoah and of anti-Semitism structured the arguments and conflicts within Jewish communities in North America and in Israel. These debates within Jewish communities can be seen as precursors to contemporary tensions in identity politics that center the question of who can know an event, the problems of epistemic privilege, and the hierarchy of social suffering that comes from the assertions of experience and the myth of direct apprehension of history.

And while Meyer Levin's struggle focused on the reception of the diary, Bruno Bettelheim suggested a different trajectory in his essay "The Ignored Lesson of Anne Frank," which first appeared in *Harper's Magazine* in November 1960, a few years after Goodrich and Hackett's play won the 1956 Pulitzer prize. The fairness of the Bettelheim's critique continues to be debated. Bettelheim's critique of the diary's popular acceptance was dual. He argued that the diary's acceptance was an enactment of the general public's denial of the magnitude of the Holocaust and further, that the diary itself was emblematic of the Frank's family's refusal to understand the Nazi policy of Jewish destruction. Bettelheim writes: "By eulogizing how they lived in their hiding place while neglecting to examine first whether it was a reasonable or an effective choice, we are able to ignore the crucial lesson of their story—that such an attitude can be fatal in extreme circumstance" (247).

Bettelheim's essay continues to be disputed. Pollack's biography of Bettelheim devotes a chapter to dispute Bettelheim's claims in his writings on the Holocaust and Bettelheim's description of his own internment in the Dachau and Buchenwald camps from 1938 through 1939. While Pollack notes that at the end of his life Bettelheim's position on the question of Jewish resistance softened, his biography seems to repeat, as opposed to work through, what Cathy Caruth calls, in her description of the belated impact of trauma, "a kind of double telling, the oscillation between a *crisis of death* and the correlative *crisis of life*: between the story of the unbearable nature of an event and the story of the unbearable nature of its survival" (*Unclaimed Experience*, 7).

33. *Linking Objects and Linking Phenomena.*

34. Cited in Graver, *An Obssesion.*

35. Frances Goodrich and Albert Hackett were best known as part of the writing team for the [MGM Frank Capra] film, *It's a Wonderful Life.* Their play went though a number of rewrites, assisted, at times, by Lillian Hellman and Garson Kanin (Graver, *An Obssesion*, 85–87). While each succeeding draft lessened the writers' attempts to highlight humor, Goodrich and Hackett continued to soften the dimension of the diary's Jewish tragedy and emphasize, instead, an abstracted human spirit capable of rising above tragedy. For Graver's discussion of the question of the play's capacity to educate audiences in Germany, see 125–31.

36. There is a contemporary literature that also engages the question of psychic work in conditions of profound difficulty. This is the work of AIDS activists and writers that draws upon and extends psychoanalytic insight into the question of individual participation in suffering. I make this assertion cautiously because psychoanalytic theories of

implication can so easily be recuperated into the formal structures of blame and moralism. On the other hand, the insistence that suffering is only the response to the bad outside forecloses the possibility of making something of suffering.

In considering the larger question of what social disavowal of AIDS means to those most affected, this writing also attempts to encourage those most affected to consider the ways individuals make themselves miserable. Douglas Crimp argues that political activists must acknowledge the unconscious and the cost of such an acknowledgment: "By ignoring the death drive, that is, by making all violence external, we fail to confront ourselves, to acknowledge our own ambivalence, to comprehend that our misery is also self-inflicted" ("Mourning and Militancy," 243). Crimp returns to this theme in a published conversation that attempts to come to terms with AIDS as a double trauma (see Cathy Caruth and Thomas Keenan, " 'The AIDS Crisis Is Not Over' "). But see also Patti Lather and Chris Smithies, *Troubling the Angels*; Silin, *Sex, Death, and the Education of Children*, and Walt Odets, *In the Shadow of the Epidemic* for discussions of psychological responses to living in the time of AIDS.

37. This metaphor of the psyche as a crystal formation is central to the psychoanalytic conceptualizations of normalcy and pathology. The pathological simply refers to the psyche's capacity to become coarser, more exaggerated in its fault lines and hence more fragile. For psychoanalysis, it is through the pathological that the normal can be understood. Psychoanalytic thought holds that anyone has the capacity to shatter; in a certain way, one can then wonder what keeps individuals together as well as what tears them apart.

38. *New Introductory Lectures on Psycho-Analysis*, 59.

39. *Group Psychology and the Analysis of the Ego*, 102.

40. These questions have been inspired by Shoshana Felman's exploration of what is at stake in learning when the curriculum is one that engages the writings of those living in times of war and catastrophe. Felman poses education as crisis when she raises the following questions in the first chapter of her study of testimony: "In a post-traumatic century, a century that has survived unthinkable historical catastrophes, is there anything that we have learned or that we should learn about education that we did not know before? Can trauma *instruct* pedagogy, and can pedagogy shed light on the mystery of trauma? Can the task of teaching be instructed by the clinical experience?" (Felman and Laub, *Testimony*, 1)

41. Miss Freud's work with evacuees and child survivors of the European Shoah culminated in the years following the war. In 1945, over one thousand orphaned Jewish children who had survived concentration camps and hiding were accepted for resettlement in the United Kingdom. Many of these children were placed in Miss Freud's nursery system. For a discussion of six of these children who survived the Theresienstadt camp, see Anna Freud, "An Experiment in Group Upbringing." But see also Anne Karpf, *The War After*, who makes the point that the needs of adult refugees in London were ignored.

42. Young-Bruehl, *Anna Freud*, 279–88.

43. This is a question that structures much of the writing on the Shoah, particularly the early accounts following the destruction, which were most concerned with document-ing the sheer magnitude of the destruction and with forcing the Allied countries to acknowledge their own insufficiency, indeed, their woeful disregard of the event as it unfolded. Here I am thinking of two very different kinds of literature: one meditates on Jewish responses to their own destruction (the early novels of Wiesel and the diary of Anne Frank); the other is historians' documentation of the apathy toward the genocide (for instance, Arthur Morse's *While Six Million Died*, Nora Levin's *The Holocaust*, and the journalistic writing of Ben Hecht).

44. For an in-depth engagement in the political and psychic stakes of the acknowledge-ment of the death drive—or that war within—see Jacqueline Rose, *Why War?* J. B. Pontalis proffers a way to consider the question of suffering in the context of analysis:

> In *every* subject under analysis we find suffering, and the movement of the treatment consists in discovering and showing by what detours this suffering is produced, induced, unconsciously sought by the individual himself, in order to obtain a premium of pleasure in some other intrapsy-chic place. The second Freudian topography in particular allows in this sense a complex series of exchanges, of which the most simple expresses itself thus: pleasure for one system (the super-ego for example), unplea-sure for another (the ego, for example). (*Frontiers in Pschoanalysis*, 197)

45. Louise Kaplan foregrounds her discussion of Anna Freud's essay in the life of Anna Freud's nephew, W. Ernest Freud, whom Anna Freud helped parent after the death in 1920 of Ernest's mother, and Anna's sister, Sophie. Ernest was five at the time of his mother's death; then, a few years later, Ernest's baby brother Heinz also died. Ernest was the inspiration of Freud's discussion in *Beyond the Pleasure Principle* of the *Fort/Da* (or Gone/Here) game. Somewhat akin to the adult version of "Peek-a-boo" or the child's revision of the "Hide and Seek" game, this early game of Ernest's was, in Freud's and Sophie's interpretation, his infantile attempt to master his anxiety during his mother's brief absences. Playing with a spool attached to a thread, Ernest would cast the spool away and then pull it back to himself. Freud noticed that Ernest seemed to have more pleasure in sending away his spool, as if the baby were saying "I shall send you away if you leave me." Years later, Ernest would elaborate on this game as an adolescent, retrieving objects others had discarded as worthless.

    Around the age of eight, Ernest went to live with the Freuds and Anna Freud took charge of his education. He was one of the members of the family who fled in exile to London in 1938. According to Kaplan's account, Ernest was finely tuned into the danger national socialism posed to Jews and had heightened anxiety over disap-pearing. As an adult, Ernest trained as an analyst in London and in midcareer shifted his efforts to studies of low-birth-weight infants in neonatal and postneonatal intensive care units in the United States and in England. Ernest Freud would not return to Vienna until fifty years after his exile, to address the International Psychoanalytic Conference with a speech entitled "Personal Reflections of the Anschluss of 1938." Kaplan's description of that speech begins with the observation that many in the audience were the sons and daughters of Nazis or Nazi sympathizers:

Though his address evoked images of loss and disappearance, Dr. Freud did not refer directly to the deaths of his loved ones or to the millions of other deaths caused by two world wars. His recollections stressed the various ways in which living people manage to go on living and caring for one another in the midst of the horrors of war. . . . As for Dr. Freud's Viennese audience, it is very likely that many of them were struggling with a conflict between their family loyalties and an unconscious need to make reparations for their parents' crimes. (83)

With this description of Ernest Freud's address we return to the heart of losing and being lost, for these actions are deeply tied to the refinding of love and the interminable work of mourning. We might also notice that Ernest played the *Fort/Da* game over the course of his life. The coincidence of history, family, and historical trauma that were the sum of Ernest Freud's life suggests that a life is made on the frontier of the psychic and the social. And as such, we might again understand the dialogic and recursive dynamics of the inside conflict and the outside conflicts.

46. See Arnold William Rachman, *Sandor Ferenczi*, 237–38.

47. My reading of Freud's essay on mourning places emphasis on what Freud names "the work of mourning" and on the ego's capacity to engage in what Melanie Klein terms "the desire to make reparation" or the offering of the gift of love to the other (*Love, Guilt, and Reparation*). This fragile and interminable work involves what Derrida calls "a learning to live . . . between life and death. . . . The time of the "learning to live," a time without tutelary present, would amount to this, to which the exordium is leading us: to learn to live *with* ghosts, in the upkeep, the conversation, the company, or the companionship, in the commerce without commerce of ghosts . . . but more justly" (xviii). For a discussion on the fragility of the work of mourning and on how this work reverses its content and becomes a hatred for "learning to live" and a disavowal of death, see William Haver, *The Body of This Death*.

48. Moses, ed., *Persistent Shadows*.

49. Doneson, "The American History."

50. For a complex discussion of Holocaust survivors' children's attempts to psychically relive their parents' massive trauma and of the term *transposition* see Louise Kaplan, *No Voice Is Ever Wholly Lost*, chapter 12, "Images of Absence, Voices of Silence." Kaplan's chapter draws upon the literature of analysts working with the second generation and the analysts's belated learning. Kaplan's work, however, may be thought of as paralleling the conference Persistent Shadows because the conference attempted to engage the question of what the Holocaust might mean to those not directly affected. This question is closer to the teaching of the diary in public schools. These two discussions meet at the point where the educator's pedagogical actions unconsciously transpose onto the student her or his own anxieties about encountering the difficulties of Anne Frank's death and the belated "massive trauma."

Kaplan also brings the term "transposition" into everyday relations and dialogues between children and parents; in doing so, she suggests a possible dynamic between teachers and students in the teaching of "difficult knowledge": "Every child cultivates a morsel of suffering absorbed from an unconscious awareness of the parent's traumas. Every child gives up some portion, however large or small, of his own life to cure a parent's trauma. However, in the child of a Holocaust survivor, where the parent suffered a *massive* trauma, transposition is omnipresent" (224).

Bibliography

Abraham, Nicolas, and Maria Torok. *The Wolf Man's Magic Word: A Cryptonymy.* Trans. Nicholas Rand. Minneapolis: University of Minnesota Press, 1986.

———. *The Shell and the Kernel.* Vol 1. Ed. and trans. Nicholas Rand. Chicago: University of Chicago Press, 1994.

Adams, Parveen. *The Emptiness of the Image: Psychoanalysis and Sexual Difference.* London: Routledge, 1996.

Adorno, Theodor. *Mahler: A Musical Physiognomy.* Trans. Edmund Jephcott. Chicago: University of Chicago Press, 1992.

Agamben, Giorgio. *The Coming Community.* Trans. Michael Hardt. Minneapolis: University of Minnesota Press, 1993.

Aichhorn, August. *Wayward Youth.* Northwestern University Press, 1983.

Als, Hinton. *The Women.* New York: Farrar, Straus and Giroux, 1996.

Appel, Stephen. "The Unconscious Subject of Education." *Discourse: Studies in the Cultural Politics of Education* 16, no. 2 (1995): 167–89.

———. *Positioning Subjects: Psychoanalysis and Critical Educational Studies.* Westport, Conn.: Bergin and Garvey, 1996.

Appignanesi, Lisa, and John Forrester. *Freud's Women.* New York: Basic Books, 1992.

Arendt, Hannah. *The Jew as Pariah: Jewish Identity and Politics in the Modern Age.* Ed. Ron H. Feldman. New York: Grove Press, 1978.

———. *Eichmann in Jerusalem: A Report on the Banality of Evil.* Revised and enlarged edition. New York: Penguin, 1979.

Austin, Regina. "'A Nation of Thieves': Consumption, Commerce, and the Black Public Sphere." *Public Culture* 15 (1994): 225–48.

Baldwin, James. "A Talk to Teachers." In *The Price of the Ticket: Collected Nonfiction, 1948–1985*. New York: St. Martin's, 1985, 325–32.

———. "Negroes Are Anti-Semitic Because They're Anti-White." Reprinted in *Blacks and Jews: Alliances and Arguments*. Ed. Paul Berman. New York: Delacorte Press, 1994, 31–41.

Balint, Alice. "Identification." *The Yearbook of Psychoanalysis* Vol. 1. International Universities Press, 1945, 317–38.

———. *The Early Years of Life: A Psychoanalytic Study*. New York: Basic Books, 1954.

Balint, Michael. *Problems of Human Pleasure and Behavior*. New York: Liveright, 1957.

———. *Thrills and Regressions*. New York: International University Press, 1959.

———. Primary *Love and Psychoanalytic Technique*. New York: Da Capo Press, 1986.

Barbin, Herculine. *Herculine Barbin: Being the Recently Discovered Memoirs of a Nineteenth-Century French Hermaphrodite*. Introduced by Michel Foucault. Trans. Richard McDougall. New York: Pantheon Books, 1980.

Bart, Pauline. "How a Nice Jewish Girl Like Me Could." In *Nice Jewish Girls: A Lesbian Anthology*. Ed. Evelyn Torton Beck. Revised and updated edition. Boston: Beacon Press, 1989, 65–68.

Bataille, Georges. *Erotism: Death and Sensuality*. Trans. Mary Dalwood. San Francisco: City Lights Books, 1986.

Bauman, Zygmut. *Modernity and the Holocaust*. Ithaca: Cornell University Press, 1989.

Beck, Evelyn Torton, ed. *Nice Jewish Girls: A Lesbian Anthology*. Revised and updated edition. Boston: Beacon Press, 1989.

Becker, Jurek. *Jacob the Liar*. Trans. Leila Vennewitz. New York: Acarade, 1996.

Benjamin, Jessica. *The Bonds of Love: Psychoanalysis, Feminism, and the Problem of Domination*. New York: Pantheon Books, 1988.

———. *Like Subjects, Love Objects: Essays on Recognition and Sexual Difference*. New Haven: Yale University Press, 1996.

Bennett, William. *Our Children and Our Country: Improving America's Schools and Affirming the Common Curriculum.* New York: Simon and Schuster, 1988.

Berman, Jeffrey. *Diaries to an English Professor: Pain and Growth in the Classroom.* Amherst: University of Massachusetts Press, 1994.

Berman, Paul, ed. *Blacks and Jews: Alliances and Arguments.* New York: Delacorte Press, 1994.

Bernfeld, Siegfried. *Sisyphus or the Limits of Education.* Trans. Frederic Lilge. Berkeley: University of California Press, 1973.

Bettelheim, Bruno. "The Ignored Lesson of Anne Frank." *Harper's Magazine* (November 1960), 45–50.

———. "Psychoanalysis and Education." *The School Review* 77, no. 2 (1969): 73–86.

———. *Surviving, and Other Essays.* New York: Vantage Books, 1979.

———. "Education and the Reality Principle." In *Surviving and Other Essays,* 127–41.

Bigelow, Maurice. *Sex-Education: A Series of Lectures concerning Knowledge of Sex in its Relation to Human Life.* New York: Macmillan, 1916.

Bion, Wilfred. *Learning from Experience.* New Jersey: Jason Aronson, 1994.

Blair, Jon. *Anne Frank Remembered.* Jon Blair Film Co. in association with the BBC and The Disney Channel. 117 min. Culver City: Columbia TriStar Home Video, 1996. Videocassette.

Bloom, Allan. *The Closing of the American Mind.* New York: Simon and Schuster, 1987.

Bogdan, Deanne. *Re-Educating the Imagination: Toward a Poetics, Politics, and Pedagogy of Literary Engagement.* Portsmouth: Heinemann, 1991.

Bollas, Christopher. *Forces of Destiny: Psychoanalysis and Human Idiom.* London: Free Association Press, 1991.

———. *Being a Character: Psychoanalysis and Self Experience.* New York: Hill and Wang, 1992.

———. *Cracking Up: The Work of Unconscious Experience.* New York: Hill and Wang, 1995.

Borch-Jacobsen, Mikkel. *The Freudian Subject.* Trans. Catherine Porter. Stanford: Stanford University Press, 1988.

Boyarin, Daniel. "Freud's Baby, Fliess's Maybe: Homophobia, Anti-Semitism, and the Invention of Oedipus." *GLQ: A Journal of Lesbian and Gay Studies* 2 (1995): 115-47.

————. *Unheroic Conduct: The Rise of Heterosexuality and the Invention of the Jewish Man.* Berkeley: University of California Press, 1997.

Britzman, Deborah P. "The Ordeal of Knowledge: Rethinking the Possibilities of Multicultural Education. *The Review of Education* 15 (1993): 123–35.

Britzman, Deborah P., and Alice J. Pitt. "Pedagogy and Transference: Casting the Past of Learning into the Presence of Teaching." *Theory into Practice* 35, no. 2 (1996): 117–23.

Bulkin, Elly, Minnie Bruce Pratt, and Barbara Smith. *Yours in Struggle: Three Feminist Perspectives on Anti-Semitism and Racism.* Brooklyn: Long Haul Press, 1984.

Burbules, Nicholas. *Dialogue in Teaching: Theory and Practice.* New York: Teachers College Press, 1993.

Burrell, Walter Rico. "*The Scarlet Letter*, Revisited: A Very Different AIDS Diary." In *Brother to Brother: New Writings by Black Gay Men.* Ed. Essex Hemphill and Joseph Beam. Boston: Alyson Publications, 1991, 121–35.

Butler, Judith. "Imitation and Gender Insubordination." *Inside/Out: Lesbian Theories, Gay Theories.* Ed. Diana Fuss. New York: Routledge, 1991, 13–31.

————. "Sexual Inversions." In *Discourses of Sexuality: From Aristotle to AIDS.* Ed. Domna Stanton. Ann Arbor: University of Michigan Press, 1992, 344-61.

————. *Bodies That Matter: On the Discursive Limits of "Sex."* New York: Routledge, 1993.

Buxbaum, Edith. "Three Great Psychoanalytic Educators." In *From Learning for Love to Love of Learning: Essays on Psychoanalysis and Education.* Ed. R. Ekstein and R. Motto. New York: Brunner/Mazel, 1969, 28–35.

Carotenuto, Aldo. *Kant's Dove: The History of Transference in Psychoanalysis.* Trans. Joan Tambureno. Wilmette: Chiron Publications, 1991.

Caruth, Cathy. *Unclaimed Experience: Trauma, Narrative, and History.* Baltimore: Johns Hopkins University Press, 1996.

Caruth, Cathy, and Thomas Keenan. " 'The AIDS Crisis Is Not Over': A Conversation with Gregg Bordowitz, Douglas Crimp, and Laura Pinsky." In *Trauma: Explorations in Memory.* Ed. Cathy Caruth. Baltimore: Johns Hopkins University Press, 1995, 256–71.

Chamoiseau, Patrick. *School Days*. Trans. Linda Coverdale. Lincoln: University of Nebraska Press, 1997.

Copjec, Joan. "Cutting Up." In *Between Feminism and Psychoanalysis*. Ed. Teresa Brennan. New York: Routledge, 1989, 227–46.

Cornell, Drucilla. *The Imaginary Domain: Abortion, Pornography and Sexual Harassment*. New York: Routledge, 1995.

Crimp, Douglas. "Mourning and Militancy." In *Out There: Marginalization and Contemporary Cultures*. Ed. Russell Ferguson et al. New York: MIT Press, 1990, 233–46.

———. "Hey, Girlfriend!" *Social Text* 33 (1992): 2-18.

Dalsimer, Katherine. *Female Adolescence: Psychoanalytic Reflections on Works of Literature*. New Haven: Yale University Press, 1986.

de Certeau, Michel. *Heterologies: Discourse on the Other*. Trans. Brian Massumi. Minneapolis: University of Minnesota Press, 1986.

———. *The Writing of History*. Trans. Tom Conley. New York: Columbia University Press, 1988.

Delany, Samuel R. *The Motion of Light in Water: Sex and Science Fiction Writing in the East Village, 1957–1965*. New York: Arbor House, 1988.

———. "Street Talk/Straight Talk." *Differences: A Journal of Feminist Cultural Studies* 5, no. 2 (1991): 21–38.

de Lauretis, Teresa. "Queer Theory: Lesbian and Gay Sexualities, An Introduction." *Differences* 3, no. 2 (1991): iii–xviii.

Denes, Magda. *Castles Burning: A Child's Life in War*. New York: W. W. Norton, 1997.

Derrida, Jacques. *Spectres of Marx: The State of the Debt, the Work of Mourning, and the New International*. Trans. Peggy Kamuf. New York: Routledge, 1994.

———. "Archive Fever: A Freudian Impression." *Diacritics* (Summer 1995): 9–63.

Dixon, Melvin. *Vanishing Rooms*. New York: Plume, 1992.

Dollimore, Jonathan. *Sexual Dissidence: Augustine to Wilde, Freud to Foucault*. Oxford: Oxford University Press, 1991.

Doneson, Judith. "The American History of Anne Frank's Diary." *Holocaust and Genocide Studies* 2, no. 1 (1987): 149–60.

Duttman, Alexander Garcia. "What Will Have Been Said about AIDS: Some Remarks in Disorder." *Public* 7 (1993): 95–115.

Dwork, Deborah. *Children with a Star: Jewish Youth in Nazi Europe*. New Haven: Yale University Press, 1991.

Edelman, Lee. *Homographesis: Essays in Gay Literary and Cultural Theory*. New York: Routledge, 1994.

Efron, John M. *Defenders of the Race: Jewish Doctors and Race Science in Fin-de-Siècle Europe*. New Haven: Yale University Press, 1994.

Eissler, K. R., ed. *Searchlights on Delinquency: New Psychoanalytic Studies*. New York: International Universities Press, 1956.

Ekstein, Rudolf, and Rocco Motto. "Psychoanalysis and Education—An Historical Account." In *From Learning for Love to Love of Learning: Essays on Psychoanalysis and Education*. Ed. R. Ekstein and R. Motto. New York: Brunner/Mazel, 1969, 3–27.

Ellsworth, Elizabeth. "Why Doesn't This Feel Empowering? Working through the Repressive Myths of Critical Pedagogy." *Harvard Educational Review* 59 (1989): 297–324.

———. *Teaching Positions: Difference, Pedagogy and the Power of Address*. New York: Teachers College Press, 1997.

Erikson, Erik. *Insight and Responsibility: Lectures on the Ethical Implications of Psychoanalytic Insight*. New York: W. W. Norton, 1964.

———. *Identity, Youth, and Crisis*. New York: W. W. Norton, 1968.

Esman, Aaron, ed. *Essential Papers on Transference*. New York: New York University Press, 1990.

Federn, Ernst. *Witnessing Psychoanalysis: From Vienna back to Vienna via Buchenwald and the USA*. London: Karnac Books, 1990.

Feinberg, Leslie. *Stone Butch Blues: A Novel*. Ithaca: Firebrand Books, 1993.

Felman, Jyl Lynn. "De Vilde Chayes—The Wild Beasts." In *The Body of Love*. Ed. Tee A. Corinne. Austin: Banned Books, 1993, 9–13.

———. "If Only I'd Been Born a Kosher Chicken." *Tikkun: A Bimonthly Jewish Critique of Politics, Culture, & Society* 9, no. 4 (July/Aug. 1994): 47–50, 78–79.

Felman, Shoshana. *Jacques Lacan and the Adventure of Insight: Psychoanalysis in Contemporary Culture*. Cambridge, Mass.: Harvard University Press, 1987.

————. *What Does A Woman Want? Reading and Sexual Difference*. Baltimore: Johns Hopkins University Press, 1993.

Felman, Shoshana, and Dori Laub. *Testimony: Crises of Witnessing in Literature, Psychoanalysis, and History*. New York: Routledge, 1992.

Fenichel, Otto. "The Means of Education." In *The Collected Papers of Otto Fenichel*. Second Series. Ed. Hanna Fenichel and David Rapaport. New York: Norton, 1954, 324–34.

Ferenczi, Sandor. "Psycho-Analysis and Education." Trans. M. Balint. *International Journal of Psychoanalysis* 20 (1949): 220–24.

Field, Kate, Bertram Cohler, and Glorye Wool, eds. *Learning and Education: Psychoanalytic Perspectives*. Madison: International Universities Press, 1989.

Finkielkraut, Alain. *The Imaginary Jew*. Trans. Kevin O'Neill and David Suchoff. Lincoln: University of Nebraska Press, 1994.

Fireweed. "Special Issue on Jewish Women." (Spring 1992).

Fletcher, John, and Martin Stanton, eds. *Jean Laplanche: Seduction, Translation, Drives*. London: Institute of Contemporary Arts, 1992.

Foucault, Michel. "Revolutionary Action: 'Until Now.'" In *Language, Counter-Memory, Practice: Selected Essays and Interviews*. Ed. Donald F. Bouchard. Trans. Donald F. Bouchard and Sherry Simon. Ithaca: Cornell University Press, 1971, 218–33.

————. *The Order of Things: An Archaeology of the Human Sciences*. New York: Vintage Books, 1973.

————. *The History of Sexuality. Volume 1: An Introduction*. Trans. Robert Hurley. New York: Vintage Books, 1980.

————. "On the Genealogy of Ethics: An Overview of Work in Progress." In Hubert Dreyfus and Paul Rabinow, *Michel Foucault: Beyond Structuralism and Hermeneutics*. 2nd ed. Chicago: University of Chicago Press, 1983, 229–52.

————. "The Subject and Power." In Hubert Dreyfus and Paul Rabinow, *Michel Foucault: Beyond Structuralism and Hermeneutics*. 2nd ed. Chicago: University of Chicago Press, 1983, 208–26.

————. *The Care of the Self. The History of Sexuality*. Vol. 3. Trans. Robert Hurley. New York: Random House, 1986.

Frank, Anne. *The Diary of a Young Girl: The Definitive Edition*. Ed. Otto Frank and Mirjam Pressler. Trans. Susan Massotty. New York: Doubleday, 1995.

Freud, Anna. *Four Lectures on Psychoanalysis for Teachers and Parents*. 1930. *The Writings of Anna Freud*. Vol. 1. New York: International Universities Press, 1974, 73–133.

————. *The Ego and the Mechanisms of Defense*. 1936. *The Writings of Anna Freud*. Vol. 2. New York: International Universities Press, 1966.

————. "An Experiment in Group Upbringing." 1951. In *Indications for Child Analysis and Other Papers, 1945–1956*. *The Writings of Anna Freud*. Vol. 4. New York: International Universities Press, 1968, 163–229.

————. "About Losing and Being Lost." 1967 (1953). In *Indications for Child Analysis and Other Papers, 1945–1956*. *The Writings of Anna Freud*. Vol. 4. New York: International Universities Press, 1968, 302–16.

————. "Psychoanalysis and Education." 1954. In *Indications for Child Analysis and Other Papers, 1945–1956*. *The Writings of Anna Freud*. Vol. 4. New York: International Universities Press, 1968, 317–26.

Freud, Anna, and Dorothy Burlingham. *War and Children: A Message to American Parents*. New York: International Universities Press, 1944.

Freud, Sigmund. *The Standard Edition of the Complete Psychological Works of Sigmund Freud*. Ed. and trans. James Strachey. In collaboration with Anna Freud. Assisted by Alix Strachey and Alan Tyson. 24 vols. London: Hogarth Press and Institute for Psychoanalysis, 1953–1974.

————. *The Interpretation of Dreams*. 2nd part. 1900. Standard Edition 5.

————. *Three Essays on the Theory of Sexuality*. 1905. Standard Edition 7, 125–243.

————. "Observations on Transference-Love (Further Recommendations on the Technique of Psycho-Analysis III)." 1915 (1914). Standard Edition 12, 158–71.

————. "On Narcissism: An Introduction." 1914. Standard Edition 14, 67–102.

————. "Instincts and Their Vicissitudes." 1915. Standard Edition 14, 111–40.

————. "The Unconscious." 1915. Standard Edition 14, 161–215.

————. "Mourning and Melancholia." 1917 (1915). Standard Edition 14, 239–58.

————. "Thoughts for the Times on War and Death." 1915. Standard Edition 14, 273–301.

————. "On Transcience." 1916 (1915). Standard Edition 14, 303–07.

————. "On the Teaching of Psycho-Analysis in Universities." 1919 (1918). Standard Edition 17, 169–74.

————. *Beyond the Pleasure Principle.* 1920. Standard Edition 18, 7–64.

————. *Group Psychology and the Analysis of the Ego.* 1921. Standard Edition 18, 67–143.

————. *The Ego and the Id.* 1923. Standard Edition 19, 3–59.

————. "On Negation." 1925. Standard Edition 19, 235–42.

————. "Inhibitions, Symptoms and Anxiety." 1926. Standard Edition 20, 77–174.

————. *Civilization and Its Discontents.* 1930. Standard Edition 21, 59–145.

————. *New Introductory Lectures on Psycho-Analysis.* 1933. Standard Edition 22, 3–182.

————. "Some Elementary Lessons in Psychoanalysis." 1940 (1938). Standard Edition 22, 279–86.

————. *An Outline of Psychoanalysis.* 1940 (1938). Standard Edition 23, 141–207.

————. "Analysis Terminable and Interminable." 1937. Standard Edition 23, 211–53.

Friedlander, Saul, ed. *Probing the Limits of Representation: Nazism and the "Final Solution."* Cambridge, Mass.: Harvard University Press, 1992.

Fung, Richard. "Looking for My Penis: The Eroticized Asian in Gay Video Porn." In *How Do I Look? Queer Film and Video.* Ed. Bad Object-Choices. Seattle: Bay Press, 1991, 145–60.

Fuss, Diana. *Identification Papers.* New York: Routledge, 1995.

Gallop, Jane, ed. *Pedagogy: The Question of Impersonation.* Bloomington: Indiana University Press, 1995.

Gies, Miep, and Alison Leslie Gold. *Anne Frank Remembered: The Story of the Woman Who Helped to Hide the Frank Family.* New York: Simon and Schuster, 1987.

Gilman, Sander. *Jewish Self-Hatred: Anti-Semitism and the Hidden Language of the Jews.* Baltimore: Johns Hopkins University Press, 1986.

————. *The Jew's Body.* New York: Routledge, 1991.

————. *Freud, Race, and Gender.* Princeton: Princeton University Press, 1993.

————. *Franz Kafka, the Jewish Patient.* New York: Routledge, 1995.

Gilroy, Paul. *The Black Atlantic: Modernity and Double Consciousness.* Cambridge, Mass.: Harvard University Press, 1993.

Giroux, Henry. *Border Crossings: Cultural Workers and the Politics of Education.* New York: Routledge, 1992.

Goldberg, David Theo. *Racist Culture: Philosophy and the Politics of Meaning.* Oxford: Blackwell Publishers, 1993.

Golding, Sue. "Sexual Manners." *Public* 8 (1993): 161–168.

Graff, Gerald. *Beyond the Culture Wars: How Teaching the Conflicts Can Revitalize American Education.* New York: Norton, 1992.

Graver, Lawrence. *An Obsession with Anne Frank: Meyer Levin and the Diary.* Berkeley: University of California Press, 1995.

Green, Andre. *On Private Madness.* Madison: International Universities Press, 1986.

———. "Instinct in the Late Works of Freud." In *On Freud's "Analysis Terminable and Interminable."* Ed. Joseph Sandler. New Haven: Yale University Press, 1991, 124–141.

Greene, Maxine. *The Public School and the Private Vision: A Search for America in Education and Literature.* New York: Random House, 1965.

———. *The Teacher as Stranger: Educational Philosophy for the Modern Age.* Belmont: Wordsworth, 1973.

———. *Landscapes of Learning.* New York: Teachers College Press, 1978.

———. *The Dialectic of Freedom.* New York: Teachers College Press, 1988.

Grumbrich-Simitis, Ilse. *Back to Freud's Texts: Making Silent Documents Speak.* Trans. Philip Slotkin. New Haven: Yale University Press, 1996.

Grumet, Madeleine. "The Beauty Full Curriculum." *Educational Theory* 39 (1989): 225–30.

Grunberger, Bela. *New Essays on Narcissism.* Trans. and ed. David Macey. London: Free Association Books, 1989.

Hacker, Marilyn. *Winter Numbers: Poems.* New York: W. W. Norton, 1994.

Hale, Nathan G. *Freud and the Americans: The Beginnings of Psychoanalysis in the United States, 1876–1917.* New York: Oxford University Press, 1971.

Hall, Stuart. "Teaching Race." In *The School in Multicultural Society.* Ed. Alan James and Robert Jeffcoate. London: Harper and Row, 1981, 58–69.

————. "New Ethnicities." *Black Film and British Cinema.* ICA Documents, London, 1988, 27–30.

Halperin, David. *Saint Foucault: Towards a Gay Hagiography.* New York: Oxford University Press, 1995.

Harper, Phillip Brian. *Are We Not Men? Masculine Anxiety and the Problem of African-American Identity.* Oxford: Oxford University Press, 1997.

Haver, William. "Thinking the Thought of That Which Is Strictly Speaking Unthinkable: On the Thematization of Alterity in Nishida-Philosophy." *Human Studies* 16 (1993): 177–92.

————. *The Body of This Death: Sociality and Historicity in the Time of AIDS.* Stanford: University of Stanford Press, 1996.

Hemphill, Essex. *Ceremonies: Prose and Poetry.* New York: Plume Books, 1992.

Henriques, Julian, Wendy Hollway, Cathy Urwin, Couze Venn, and Valerie Walkerdine, eds. *Changing the Subject: Psychology, Social Regulation and Subjectivity.* London: Methuen, 1984.

hooks, bell. "Keeping a Legacy of Shared Struggle." In *Blacks and Jews: Alliances and Arguments.* Ed. Paul Berman. New York: Delacorte Press, 1994, 229–38.

Horney, Karen. *Self-Analysis.* New York: W. W. Norton, 1942.

————. *Final Lectures.* Ed. Douglash Ingram. New York: W. W. Norton, 1987.

Ignatieff, Michael. "Nationalism and the Narcissism of Minor Differences." *Queens Quarterly* 102 (1995): 13–26.

Irvine, Janice, ed. *Sexual Cultures and the Construction of Adolescent Identities.* Philadelphia: Temple University Press, 1994.

Jersild, Arthur. *When Teachers Face Themselves.* New York: Teachers College Press, 1955.

Kaplan, Louise. *No Voice Is Ever Wholly Lost.* New York: Simon and Schuster, 1995.

Karpf, Anne. *The War After: Living with the Holocaust.* London: Heinemann, 1996.

Katz, Judith. *Running Fiercely toward a High Thin Sound.* Ithaca: Firebrand Books, 1992.

Kaufman, Sarah. *Rue Ordener Rue Labat.* Trans. Ann Smock. Lincoln: University of Nebraska Press, 1996.

Kaye/Kantrowitz, Melanie. *The Issue Is Power: Essays on Women, Jews, and Violence.* San Francisco: Aunt Lute, 1992.

Kaye/Kantrowitz, Melanie, and Irena Klepfisz, eds. *The Tribe of Dina: A Jewish Women's Anthology.* Boston: Beacon Press, 1989.

Kincaid, Jamaica. *Lucy.* New York: Farrar, Straus and Giroux, 1990.

Kincheloe, Joe and William Pinar, eds. *Curriculum as Social Psychoanalysis: The Significance of Place.* Albany: State University of New York Press, 1991.

Klein, Dennis. *Jewish Origins of the Psychoanalytic Movement.* New York: Praeger, 1981.

Klein, Melanie. *Envy and Gratitude, and Other Works, 1946–1963.* London: Virago, 1993.

———. *Love, Guilt, and Reparation and Other Works, 1921–1945.* London: Virago Press, 1994.

———. "The Role of the School in the Libidinal Development of the Child." 1923. In *Love, Guilt and Reparation,* 59–76.

Klepfisz, Irena. *Dreams of an Insomniac: Jewish Feminist Essays, Speeches, and Diatribes.* Portland: Eighth Mountain Press, 1990.

Kurzweil, Edith. *The Freudians: A Comparative Perspective.* New Haven: Yale University Press, 1989.

Kushner, Tony. *Angels in America. Part I: Millennium Approaches. Part II: Perestroika.* New York: Theatre Communications Group, 1993.

LaCapra, Dominick. *Representing the Holocaust: History, Theory, and Trauma.* Ithaca: Cornell University Press, 1994.

———. "Lanzmann's *Shoah*: 'Here There Is No Why.' " *Critical Inquiry* 23, no. 2 (Winter 1997): 231– 69.

Laplanche, Jean. *Life and Death in Psychoanalysis.* Trans. Jeffrey Mehlman. Baltimore: Johns Hopkins University Press, 1976.

———. *New Foundations for Psychoanalysis.* Trans. David Macey. Cambridge, Mass.: Basil Blackwell, 1989.

Laplanche, Jean, and J. B. Pontalis. *The Language of Psychoanalysis.* Trans. Donald Nicholson-Smith. London: Karnac Books and the Institute of Psycho-Analysis, 1988.

Lather, Patti and Chris Smithies. *Troubling the Angels: Women Living with HIV/AIDS.* Boulder: Westview Press, 1997.

Lavender, Abraham, ed. *A Coat of Many Colors: Jewish Subcommunities in the United States*. Westport: Greenwood Press, 1977.

Lesko, Nancy. "Denaturalizing Adolescence: The Politics of Contemporary Representations."*Youth and Society* 28, no. 2 (1996): 139–161.

Lester, Julius. *Lovesong: Becoming a Jew*. New York: Henry Holt, 1988.

————. "The Stone That Weeps." In *Testimony: Contemporary Writers Make the Holocaust Personal*. Ed. David Rosenberg. New York: Random House, 1989, 192–210.

Levin, Meyer. *The Obsession*. New York: Simon & Schuster, 1974.

Linenthal, Edward. *Preserving Memory: The Struggle to Create America's Holocaust Museum*. New York: Viking, 1995.

Lowenstein, Andrea Freud. *This Place*. Boston: Pandora Press, 1984.

Luel, Steven. "Bettelheim on Education." *Psychoanalytic Review* 81, no. 3 (1994): 565–79.

Luke, Carmen, and Jennifer Gore, eds. *Feminisms and Critical Pedagogy*. New York: Routledge, 1992.

Lyotard, Jean-François. *The Inhuman: Reflections on Time*. Trans. Geoffrey Bennington and Rachel Bowlby. Stanford: Stanford University Press, 1991.

McBride, James. *The Color of Water: A Black Man's Tribute to His White Mother*. New York: Riverhead Books, 1996.

McCarthy, Cameron, and Warren Crichlow, eds. Special Issue: "Toni Morrison and the Curriculum." *Cultural Studies* 9, no. 2 (May 1995).

McLaren, Angus. *Our Own Master Race: Eugenics in Canada, 1885–1945*. Toronto: McClelland and Steward, 1990.

Mannoni, Maud. *The Child, His "Illness," and the Others*. New York: Random House, 1970.

Marks, Elaine. *Marrano as Metaphor: The Jewish Presence in French Writing*. New York: Columbia University Press, 1996.

Mayer, Hans. *Outsiders: A Study in Life and Letters*. Trans. Denis M. Sweet. Cambridge, Mass.: MIT Press, 1982.

Melnic, Jeffrey. "Black and Jew Blues." *Transitions* 62 (1993): 106–21.

Mercer, Kobena. "Skin Head Sex Thing: Racial Difference and the Homoerotic Imaginary." In *How Do I Look? Queer Film and Video*. Ed. Bad Object-Choices. Seattle: Bay Press, 1991, 196–210.

Merck, Mandy. *perversions: deviant readings.* London: Verso, 1993.

Miller, D. A. *Bringing Out Roland Barthes.* Berkeley: University of California Press, 1992.

Miller, Janet. *Creating Spaces and Finding Voices: Teachers Collaborating for Empowerment.* Albany: State University of New York Press, 1990.

Mitchell, Stephen, and Margaret Black. *Freud and Beyond: A History of Modern Psychoanalytic Thought.* New York: Basic Books, 1995.

Mohr, George. "August Aichhorn: Friend of the Wayward Youth." In *Psychoanalytic Pioneers.* Ed. Franz Alexander, Samuel Eisenstein, and Martin Grotjahn. New York: Basic Books, 1966, 348–59.

Morrison, Toni. *The Bluest Eye.* New York: Pocket Book, 1974.

———. *Playing in the Dark: Whiteness and the Literary Imagination.* Cambridge, Mass.: Harvard University Press, 1992.

Morse, Arthur. *While Six Million Died: A Chronicle of American Apathy.* New York: Random House, 1968.

Morton, Donald, and Mas'ud Zavarzadeh, eds. *Theory/Pedagogy/Politics: Texts for Change.* Urbana: University of Illinois Press, 1991.

Moses, Rafael, ed. *Persistent Shadows of the Holocaust: The Meaning to Those Not Directly Affected.* Madison: International Universities Press, 1993.

Muñoz, Victoria. *Where "Something Catches": Work, Love, and Identity in Youth.* Albany: State University of New York Press, 1995.

Nelson, Cary, ed. *Theory in the Classroom.* Urbana: University of Illinois Press, 1986.

Nestle, Joan. *A Restricted Country.* Ithaca: Firebrand Books, 1987.

New Formations: A Journal of Culture/Theory/Politics 19. "Special Issue on "Perversity." (Spring 1993).

Odets, Walt. *In the Shadow of the Epidemic: Being HIV-Negative in the Age of AIDS.* Durham: Duke University Press, 1995.

Pagano, Jo Anne. *Exiles and Communities: Teaching in the Patriarchal Wilderness.* Albany: State University of New York Press, 1990.

Patton, Cindy. *Inventing AIDS.* New York: Routledge, 1990.

———. "Visualizing Safe Sex: When Pedagogy and Pornography Collide. In *Inside/Out: Lesbian Theories, Gay Theories.* Ed. D. Fuss. New York: Routledge, 1991, 373–86.

————. *Last Served? Gendering the HIV Pandemic.* Bristol: Taylor and Francis, 1994.

Pearl, Daniel. "The Bitter War over Anne Frank's Soul." *Toronto Globe and Mail.* 1 February, 1997, C 16. (Reprinted from the *Wall Street Journal,* Amsterdam.)

Pellegrini, Ann. *Performance Anxieties: Staging Psychoanalysis, Staging Race.* New York: Routledge, 1997.

Penley, Constance. *The Future of an Illusion: Film, Feminism, and Psychoanalysis.* Minneapolis: University of Minnesota Press, 1989.

Phelan, Peggy. *Unmarked: The Politics of Performance.* London: Routledge, 1993.

Phillips, Adam. *On Kissing, Tickling and Being Bored: Psychoanalytic Essays on the Unexamined Life.* Cambridge, Mass.: Harvard University Press, 1993.

————. *Terrors and Experts.* Cambridge, Mass.: Harvard University Press, 1996.

Phillips, Caryl. *The Nature of Blood.* New York: Alfred A. Knopf, 1997.

Pinar, William. *Autobiography, Politics, and Sexuality: Essays in Curriculum Theory, 1972–1992.* New York: Peter Lang, 1994.

Pinar, William, William Reynolds, Patrick Slattery, and Peter Taubman. *Understanding Curriculum: An Introduction to the Study of Historical and Contemporary Curriculum Discourses.* New York: Peter Lang, 1995.

Pitt, Alice. "Subjects in Tension: Engaged Resistance in the Feminist Classroom." Ph.D. diss., Ontario Institute for Studies in Education, University of Toronto, 1995.

————. "Fantasizing Women in the Women's Studies Classroom: Toward a Symptomatic Reading of Negation." *Journal of Curriculum Theorizing* 12, no. 4 (1996): 32–40.

Pollack, Richard. *The Creation of Dr. B: A Biography of Bruno Bettelheim.* New York: Simon and Schuster, 1997.

Pontalis, J. B. *Frontiers in Psychoanalysis: Between the Dream and Psychic Pain.* Trans. Catherine Cullen and Philip Cullen. New York: International Universities Press, 1981.

Prager, Emily. *Eve's Tattoo.* New York: Vintage Press, 1991.

Rachman, Arnold William. *Sandor Ferenczi: The Psychotherapist of Tenderness and Passion.* North Vale, New Jersey: Jason Aronson, 1997.

Rank, Otto. *Modern Education: A Critique of Its Fundamental Ideas.* Trans. Mabel Moxon. New York: Agathon Press, 1968.

———. "The Prometheus Complex (1927)." In *A Psychology of Difference: The American Lectures.* Ed. Robert Kramer. Princeton: Princeton University Press, 1996, 201–10.

Ravitch, Diane. *The Schools We Deserve: Reflections on the Educational Crises of Our Times.* New York: Basic Books, 1985.

Readings, Bill. *The University in Ruins.* Cambridge, Mass.: Harvard University Press, 1996.

Reed, Gail. *Transference Neurosis and Psychoanalytic Experience.* New Haven: Yale University Press, 1994.

Riley, Denise. *War in the Nursery: Theories of the Child and Mother.* London: Virago, 1983.

Robertson, Judith. "Cinema and the Politics of Desire in Teacher Education." Ph.D. diss., Ontario Institute for Studies in Education, University of Toronto, 1994.

Roith, Estelle. *The Riddle of Freud: Jewish Influences on His Theory of Female Sexuality.* London: Tavistock, 1987.

Rose, Gillian. *Love's Work: A Reckoning with Life.* New York: Schocken Books, 1995.

Rose, Jacqueline. *Why War?—Psychoanalysis, Politics, and the Return to Melanie Klein.* Oxford: Blackwell, 1993.

———. *States of Fantasy.* Oxford: Claredon Press, 1996.

Rosenblatt, Louise. *Literature as Exploration.* New York: Noble and Noble, 1968.

Rosenfeld, Alvin. "Popularization and Memory: The Case of Anne Frank." In *Lessons and Legacies: The Meaning of the Holocaust in a Changing World.* Ed. Peter Hayes. Evanston: Northwestern University Press, 1991, 243–78.

———. "Anne Frank—And Us: Finding the Right Words." *Reconstruction* 2, no. 2 (1993): 86–92.

Rukeyser, Muriel. *Breaking Open.* New York: Random House, 1973.

Sachs, Hans. "Community of Daydreams." *Yearbook of Psychoanalysis.* vol. 1. New York: International Universities Press, 1945, 281–302.

Santer, Eric L. *My Own Private Germany: Daniel Paul Schreber's Secret History of Modernity.* Princeton: Princeton University Press, 1996.

Schulman, Sarah. *My American History: Lesbian and Gay Life during the Reagan/Bush Years*. New York: Routledge, 1994.

Scott, Darieck. "Jungle Fever? Black Gay Identity Politics, White Dick, and the Utopian Bedroom." *GLQ: A Journal of Lesbian and Gay Studies* 1, no. 2 (1994): 299–322.

Sedgwick, Eve Kosofsky. *Epistemology of the Closet*. Berkeley: University of California Press, 1990.

———. "White Glasses." *Yale Journal of Criticism* 53, no. 3 (1992): 193–208.

Segal, Josylyn. "Interracial Plus." In *Nice Jewish Girls: A Lesbian Anthology*. Ed. Evelyn Torton Beck. Revised and updated edition. Boston: Beacon Press, 1989, 61–64.

Seidman, Naomi. "Theorizing Jewish Patriarch *in extremis.*" In *Judaism since Gender*. Ed. Mariam Peskowitz and Laura Levitt. New York: Routledge, 1997, 40–48.

Silberfeld, Michael. "The Psychology of Hope and the Modification of Entitlement Near the End of Life." In *Attitudes of Entitlement: Theoretical and Clinical Issues*. Ed. V. Volkan and T. Rodgers. Charlottesville: University Press of Virginia, 1988, 41–52.

Silin, Jonathan. *Sex, Death, and the Education of Children: Our Passion for Ignorance in the Age of AIDS*. New York: Teachers College Press, 1995.

Simon, Roger. *Teaching against the Grain: Texts for a Pedagogy of Possibility*. New York: Bergin & Garvey, 1992.

Simon, Roger, and Cynthia Eppert. "Remembering Obligation: Pedagogy and the Witnessing of Testimony of Historical Trauma." *Canadian Journal of Education* 22, no. 4 (Fall 1997): 175–191.

Sinclair, Jo. *Wasteland*. Philadelphia: Jewish Publication Society, 1987.

Singer, Isaac Bashevis. *Meshugah*. Trans. by the author and Nili Wachtel. New York: Farrar Straus and Giroux, 1994.

Spanos, William. *The End of Education: Toward Posthumanism*. Minneapolis: University of Minnesota Press, 1993.

Spiegelman, Art. *Maus: A Survivor's Tale*. Vol. 1. New York: Pantheon, 1986.

———. *Maus: A Survivor's Tale: And Here My Troubles Begin*. Vol. II. New York: Pantheon, 1991.

Spivak, Gayatri Chakravorty. "Acting Bits/Identity Talk." In *Identities*. Ed. Kwame Anthony Appiah and Henry Louis Gates, Jr. Chicago: University of Chicago Press, 1995, 147–80.

————. *Outside in the Teaching Machine.* New York: Routledge, 1993.

Steedman, Carolyn. *Strange Dislocations: Childhood and the Idea of Human Interiority, 1780–1930.* Cambridge, Mass.: Harvard University Press, 1995.

Sterba, Editha. "Interpretation and Education." *Psychoanalytic Study of the Child.* Vol. 1. New York: International Universities Press, 1945, 309–18.

Stern, Anne-Lise. "'Mending' Auschwitz, Through Psychoanalysis?" *Strategies: A Journal of Theory, Culture and Politics* 8 (1995/1996): 41–52.

Sutton, Nina. *Bruno Bettelheim: A Life and Legacy.* New York: Basic Books, 1996.

Thompson, Audrey, and Andrew Gitlin. "Creating Spaces for Reconstructing Knowledge in Feminist Pedagogy." *Educational Theory* 45, no. 2 (Spring 1995): 125–50.

Todd, Sharon. "Pedagogical Imaginary and the Politics of Identity." Ph.D. diss., Concordia University, 1995.

Volkan, Vamik. *Linking Objects and Linking Phenomena: A Study of the Forms, Symptoms, Metapsychology, and Therapy of Complicated Mourning.* New York: International Universities Press, 1981.

————. *The Need to Have Enemies and Allies: From Clinical Practice to International Relationships.* Northvale: Jason Aronson, 1988.

Walcott, Rinaldo. *Black Like Who?: Writing Black Canada.* Toronto: Insomniac Press, 1997.

Waller, Willard. *The Sociology of Teaching.* New York: Russell and Russell, 1961.

Warner, Michael. "Something Queer about the Nation State." *Alphabet City* 3 (1993): 14–17.

————. "Introduction." In *Fear of a Queer Planet.* Ed. Michael Warner. Minneapolis: University of Minnesota Press, 1993, vii–xxxi.

Washington, Eric K. "Sculpture in Flight: A Conversation with Bill T. Jones." *Transition* 62 (1994): 188–202.

Watney, Simon. "Schools Out." In *Inside/Out: Lesbian Theories, Gay Theories.* Ed. D. Fuss. New York: Routledge, 1991, 387–404.

Wickham, Gary, and William Haver. "Come Out, Come Out, Wherever You Are: A Guide for the Homoerotically Disadvantaged." Unpublished paper, 1992.

Wilkomirski, Binjamin. *Fragments: Memories of a Wartime Childhood.* Trans. Carol Brown Janeway. New York: Shocken Books, 1996.

Williams, Raymond. *Keywords: A Vocabulary of Culture and Society.* New York: Oxford University Press, 1976.

Willis, Ellen. "The Myth of the Powerful Jew." In *Blacks and Jews: Alliances and Arguments.* Ed. Paul Berman. New York: Delacorte Press, 183–209.

Winnicott, D. W. "Aggression, Guilt and Reparation." In *Home Is Where We Start From: Essays by a Psychoanalyst.* New York: W. W. Norton, 1986, 80–89.

———. *Playing and Reality.* London: Routledge, 1993.

Wood, Joe. "The Problem Negro and Other Tales." In *Blacks and Jews: Alliances and Arguments.* Ed. Paul Berman. New York: Delacorte Press, 97–128.

Yerushalmi, Yosef Hayim. *Freud's Moses: Judaism Terminable and Interminable.* New Haven: Yale University Press, 1991.

Yon, Daniel. "Pedagogy and the 'Problem' of Difference: On Reading Community in 'The Darker Side of Black.'" *Qualitative Studies in Education,* forthcoming.

———. *Elusive Culture: An Ethnography of Youth and Identity.* Albany: State University of New York Press, forthcoming.

Young-Bruehl, Elisabeth. *Anna Freud: A Biography.* New York: W.W. Norton, 1988.

———. "Discriminations." *Transition: An International Review* 60 (1993): 53–69.

———. *The Anatomy of Prejudices.* Cambridge, Mass.: Harvard University Press, 1996.

Index

P°IT

Printed in the United States
25604LVS00004B/76-81